Sally Fountain and Linda Goodwin

PE to 16

SECOND EDITION

OXFORD

UNIVERSITY PRESS

SEC

OXFORD
UNIVERSITY PRESS

Great Clarendon Street, Oxford OX2 6DP

Oxford University Press is a department of the University of Oxford.
It furthers the University's objective of excellence in research,
scholarship, and education by publishing worldwide in

Oxford New York

Auckland Bangkok Buenos Aires Cape Town Chennai
Dar es Salaam Delhi Hong Kong Istanbul Karachi Kolkata
Kuala Lumpur Madrid Melbourne Mexico City Mumbai Nairobi
São Paulo Shanghai Taipei Tokyo Toronto

Oxford is a registered trade mark of Oxford University Press
in the UK and in certain other countries

British Library Cataloguing in Publication Data

Data available

ISBN 0 19 913444 8

10 9 8 7 6

Printed by Gráficas Estella, Spain.

Acknowledgements
The publisher and authors would like to thank the following for their permission
to reproduce photographs and other copyright material:

p1 Corbis; p6 (l) Gabe Palmer/Ace, (r) Colorsport; p7 (l) Neil Tingle/Action
Plus (r) Andrew Cowie/Colorsport; p8 Soccer AM/British Sky Broadcasting; p9
Tony Marshall/Empics; p11 Nick Kidd/Sporting Pictures (UK) Ltd; p12 (t)
Image Bank/Getty Images, (b) Oxford University Press; p13 (tl) Andy
Budd/Action Images,(tr) FPG International/Getty Images, (b) Richard
Francis/Action Plus p14 (tl) Anton Want/ Getty Images/Allsport (UK) Ltd. (tr)
Mike Powell/Allsport (UK) Ltd.(b) Tony Marshall/Empics; p17 (t) Allsport
Australia/Allsport (UK) Ltd., (b) Colorsport; p18 Colorsport; p19 (t) Stewart
Fraser/Colorsport, (b) Matthew Impey/Colorsport; p22 Duomo/Corbis UK
Ltd.; p25 (t) James Stevenson/Science Photo Library, (c) James
Stevenson/Science Photo Library, (b) James Stevenson/Science Photo Library;
p27 (l) Oxford University Press, (r) Oxford University Press; p30 Ian
West/Bubbles; p32 (tl) Oxford University Press, (bl) Oxford University Press,
(tc) Oxford University Press, (bc) Oxford University Press, (tr) Oxford
University Press, (br) Oxford University Press, (c) Oxford University Press; p33
(tl) Oxford University Press, (tc) Neal Preston/Corbis UK Ltd., (tr) Oxford
University Press (b) Clive Brunskill/Allsport (UK) Ltd.; p38 (t) Manfred
Kage/Science Photo Library, (b) Professor P.M. Motta & E. Vizza/Science Photo
Library; p41 Oxford University Press; p43 (tl) Ben Radford/Allsport (UK) Ltd.,
(bl) Oxford University Press, (bc) Oxford University Press, (tr) Colorsport, (br)
Oxford University Press; p44 (t) Oxford University Press, (b) Oxford

University Press; p45 (tl) Oxford University Press, (cl) Oxford University Press,
(bl) Oxford University Press, (tr) Oxford University Press, (cr) Oxford
University Press, (br) Oxford University Press; p46 (t) Andrew
Cowie/Colorsport, (b) Neil Tingle/Action Plus; p47 Mike King/Action Plus;
p48 (t) Oxford University Press, (b) Oxford University Press; p49 (t) Oxford
University Press, (b) Oxford University Press; p50 (t) Allsport (UK) Ltd., (b)
Ben Radford/ Getty Images/Allsport (UK) Ltd.; p51 (t) Oxford University
Press, (b) Oxford University Press; p52 (t) Oxford University Press, (b) Oxford
University Press; p53 (l) Oxford University Press, (c) Oxford University Press,
(r) Oxford University Press; p54 Duomo/Corbis UK Ltd.; p56 Science Photo
Library; p58 (l) Oxford University Press, (c) Oxford University Press, (r)
Oxford University Press; p62 BSIP, LBL/Science Photo Library; p63 (t) Dr. P.
Marazzi/Science Photo Library, (b) Dr. H.C. Robinson/Science Photo Library;
p64 Jim Selby/Science Photo Library; p65 Sheila Terry/Science Photo Library;
p68 (l) J.C. Revy/Science Photo Library, (r) Oxford University Press; p71 (t)
Nathan Benn/Corbis UK Ltd., (b) Duomo/Corbis UK Ltd.; p73 (t) Colorsport,
(b) Nick Wilson/Allsport (UK) Ltd.; p74 Colorsport; p75 Colorsport; p78 (t)
Colorsport,(b) Oxford University Press; p79 (t) Richard Hamilton
Smith/Corbis UK Ltd., (b) Education Photos; p80 (t) Warren Morgan/Corbis
UK Ltd., (b) Oxford University Press; p81 Larry Mulvehill/Science Photo
Library; p82 Matthew Impey/Colorsport; p84 (t) Oxford University Press, (b)
Mike Powell/Allsport (UK) Ltd.; p86 Oxford University Press; p87 Oxford
University Press;p90 Oxford University Press;p91 (t) Peter Turnley/Corbis UK
Ltd.,(b) Education Photos; p92 (t) Oxford University Press, (b) Addict Ltd;
p96 (t) Neil Rabinowitz/Corbis UK Ltd., (c) FPG International/Getty Images,
(b) Karl Weatherly/Corbis UK Ltd.; p97 Steve Morton/Empics; p99 Darren
Walsh/Action Images; p102 (t) Oxford University Press, (c) Oxford University
Press, (b) Oxford University Press; p103 Oxford University Press; p104 Prof. P.
Motta/ Dept. of Anatomy/ University "La Sapienza", Rome/Science Photo
Library; p105 (t) Oxford University Press, (c) Oxford University Press, (b)
Oxford University Press; p106 (t) Oxford University Press, (b) Oxford
University Press; p107 Colorsport; p108 Oxford University Press; p110
Colorsport/Colorsport; p111 Science Photo Library; p112 (t) Eye of
Science/Science Photo Library, (b) Duomo/Corbis UK Ltd.; p113 (bl) Dr. P.
Marazzi/Science Photo Library, (bc) Dr. P. Marazzi/Science Photo Library, (br)
Phil Schermeister/Corbis UK Ltd., (t) Dr. P. Marazzi/Science Photo Library;
p116 (t) Action Images, (b) Action Images; p117 (l) Addject Ltd, (r) Action
Images; p119 Oxford University Press; p120 Shout; p121 Oxford University
Press; p122 (t) Science Photo Library, (b) Shaun Botterill/Allsport (UK) Ltd.;
p123 Oxford University Press; p124 Oxford University Press; p125 Stuart
MacFarlane/Colorsport; p126 John Callan/Shout; p127 Juha Tamminen/Action
Images; p130 TempSport/Corbis UK Ltd.; p131 (l) Stuart
MacFarlane./Colorsport, (c) Action Images, (r) Oxford University Press; p132
Oxford University Press; p133 Glyn Kirk/Action Plus; p134 Oxford University
Press; p135 Oxford University Press; p136 Gary M Prior/Allsport (UK) Ltd.;
p137 (l) Mark Thompson/Allsport (UK) Ltd., (r) Shaun Botterill/Allsport (UK)
Ltd.; p138 Michael S. Yamashita/Corbis UK Ltd.; p139 Mike Cooper/Allsport
(UK) Ltd.; p142 Matthew Impey/Colorsport; p143 Oxford University Press;
p144 Oxford University Press; p145 Neil Tingle/Action Plus; p146 (l) Neil
Tingle/Action Plus, (r) Glyn Kirk/Action Plus; p147 Bettmann/Corbis UK
Ltd.; p151 (t) Matthew Clarke/Action Plus, (b) Stu Forster/Allsport (UK) Ltd.;
p152 Bob Krist/Corbis UK Ltd.; p153 Mike Hewitt/Allsport (UK) Ltd.; p155
Action Images; p156 (t) Oxford University Press, (b) Oxford University Press;
p158 Lilleshall National Sports Centre; p159 Gary M Prior/Allsport (UK) Ltd.;
p163 British Sports Trust; p164 (t) Allsport (UK) Ltd., (b) British Olympic
Association; p165 (l) Popperfoto, (r) Patrick Ward/Corbis UK Ltd.; p169
Andrew Cowie/Colorsport; p170 Colorsport; p175 (t) Matthew
Impey/Colorsport, (b) Colin Elsey/Colorsport; p176 Clive Mason/Allsport
(UK) Ltd.; p177 Clive Brunskill/Allsport (UK) Ltd.; p178 Andrew
Cowie/Colorsport; p179 Allsport (UK) Ltd.; p180 (t) Bubbles, (b) Roger
Howard/Ace; p182 Stu Forster/Allsport (UK) Ltd.; p183 Patrick Ward/Corbis
UK Ltd.; p184 Andrew Cowie/Colorsport; p185 Mike
Hewitt/Action Plus.

Logos courtesy of organizations concerned.

Illustrations by IFA Design. Cartoons by Steve Evans.

Front cover photographs by Corbis (main, centre and right insets). Corel (left
inset).
Back cover Corbis.

Introduction

PE continues to be one of the most interesting subjects at GCSE. It is the only subject where what you learn and do can directly influence your life and health.

In 2001 the GCSE specifications for PE were changed. This Second Edition of *PE to 16* takes account of the revised specifications and their different approach to questioning. The specifications no longer tend to isolate topics, but instead bring all the areas of the subject together. This helps you to realise how topics are related but does mean that you need to practise drawing information from many sources. As you progress through this book, your understanding will be tested increasingly and, for some questions, you will need to remember work from previous chapters. Don't worry though, these 'thinking style' questions will be introduced to you gradually, chapter by chapter.

Throughout this book, the theory behind PE is related to practical examples, to help you understand and remember it. The chapters are displayed in easy-to-use double-page spreads, which end with a small set of questions. Most of these questions can be answered from the double page. They are designed to help you become more familiar with the work you have just covered and to test your understanding. There will usually be a question that will require you to think for yourself.

The end-of-chapter questions reinforce the work that you have just completed in that chapter, and also encourage you to bring in knowledge from other chapters to reflect the new-style exam questions. You will also find that ICT extension work is included in the end-of-chapter questions.

Good luck with your GCSE and use the information to keep yourself fit and healthy for life.

CONTENTS

Section 1 The body

Section 2 Getting and staying fit

Section 3 Sport and you

Section 4 Sport in society

1.1   Health and fitness

You have no colds, flu, aches or pains, and you can run a mile in six minutes. But does that mean you are healthy and fit?

What is health?

Health does not just mean the absence of sickness.
Health is a state of complete physical, mental and social well-being, and not merely the absence of disease or infirmity.
It means you feel good all round.

Physical activity helps:

1. your physical well-being

◎ Your heart, lungs and other body systems grow strong and healthy and lack of illness contributes to your enjoyment of life.

◎ Your body shape improves – if you look good you feel good.

2. your mental well-being

◎ You learn how to cope with stress and difficult situations in sport and can then use this in real life, e.g. coping with the pressures of exams.

◎ You learn to control emotions, as in sport there is an immediate penalty for the breaking of rules. It then helps you in real life, e.g. even if you feel really angry you still do not become violent.

◎ You get the chance to feel emotions and experiences that you might not get elsewhere, e.g. success, skilfulness and the feeling of being important and worthwhile. Sport helps to give you self-esteem.

3. your social well-being

◎ Humans live in groups and we must learn social or group behaviour to fit in. Sport helps us with this by teaching us confidence, co-operation, communication and teamwork.

◎ You meet people and learn friendship and support.

◎ You get a feeling of worth, i.e. that you are of some value in society.

These kinds of well-being are all related. If you get injured in a car accident it may affect your mental well-being. It may also affect your social well-being, if you can't work and lose touch with your friends.

Having fun with your friends is part of a healthy lifestyle. But are you as fit as a top-class athlete? Do you need to be? Could you be?

People's environments make different demands on them. The demands of a top sportsperson will include many hours of training a day.

What is fitness?

Fitness isn't just being able to do sit-ups or run fast. **Fitness is the ability to meet the demands of the environment.**
Your environment is everything around you. It includes home, school, family and friends. All of them make demands on you. Meeting the demands means carrying out tasks and activities. If you can carry out these tasks and activities *without getting too tired*, and still have energy left over for emergencies, then you are fit.

For example:
cycling to and from school every day
concentrating on lessons all day
doing two hours of school work every evening
helping at home with cleaning and shopping
playing for a team twice a week
working in the supermarket on Saturday
going out with friends at the weekend to a party or club.

The link between health and fitness

Health and fitness are closely linked. You cannot be healthy without being fit enough to meet the demands of your environment, e.g. a broken arm (poor physical health) means not being able to do your school work (i.e. not coping with the demands of your environment). However, it is possible to be fit but not healthy, e.g. you can physically manage your everyday tasks (so you are fit) but are constantly depressed about being no good at anything. Remember, health is complete physical, social and MENTAL well-being. Don't forget this when you plan your PEP (pages 94-95).

The more easily you can meet the demands on you, the less likely you are to suffer stress, or fall ill, or injure yourself. But if you are ill, you will not be able to meet those demands. You may have to stay off school, give up your Saturday job, and stay in bed for a week or two.

QUESTIONS

1 What is health?

2 Give two ways in which sport can help your 'physical well-being'.

3 How can sport help you mentally? Give two examples.

4 Body shape can be improved for very slim people and those who are overweight. Explain how this would differ.

5 What is meant by the word environment?

6 Why is teamwork a useful thing to learn in sport? Give an example from your non-sporting life where you need it.

7 What is fitness?

8 In terms of physical exercise, compare the environment for one week between yourself, a non-sporty adult you know and a high-level sportsperson.

1.2 Why exercise?

Exercise is a form of physical activity, done primarily to improve one's health and physical fitness.

There are many ways to take exercise. Walking, swimming, climbing, aerobics, rugby, golf and judo are just some of them. What can exercise do for you? Lots, as you'll see below.

Physical benefits

Exercise helps you to look good and feel good.

◎ It burns up stored body fat so your shape improves and you won't be overweight. For thin people it builds muscles and gives you a nice shape.
◎ It tones up the muscles of your back and abdomen so your posture improves.
◎ It strengthens your bones.
◎ It keeps your joints flexible so you can move efficiently.

◎ It makes your heart and lungs work more efficiently, so you don't get tired so easily.
◎ It helps to prevent heart disease, high blood pressure, back pain and cancers. Swimming and walking help people with asthma.
◎ All the above give you an increased life expectancy.

This shows the number of deaths per 10 000 people per year.

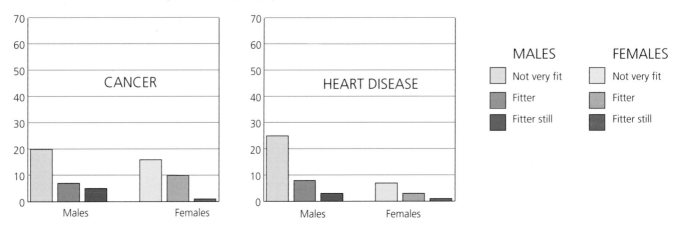

Social benefits

Exercise increases your social well-being, and especially if it's in the form of a sport.

◎ Exercise helps to make you confident. That means you can cope better with difficult people and difficult situations.
◎ Playing sport is a way to meet people and make good friends.
◎ Sport develops teamwork and co-operation. These qualities will help you in your working life.
◎ You may find you are talented at a sport. You may be able to make a career of it or be a part-time professional.
◎ You can choose a sport that suits your personality and makes you feel fulfilled. For example, rock climbing might suit if you like to get away from it all and enjoy a challenge.

Tim Lovejoy and Helen Chamberlain are presenters for Sky TV's SoccerAM. An interest in sport can lead to a career related to sport.

Mental benefits

Exercise helps your mental well-being too.

◎ It is stimulating and enjoyable. It peps you up.
◎ It relieves tension and stress, which can cause high blood pressure and heart disease. A lively game or workout helps you get rid of the tensions from a difficult day.
◎ It gets rid of aggression. You can take out angry feelings on a ball or bike pedals instead of a person.
◎ It helps you forget your problems. When you think about them later, they won't seem so bad.
◎ It relieves boredom and provides a challenge.
◎ It helps you sleep better, so you feel more rested.
◎ If you look and feel better, your self-confidence increases.
◎ Success at a sport is good for your self-esteem. Success is not just about winning, it can be the satisfaction that comes with any good performance.

Exercise and fitness

All those benefits mean that exercise helps you meet the demands of your environment more easily. In other words it makes you fitter. You can work harder, feel less tired and enjoy life more. The way to improve your fitness is through exercise.

Performance

This is how well a task is completed. If you have a good performance, you will feel satisfied and successful. Everyone's idea of a good performance differs. For example, in the London Marathon, a person may feel that they have achieved a good performance by finishing. Some people will want to improve their time, some will want to beat rivals and some will want to win or even to break the time record.

Even watching sport can provide plenty of benefits. We learn to appreciate a good performance. If the move was creative and beautiful it is called AESTHETIC. Whole sports, gymnastics, for example, can be aesthetic.

QUESTIONS

1 Look at the graphs on page 8. Which group of males and females is most at risk of dying?

2 Why is this so?

3 Exercise can also give you mental benefits. How could this help prevent heart disease?

4 Give two more mental benefits of exercise.

5 Some people like being in groups and some people like being on their own for a while. For each type of person list three sports that they might enjoy.

6 If Sheffield Wednesday drew 0-0 with Manchester Utd they might think that a good performance. If they drew 0-0 with Astor School first XI they might not. Why?

7 Give two ways in which playing sport could help you learn social skills that would be useful when you start work.

1.3 Exercise and the body systems

A car has an ignition system, a brake system, a cooling system and so on. Your body also has different systems. They work together to make the body a truly brilliant machine.

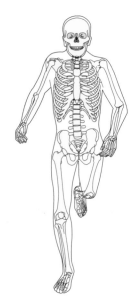

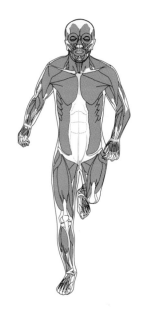

When you run, it's not just a case of moving your arms and legs. All your **body systems** work together.

Your **skeletal system**: bones and joints. Without bones you'd be a shapeless heap. Your joints allow movement.

Your **muscular system**: muscles. Muscles are the red meat around bones. They pull on bones and make them move.

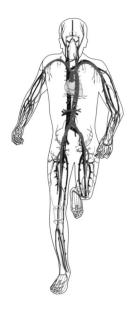

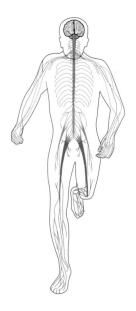

Your **circulatory system**: blood, heart and blood vessels. Blood carries food and oxygen round the body and carries waste away.

Your **respiratory system**: the lungs and breathing tube. It's how you take in oxygen and get rid of carbon dioxide.

Your **nervous system**: the brain, spinal cord and a network of nerves. It controls and co-ordinates movement.

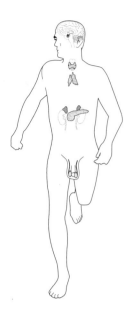

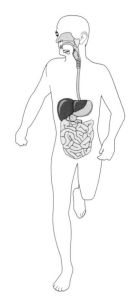

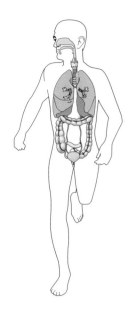

Your **hormonal system**: a set of glands which make **hormones**. These chemicals help to control activities going on in your body.

Your **digestive system**: the stomach and gut, where the food you eat gets broken down. You use digested food as fuel.

Your **excretory system**: the lungs, kidneys and intestine. They get rid of or **excrete** the waste from your body.

How body systems work together: an example

Warming up for an important game? This shows how body systems work together:

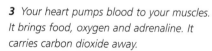

1 Signals from the eyes, ears, muscles and skin tell your brain you're on the way. It responds by sending signals around your body along the nervous system.

*2 At a signal, a gland pumps **adrenaline** into your blood. This hormone makes your heart and lungs work faster and gets your muscles ready for action.*

3 Your heart pumps blood to your muscles. It brings food, oxygen and adrenaline. It carries carbon dioxide away.

6 The lungs take in oxygen, which you also need for energy. They excrete carbon dioxide, a waste material, at the same time.

*5 Food from your digestive system is stored as **body fat** and as **glycogen** in muscles. Your muscles use these as fuel to get energy for movement.*

4 Signals from your brain tell your muscles to shorten. When they shorten they pull on your bones. This makes you move.

QUESTIONS

1 List eight systems that act together to keep your body going. Say what each does.

2 What does *excrete* mean?

3 What is *adrenaline*? What does it do?

4 Look at note 4 for the photograph above.
It shows the nervous and muscular systems at work together.
For each of the other notes say which system or systems are at work.

1.4 General fitness

Fitness is the ability to meet the demands of the environment, and can be divided into two areas – general and specific.

General fitness

This is the ability of your body to carry out everyday activities without excessive tiredness and still have enough energy to cope with emergencies.

It is the last part of this definition that causes many people to be unfit. Imagine an adult who does little exercise. (I'm sure you know someone!) They get up, drive to work, work sitting down, drive home, do some housework and go to bed. They may cope with this with no problem for years. Suddenly their car doesn't start in the morning – they have to run to the bus stop quickly. Their heart is not used to beating quickly, their lungs hurt, their joints and muscles ache due to the exercise. In extreme cases they may even have a heart attack. These sort of people are not fit because they do not have enough energy to cope with emergencies.

There are five aspects of general fitness:

1 *Stamina / endurance / cardiovascular fitness*. This is the ability to exercise the entire body for long periods of time, e.g. walking to the train station, jogging, aerobics. The word cardiovascular means heart and blood vessels. You can never separate these areas as they are interdependant to get oxygen into the body, distribute it and get carbon dioxide out.

2 *Muscular endurance*. This is the ability of muscles to maintain and repeat contractions without getting tired. Many activities need both kinds of endurance. For example, stacking shelves all day long in a shop, swimming or jogging.

3 *Strength*. This is the amount of force a muscle can exert against a resistance. You need strength to lift a suitcase or push in a rugby scrum. If you have too little strength you risk injury when you lift, pull or push things.

4 *Flexibility or suppleness.* This is the range of movement at a joint. You need flexibility for tying your shoe laces, reaching up to a shelf, or playing sports. If you have poor flexibility you move stiffly and are more likely to injure your tendons and ligaments in violent movements.

5 *Body composition*. This is the percentage of body weight which is fat, muscle and bone. If we have too much fat or excess weight we put a strain upon our vital organs. It also leads to a greater chance of disease. This area will be discussed in greater detail on pages 18 and 105.

General fitness includes being able to cope with emergencies.

Fetching, carrying, stacking. All in a day's work for some people, and all demanding general fitness.

General fitness and health

General fitness is sometimes called **health-related fitness** because it helps to keep you healthy. It helps to protect you against accidents, heart disease, stress, muscle injury and other health problems. We all need a minimum level of general fitness, just to cope with everyday life. Methods of training will be discussed in a later chapter but,

A PE or games lesson.

Doing everyday chores with extra effort.

briefly, three lots of exercise lasting at least twenty minutes per week is really the minimum we need. This exercise should use as much of the body as possible and make you out of breath. It should include a stretching session before or afterwards. A good example of this type of exercise is a sport such as netball. It lasts from thirty minutes (school game) to an hour and makes you out of breath (improves stamina). You use your muscles repeatedly (muscular endurance). You jump, sprint and throw (strength). You use energy and burn up calories (helps you towards a good body composition) and you warm up and cool down (improves flexibility).

Remember you must do exercise three times a week. PE is compulsory at school so that is one occasion. Join at least one club that practises weekly, e.g. badminton. Finally, do something at the weekend. Join up with a friend to make it enjoyable. If you are going shopping, walk there quickly or get off the bus a couple of stops early. Twenty minutes FAST walking is ideal.

For a higher level of sport you need a higher level of fitness in the areas mentioned, e.g. if you are a long-distance walker/runner you will need to work hard on your cardiovascular fitness. In most sports increased flexibility not only prevents injury but also improves performance, e.g. good flexibility around the shoulder will improve technique for javelin throwing or the butterfly swimming stroke, which will allow greater force to be transmitted. You also need specific skills or skill-related fitness which is discussed on the next page.

A club match.

QUESTIONS

1 What are the two areas of fitness?

2 Which one helps with our everyday life and health?

3 Give a definition of your answer to question 2.

4 Give your own example of an emergency that may occur in our lives.

5 What are the five aspects of general fitness?

6 Which of the following would you say need stamina: aerobics, swimming, press-ups, skiing, sit-ups? Explain each answer.

7 Why would jogging need cardiovascular fitness and muscular endurance?

8 Elderly people lose flexibility if they do not exercise. Why would this be a problem in their everyday lives?

9 We know that there is a danger in having too much fat. Do you think it could be possible to have too much muscle? Explain your answer.

10 What aspect of general fitness are you discussing in question 9?

1.5 Specific fitness

This needs an exceptionally good sense of balance . . .

. . . this needs explosive strength . . .

Specific fitness

This is the ability of the body to carry out set tasks effectively and efficiently. It usually requires some sort of learning and so can also be called skill-related fitness.

◎ **Power** or **explosive strength.** This is the ability to do strength performances quickly. Power = strength x speed. For example, you need power to hit the ball hard in tennis, to throw a discus or do a karate chop.

◎ **Agility.** This is the ability to change the position of the body quickly whilst keeping the whole body under control, e.g. dodging an opponent in rugby or netball.

◎ **Coordination.** This is the ability to move two or more body parts together smoothly and accurately in response to what your senses tell you, e.g. when climbing you see a hold, or small ledge, and then you move a hand or foot to it. You feel if it is firm and then transfer your body weight to it.

◎ **Speed of reaction.** This is the time taken between the presentation of a stimulus and the onset of movement. A stimulus is something that causes us to act in some way, e.g. a hot oven could be the stimulus that makes us move our hands quickly. The gun making a noise is the stimulus that makes us start running in the sprints. The quicker we can move in response to the stimulus, the quicker our reactions are.

◎ **Timing.** This is the ability to coincide movements in relation to external factors, e.g. choosing to tackle when the ball is slightly away from your opponent's feet in football.

◎ **Speed.** This is the different rates at which a person is able to perform a movement or cover a distance in a short period of time. This means speed is needed to move either your whole body (e.g. the run up in long jump) or just a bit of it (e.g. upper body, shoulder and arm for a strong shot in tennis).

. . . and this needs good reactions.

◎ **Balance.** This is the ability to retain the centre of mass above the base of support.

The base of support is the area in touch with the ground or an object. The bigger your base of support, the more stable you are, i.e. you are better balanced.

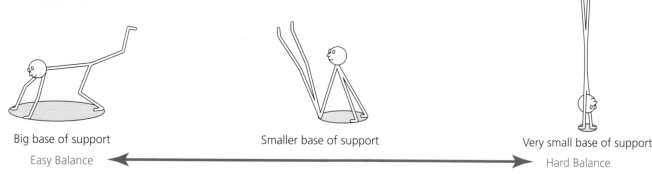

Big base of support — Easy Balance ←——————————→ Very small base of support — Hard Balance

Smaller base of support

Your centre of mass is the part of you that is the middle of your weight. The centre of mass of a ruler:

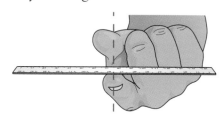

If you do this, i.e. balance a ruler on your finger, you have to find its centre of mass. Only a small amount is touching your finger (small base of support). When the centre of mass (the middle of the ruler) is directly above the base of support you get a balance. If you put the centre of mass outside/away from the base of support it falls off, i.e. overbalances.

Centre of mass

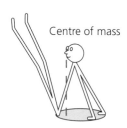

Centre of mass

Centre of mass

In all the above diagrams the centre of mass is directly over the base of support so the gymnast can balance.

If the person doing the handstand leans too far one way, their centre of mass is no longer over the base of support and they overbalance. Remember – balance can be static (still) as the examples above or dynamic (moving), e.g. a sequence on the beam in gymnastics.

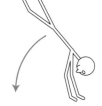

QUESTIONS

1 In the sport you are doing now, try to give a good example of when you require power, agility, co-ordination, quick reactions, speed, timing and balance.

2 In contact sports (e.g. rugby) when a player expects to be tackled they normally put their feet wide apart and lower their centre of mass. Why do you think this is?

3 Give two examples from a team game and two from athletics where you need good reactions.

4 If you wanted to be a top-level player in the sports below, list the areas of specific fitness you would require:
a Sprint swimming **b** Ice skating **c** Judo **d** Long jumping

1.6 Factors affecting fitness

How fit are you right now? That depends on several factors.
Not all of them are under your control!

1 Age

You are usually at your fittest in your twenties. The graph below shows
fitness in terms of oxygen used per kilogram of body weight. The more
you use, the fitter you are (page 70).

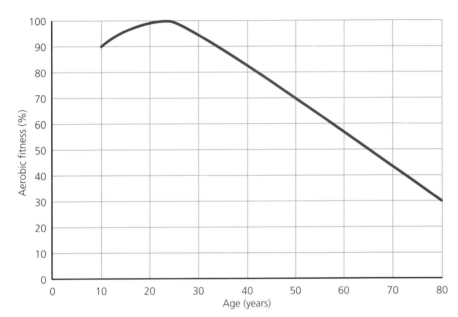

From your thirties onwards,
fitness falls because:

◉ muscles get weaker
◉ bones get lighter
◉ heart rate decreases
◉ joints get stiffer
◉ movements get slower
◉ body fat increases.

But exercise can slow these
changes down and even reverse
them.

2 Gender

Up to about age 11, males and females are equal in terms of general
fitness.
But things change from then on . . .

◉ **Strength.** Males grow about 50% stronger than females because they
have more muscle. The male hormone testosterone promotes the
growth of muscle and bone. It is released at puberty.

◉ **Cardiovascular endurance.** Males are better than females at
transporting oxygen. They have larger hearts and lungs and more
blood. Their red blood cells contain more haemoglobin, which is the
oxygen carrier.

◉ **Bone structure.** Males are usually larger and heavier than females
because they have bigger bones. They also have a narrower pelvis. This
makes it easier to transmit power between the legs and trunk, an
advantage in most sports.

◉ **Speed.** Because they have longer bones and bigger muscles, males can
move faster. This means they also generate more power.

◉ **Flexibility.** Females score higher for flexibility. Females of all ages
tend to be more flexible than males.

◉ **Body composition.** Females usually have more body fat than males.
Fat acts as padding and keeps you warm, but it is extra weight to carry
round. It puts extra strain on the heart, joints and muscles.

3 Physique

Your build and shape make you fitter for some sports than others.
A tall thin person is probably more suited to basketball than boxing. Find out more about sport and build in the next unit.

4 Diet

Your body needs certain substances for energy, growth and repair.
You get them from food. If you don't eat a healthy diet your body won't function properly.
You can find out about eating for fitness on pages 102-107.

5 Exercise

No matter how unfit you are, regular exercise will make you fitter.
Discover how training affects your body on pages 74-75.

6 Physical disability

A disability means part of your body does not function properly.
But exercise can keep the rest of the body very fit. Many disabled people are first-class athletes.

7 Illness and fatigue

When you are tired or ill you are less fit for any activity.

8 Drug-taking

Alcohol, cigarettes and many other substances lower your fitness.
See pages 108-111 for more about drugs.

9 Stress

Exams, quarrels, overwork, money problems – all these can lead to stress. Continual stress will affect your health, causing high blood pressure and heart disease. It is also linked to cancer.
Short-term stress can affect your perfomance in sports events.
Your muscles are tense, you can't concentrate, you make mistakes.
One good way to deal with stress is to practise relaxation.

10 The environment

Fumes from traffic and factories, over long periods of time, will damage your lungs and make breathing difficult. This means your fitness suffers.
Your performance in a sports event is also affected by the environment.
For example on a hot, humid day you can overheat, which makes you weak and dizzy. And think what a windy day can do to a tennis match.
At high altitudes the air is 'thinner', so you must breathe harder to get enough oxygen. To perform well in sport at high altitudes you first need time to adapt.

Tanni Grey-Thompson – Olympic gold medal winner, Sydney Olympics 2000.

In windsurfing, wind speed has a dramatic effect on performance.

QUESTIONS

1 About what age are people usually at their fittest?
2 Explain how males and females differ in terms of:

   a strength **b** oxygen transport **c** body fat

3 How might stress affect your performance in sport?
4 Explain how pollution can affect fitness.
5 Could a person be fitter at 40 than at 20? Explain.

1.7 Somatotyping

Would you make a good gymnast? Or a good wrestler? Success in a sport depends to a large extent on your build.

We inherit our body shape from our parents but we can train to get stronger bone and muscle and reduce fat.

Somatotyping is a way to describe build. It looks at how fat, how muscular and how linear you are, in that order. This shows the extreme examples:

Extreme endomorph

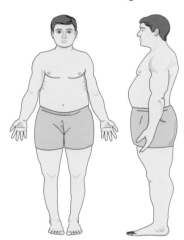

- ◉ wide hips and narrow shoulders (pear-shaped)
- ◉ a lot of fat on the body
- ◉ a lot of fat on the upper arms and thighs
- ◉ quite slim wrists and ankles

Endomorphs stay pear-shaped even when they lose weight.

Extreme mesomorph

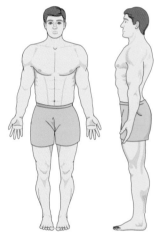

- ◉ broad shoulders and narrow hips (wedge-shaped)
- ◉ a large head
- ◉ a muscular body
- ◉ strong forearms and thighs
- ◉ very little body fat

***M**esomorphs have **m**uscles.*

Extreme ectomorph

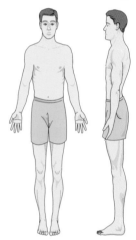

- ◉ narrow shoulders and hips
- ◉ a thin face and high forehead
- ◉ a thin narrow chest and abdomen
- ◉ thin legs and arms
- ◉ very little muscle or body fat

*Ec**t**omorphs are **t**hin and often **t**all.*

Sport and somatotypes

In any sport where you have to lift your body weight (jumping) or take it over long distances, you want to be as light as possible whilst still retaining muscle strength. Look at the sizes of people's wrists in your group. This is an indicator of frame size. Bone and muscle are very heavy and you would waste a lot of energy carrying large ones when doing long distance running. On the other hand, if you have too little muscle you would not have the muscular endurance to run long distances. The ideal build for a long-distance runner is ectomorph with some mesomorph.

Long-distance runners need strength with no excess body weight.

People whose sports require throwing or jumping need long levers (long bones). The longer the lever the more force or power you can give to the throwing object. Think of the differences in power when hitting with a rounders bat compared to a softball bat, i.e. a short lever compared to a long one. However, you still require muscles to help you generate the explosive strength. The ideal build is mesomorph with ectomorph.

In sports requiring balance, e.g. gymnastics, it is best to have short levers because then your centre of mass stays nearer to the middle of your body and helps you balance. The ideal build is mesomorph.

Finally, in sports where there is contact, it is better to have plenty of body weight. In just about every sport it is best if this extra weight is muscle rather than fat. Rugby players who are in the front row of the scrum tend to be very muscular, heavy and shorter than the rest of the team. This helps them to knock others over and keep well balanced themselves.

Somatotyping top athletes

The chart below shows average ratings for top male athletes.

They are all towards the mesomorph end. That proves the importance of muscle at this level! As you'd expect, weight lifters, wrestlers and weight throwers are more endomorphic than other athletes.

Javelin throwers need long levers.

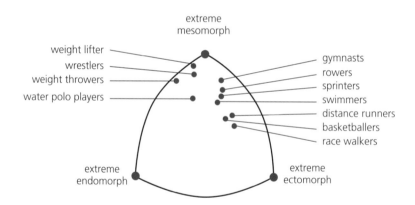

extreme mesomorph

weight lifter
wrestlers
weight throwers
water polo players

gymnasts
rowers
sprinters
swimmers
distance runners
basketballers
race walkers

extreme endomorph

extreme ectomorph

Rugby prop forwards need a low centre of mass.

QUESTIONS

1 What is *somatotyping*?

2 Which body build has: **a** most muscle? **b** most fat? **c** least muscle and fat?

3 Can you change your build completely? Explain.

4 What do you think would be the ideal build for: **a** a hurdler? **b** a long jumper? **c** a jockey?

5 Draw a little diagram that helps you to remember the differences between somatotypes. Label each one.

Questions on chapter 1

1   Katherine is a good footballer.
   a   Give three specific areas of fitness she would want to improve during training and explain why.
   b   She has good all round general fitness but what two areas might she want to improve further and why?
   c   Katherine's build is mainly ectomorph. Can she change this to make herself more suitable for football? Explain your answer fully.
   d   Katherine and her friend Paul are similar in their ability in Year 7. Will this stay the same as they become adults? Give three reasons to explain your answer.
   e   As stated earlier, Katherine's build is mainly ectomorph. Name two other sports that this suggests she might be good at?
   f   Obviously your build only suggests what you might excel at. A tall mesomorph might be good at discus.
      i   What is there to suggest this?
      ii   What other areas of fitness would they also need to be good at?
   g   Katherine's dad, Mike, is forty years old. He does no exercise. List three changes that will be occurring in his body that will cause his fitness to drop.
   h   Mike's friend Pete is fifty-five years old. He is a marathon runner and much fitter than Mike. How can this be when he is fifteen years older than him?

2   Jamie is a shy fourteen-year-old. He is slightly overweight and does not really enjoy games where he has to run long distances and get muddy and wet. He has just moved to a new area and has no real hobbies.
   a   Name three sports he could take up in or out of school.
   b   Which physical benefit would he gain the most from?
   c   What three mental benefits would really help him?
   d   What two social benefits would help him?
   e   If Jamie took up swimming to get fitter, how often and for how long should he do it?
   f   What might Jamie consider a good performance from himself?

3   Say whether the statements below are true or false.
   a   Gardening and cleaning are forms of exercise.
   b   It is not possible for a seventy-year-old to be fit.
   c   There is no connection between health and fitness.
   d   Environment just means the air around you.
   e   Exercise improves your fitness.
   f   The fitter you are, the more demands you can meet.
   g   If your normal activities make you feel worn out, that means you are unfit.

4   Nathan is sixteen. He has not enjoyed school and has many difficulties at home. He used to have many problems with getting into fights until he started playing rugby on a regular basis.
   a   Why is rugby a good sport for Nathan?
   b   Give two other mental benefits that will aid his well-being.
   c   Do you think it would be good for a rugby player to work on all-over flexibility? At what joints should rugby players have good flexibility and where do they not want it? Explain your answer.
   d   In the following scenario, state the area of fitness Nathan needs:
      i   From the kick-off Nathan sprints after the ball.
      ii   It unexpectedly bounces off the opposition and goes sideways. Nathan immediately responds and gets to the ball first.
      iii He picks up the ball, dodges a tackle,
      iv   and then passes a long ball out to the wing.

5   a   What is fitness?
   b   A county tennis player and an international tennis player both need to be fit. But the international player needs a higher level of fitness. Do you agree? Explain your answer.

6   The physical demands on each of the people below are different. Arrange them in order, with the least demanding first.
   •   a member of the England rowing team
   •   a bus conductor
   •   an office worker who sits at a desk all day
   •   an under-sixteen county football player
   •   a seventy-year-old bedridden person
   •   an Olympic triathlon champion

7   Your physical surroundings, and what you eat, affect your health and therefore your fitness. Think of one example where people's health has been affected by:
   a   air pollution
   b   water pollution
   c   noise
   d   sunshine
   e   infected food

8   For each of the following systems say:
   a   what it is made up of
   b   what its job is.
   Skeletal   Circulatory   Respiratory
   Digestive   Nervous   Muscular

9

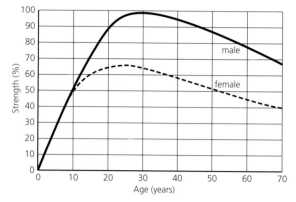

The graph above shows how strength changes with age for people who don't do much exercise.

a From the age of 11 onwards, males become stronger than females. Why is this?

b Around what age are both at their strongest?

c Why do people lose strength as they get older?

d By the age of seventy, people have lost a lot of strength. Give three examples of problems this might cause in everyday life.

e What can you do to slow down strength loss as you get older?

10 a What is body composition?

b How do males and females differ in terms of:
  i body fat?
  ii muscle?
  iii bone?
  iv volume of blood?
  v amount of haemoglobin?

11 A comparison of world records for male and female athletes shows that:
- in the 100 m sprint, males are about 5% faster.
- in the marathon, males are about 10% faster.
- in the long jump, males jump nearly 16% further.

a Why do males do better in running events than females?

b Why is the difference bigger for the marathon than for the 100 m sprint?

c Why can male long jumpers jump further?

12 The three body types are:
A endomorph
B mesomorph
C ectomorph
Match each description below to A, B or C.
i broad muscular shoulders and narrow hips
ii plump and pear-shaped
iii thin narrow chest and shoulders

13 Look again at the body systems in question 8. Which do you think are affected by exercise?

14 Smoking affects your health and fitness. Below are figures from research carried out some years ago.

	Deaths from lung cancer per 100 000 people
non-smokers	7
light smokers	47
moderate smokers	86
heavy smokers	166

What can you say about the relationship between smoking and lung cancer?

15 In 1996 the UK health care system spent £1,600 million helping those with heart disease. 1% of this was spent on preventing it. Imagine you are the Minister for Health. Try to think of five things you would do to make the population of the UK more healthy.

16 In most sports, winners and losers are easily identified.
  a How are points awarded in sports like gymnastics?
  b What name is given to these creative, artistic sports?

USE OF INFORMATION TECHNOLOGY

17 Half the group should find data relating exercise to age. In pairs, or small groups, choose one of the following 4 areas to find data on:
i age and cardiovascular
ii age and bones
iii age and muscles (strength)
iv age and flexibility
(Typing these words into a search engine on the internet can produce a lot of resource material.)

The other half of the group should find data relating exercise to gender. In pairs, or small groups, choose one of the following 4 areas to find data on:
i gender and cardiovascular
ii gender and bones
iii gender and muscles (strength)
iv gender and flexibility

All groups should produce a report, one paragraph or so but no more than half a page, ready for presentation to the others. If facilities allow, then presentation through software such as Powerpoint could be used.

Other useful words for use in search engines:
Age: "old age", "growth". Gender: "male" ,"female", "difference". Cardiovascular: "heart", "lungs". Bones: "osteo" (bones on its own will turn up many sites to do with fossils, exclude these. Yahoo uses the "-" to exclude words so putting "-fossils" or "-prehistoric" in the search engine will get rid of these sites. Other search engines will have similar exclude facilities.)

2.1 Bones

How tall will you be? Will you be petite or will you have thick, heavy bones? As mentioned in the previous chapter, bone/body size is an important factor in high-level sports. Bones don't stop growing completely until you are in your early twenties.

The composition of a typical adult long bone

The arm and leg bones of an adult look like this:

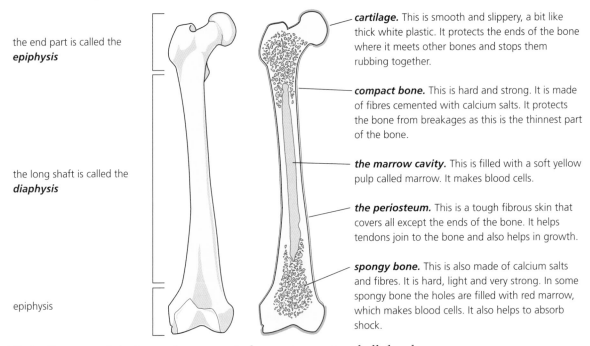

the end part is called the **epiphysis**

the long shaft is called the **diaphysis**

epiphysis

cartilage. This is smooth and slippery, a bit like thick white plastic. It protects the ends of the bone where it meets other bones and stops them rubbing together.

compact bone. This is hard and strong. It is made of fibres cemented with calcium salts. It protects the bone from breakages as this is the thinnest part of the bone.

the marrow cavity. This is filled with a soft yellow pulp called marrow. It makes blood cells.

the periosteum. This is a tough fibrous skin that covers all except the ends of the bone. It helps tendons join to the bone and also helps in growth.

spongy bone. This is also made of calcium salts and fibres. It is hard, light and very strong. In some spongy bone the holes are filled with red marrow, which makes blood cells. It also helps to absorb shock.

All the features of the bone above are vital to us in sport and all develop with training.

Cartilage. Imagine how our bones would rub together if we did not have cartilage. Exercise causes cartilage to become thicker, so our joints move smoothly and absorb shock better as we jump or run.

Compact bone. This becomes thicker as we train and exercise. This means we are better protected against impact injuries and thicker bones mean we can train with heavier weights.

Marrow cavity. This produces red and white blood cells. With regular exercise this process is speeded up. More blood cells means more blood, and this means more oxygen can be carried round the body. This in turn means more exercise can be performed.

Periosteum. One of the functions of the periosteum is to lay down bone cells so the bone grows in width. With exercise this process is increased so our bones are thicker and stronger.

Spongy bone. If our bones grow thicker we must also have more spongy bone. This helps with shock absorption and making more blood cells.

The skeleton

Without your skeleton you'd be just a shapeless sack of flesh. The skeleton has 206 bones, held together at **joints** by strong fibres called **ligaments**. These are its main bones:

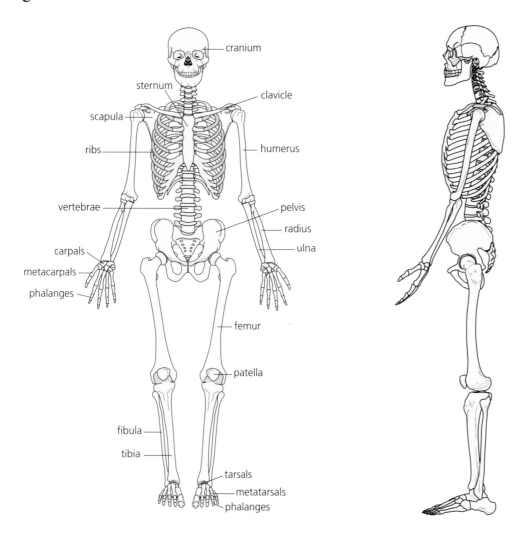

Each arm and leg has three long bones. Look at the bone sticking out at the end of the backbone, in the side view. It's the remains of a tail!

QUESTIONS

1 Imagine you had just played a game of hockey. How would the composition of your bones have aided you in this game?

2 Without looking at the diagram, see if you can quickly sketch a typical long bone and put on all five labels.

3 Why should jockeys not do a vast amount of strength training?

4 Thicker bones mean we can lift heavier weights when training. What lays down bone cells to make the bone grow in width?

5 Why do American footballers and rugby players need thick strong bones?

6 Name the bones that make up the **a** knee joint **b** hip joint **c** shoulder joint

7 What do you think happens to bone if you are in hospital for a long time or do hardly any exercise?

2.2 The functions of the skeleton

1 **Shape and support.** These two functions are similar. The bones form a framework to support your body just like steel girders in a building. The different length and thickness of the bones determine our individual shape and what sports we are most suitable for, although when playing for fun or at a low level it does not matter. Remember the information from the last chapter about this.

2 **Protection.** Bones surround the areas that are delicate and could get damaged. The vertebral bones surround our spinal cord, and our skull acts as an internal crash helmet to protect our brain. Our ribs and sternum act as a flexible but strong surround to protect lungs, heart, kidneys, etc.

3 **Movement.** Your muscles are firmly attached to your skeleton. Muscles work by contracting or getting shorter. When they contract they pull on bones. This makes the bones move. The longer the bones, the greater the range of movement possible. The shorter the bone, the easier it is to generate power.

4 **Blood production.** Bones make blood cells in the marrow cavity and spongy bone. These cells are then used to transport gases around the body.

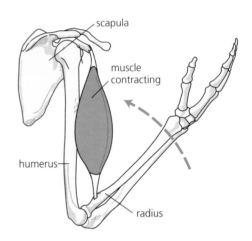

Bones move when muscles contract.

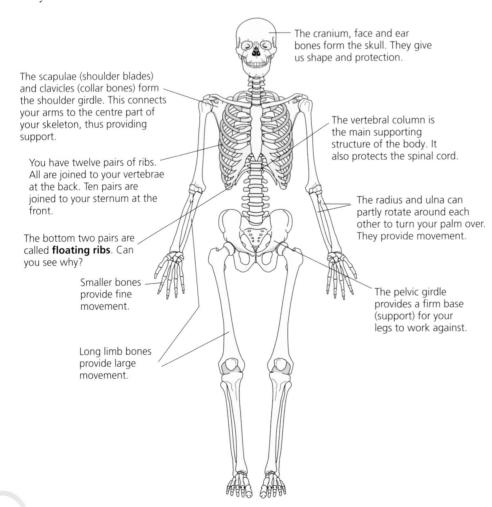

The cranium, face and ear bones form the skull. They give us shape and protection.

The scapulae (shoulder blades) and clavicles (collar bones) form the shoulder girdle. This connects your arms to the centre part of your skeleton, thus providing support.

You have twelve pairs of ribs. All are joined to your vertebrae at the back. Ten pairs are joined to your sternum at the front.

The bottom two pairs are called **floating ribs**. Can you see why?

Smaller bones provide fine movement.

Long limb bones provide large movement.

The vertebral column is the main supporting structure of the body. It also protects the spinal cord.

The radius and ulna can partly rotate around each other to turn your palm over. They provide movement.

The pelvic girdle provides a firm base (support) for your legs to work against.

The four types of bones in your skeleton

Your bones are different shapes and sizes because they have different jobs to do. They are divided into four groups:

1 **Long bones.** These are shaped like the bone on page 22. They have a diaphysis, epiphyses and a hollow centre. Your height, shoe size and glove size depend on long bones.
Examples: the bones of the upper and lower arms and legs, the collar bone, the ribs, the metatarsals, metacarpals and phalanges.

2 **Short bones.** These are small and squat. They are spongy bone covered with a thin layer of compact bone. So they are light and very strong.
Examples: the carpals of the wrist, the tarsals of the feet.

3 **Flat bones.** These are spongy bone between two layers of compact bone. They have a large surface area.
Examples: the scapula, pelvis and cranium. The scapula and pelvis need a large area for all the muscles that attach to them. The cranium needs a large area to protect the brain.

4 **Irregular bones.** These are spongy bone inside and compact bone outside. They are specially shaped to suit the job they have to do.
Examples: the vertebrae.

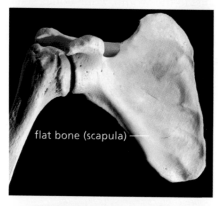
short bone (carpal)
long bone (radius)
long bone (phalange)

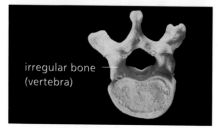
flat bone (scapula)

irregular bone (vertebra)

Functions

◎ **Long bones.** These mainly act as levers for a large range of movement, e.g. the very long ones (radius, ulna and humerus) all work together to allow you to hit a shuttlecock a long way in badminton. The smaller long bones, e.g. phalanges and metacarpals, allow you to perform more delicate movements, like net shots. People who do sports where you need to impart momentum to things, often have long levers.

◎ **Short bones.** These provide movement where it is needed in lots of directions but also give strength.

◎ **Flat bones.** These protect delicate organs and give a big surface area for muscle attachment.

◎ **Irregular bones.** These protect for example the spinal cord, and provide support.

QUESTIONS

1 In some sports the bones alone cannot provide enough protection. Name three sports and three pieces of extra protective equipment that are used in them.

2 Apart from identical twins, all fifty-eight million of us in Britain look different. Why?

3 What bones protect **a** our brain **b** our spinal cord **c** our heart?

4 Bones cannot move on their own and yet this is a function of the skeleton. How do they provide movement?

5 Name two sports where it would be good to have long thin bones. Explain.

6 Name a sport where it would be good to have long thick bones. Explain.

7 Name a sport where it would be good to have short thick bones. Explain.

8 Are the following bones long, short, flat or irregular? **a** radius **b** cranium **c** carpal **d** humerus **e** vertebra **f** metatarsal **g** phalange **h** scapula.

2.3 Bone growth

How bones grow

Inside the womb, your bones start life as **cartilage**. Over the years this turns into bone in a process called **ossification**. **Ossification is the development and growth of bone.** This shows what happens:

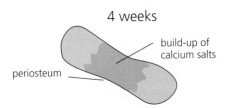

4 weeks

periosteum

build-up of calcium salts

A periosteum grows round the cartilage. It will control the shape and thickness of the bone. Then calcium salts build up.

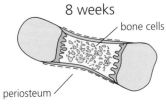

8 weeks

bone cells

periosteum

Bone cells appear in the middle. They start changing the cartilage into bone. The periosteum also lays down bone.

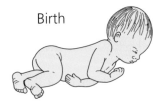

Birth

By the time you are born, bones are still mostly cartilage. They are quite soft and easily bent.

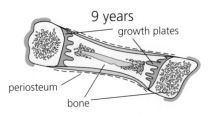

9 years

growth plates

periosteum

bone

Next, bone cells appear at the ends and change these to bone. Two bands of cartilage remain. They are called **growth plates** *or* **EPIPHYSEAL PLATES.**

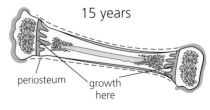

15 years

periosteum

growth here

The plates grow at the outer edge so the bone gets longer. At the same time the inner edge is being turned into bone. The periosteum continues to lay down cells so the width grows slowly.

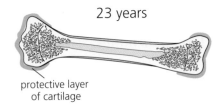

23 years

protective layer of cartilage

Growth stops when the plates are all bone. Now the only cartilage left in the bone is the thin layer at each end.

The whole process is controlled by hormones. If there is too much **growth hormone**, the cartilage in the plates grows too fast and the person could end up a giant. If there is too little the person fails to grow.

It is vital at these ages that children do not overdo certain kinds of exercise. Weight training, hard contact sports and long-distance road running could cause the bone – still cartilage in places – to grow unevenly, causing problems such as bow legs. It is equally important that exercise is done regularly to promote good bone growth.

Diet and bone growth

Diet will be discussed in Chapter 8 in greater detail. The most important nutrients for growth are proteins, vitamins and minerals.

Proteins. These build cells and repair damage and are found in milk, cheese, meats, eggs, fish, pulses, and nuts.

Vitamins. There are many kinds. Vitamin D helps you to absorb calcium into your body and is found in milk, fish, liver, and eggs. Our body can also make it when we are in sunshine.

Minerals. Again there are many of these. Calcium gives us strong bones and teeth and is found in milk, cheese, fish, and green vegetables.

Vitamins and **minerals** cannot be stored in the body so we need a regular supply.

Bone cells and exercise

Even when a bone has stopped growing, it is full of life. Bone cells called **osteoblasts** make new bone and at the same time cells called **osteoclasts** break it down. Exercise causes osteoblasts to work harder and makes bones strong and thick.

Press-ups get those osteoblasts going! But in space, weightlessness means both bones and muscles will weaken. So an exercise machine is part of the astronaut's space kit.

Bones and ageing

Bones get lighter as you age; exercising to make the osteoblasts work is vital. Men's bones tend to be thicker than women's and many older women suffer from osteoporosis, where bones get so weak they break easily. Gentle cardiovascular exercise (avoiding high impact) can help prevent this. It is very important to keep exercising when you get old.

Optimum weight

We looked at the importance of bone size for specific sports in the last chapter. In some sports you may even want to develop and strengthen some bones but not others. Boxers do a lot of upper body strength work, thickening their arm bones, but do not want to do this to their legs. Can you think why?

Ideal weight for everyday life varies. An adult who is 1.7m tall could weigh anywhere between 57kg (small frame with small bones) and 76kg (big frame).

QUESTIONS

1 Name the skin-like substance that causes bone to grow in width.

2 Name the plates that cause it to grow in length.

3 Why is it correct for an adult to lift heavy weights repeatedly but not a child?

4 Name two other types of training that are bad for youngsters.

5 Why would you recommend to an elderly person that they should take a little walk each day.

6 Name the three most important nutrients for bone growth.

7 The optimum weight for a person who is 1.7m tall can vary by up to 19 kilograms. How can this be?

8 If you were a marathon runner do you think it would be good to do lots of training to make your bones really strong and thick? Explain your answer.

2.4 The vertebral column

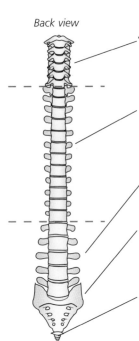

Back view

Side view

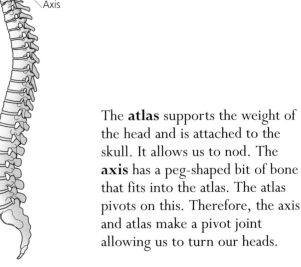

CERVICAL VERTEBRAE – (7) [*say:* 'sir vic all']
This is your neck. It provides the attachment for neck muscles. It also includes the two bones called the **ATLAS** and **AXIS**.

THORACIC VERTEBRAE – (12) [*say:* 'thaw rass ick']
The ribs are attached to these. They form part of the chest area.

LUMBAR VERTEBRAE – (5)
These are the largest individual vertebrae. They support the weight of the others and lots of movement occurs here.

SACRUM – (5) [*say:* 'say crumb']
These are FUSED together to make a large triangular bone. This is also fused to your pelvis. (Fused = stuck together.)

COCCYX – (4) [*say:* 'cock ix']
These are fused together as well. This is the remains of our tail. Now it is used for muscle attachment.

How many pieces are there?

A little trick to remember:

Keep saying the numbers to a beat:
7 12 5 5 4

Now use the rhyme opposite to remember their order

Cute	Cervical	(neck)	7
Teddies	Thoracic	(attached to ribs)	12
Love	Lumbar	(lower back)	5
Some	Sacrum	(pelvis)	5
Cuddles	Coccyx	(tail remains)	4

The parts of a vertebra

A single vertebra, seen from above.

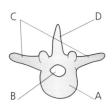

The spinal cord.

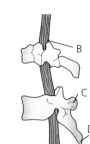

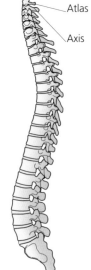

A The bit of the bone which supports the weight of the other vertebrae

B The gap through which the spinal cord passes

C
D Muscles attach to these

Atlas and Axis

Atlas

Axis

The top two bones of the cervical vertebrae.

The **atlas** supports the weight of the head and is attached to the skull. It allows us to nod. The **axis** has a peg-shaped bit of bone that fits into the atlas. The atlas pivots on this. Therefore, the axis and atlas make a pivot joint allowing us to turn our heads.

Why the spine may be regarded as weak for some activities

Look at the spine's shape. It is fairly thin for the weight we expect it to carry and support. Any activity where we have to lift or carry additional weight can be dangerous. If we break our spine we will damage our spinal cord. This can result in paralysis or death.

Look at the shape of the neck area. This is particularly vulnerable to injury. Lower down, the spine is supported by ribs and it becomes thicker. In rugby, if the scrum collapses, the front row can easily damage their necks.

Look at the movement the back does. It looks very flexible . . .

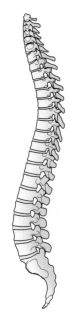

. . . but in fact it's not!

Between each vertebra you have a disc of cartilage. When you bend over there is a small amount of movement between each one. Because we have so many vertebrae, a small amount of movement between each one allows a lot of movement overall.

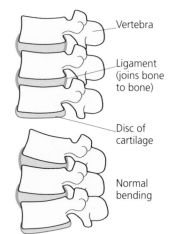

Vertebra

Ligament
(joins bone
to bone)

Disc of
cartilage

Normal
bending

If you lift something badly or bend over or twist unexpectedly you can tear or strain the ligaments holding the vertebrae together. You may slip a disc.

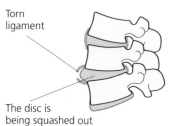

Torn
ligament

The disc is being squashed out of position by bending too far

A slipped disc in the normal standing position is pressing on the spinal cord causing pain

Slipped disc

Spinal cord

QUESTIONS

1 Copy the table below and add 2 neck-related examples of your own.

Sport	Incident	Possible result
Rugby	Collapsed scrum	Body weight lands on your neck at a bad angle and breaks it

2 When we play golf, the spine seems to move a lot. How can this be?

3 List the four functions of the skeleton. (Try not to look them up!)

4 Using the above answers as headings, explain how the vertebrae help to fulfil those functions.

5 a What are the top two bones of the cervical vertebrae called? b What is the job/function of each?

2.5 Different kinds of joints

Your skeleton is made up of bones. **Joints are where two, or more, bones meet.** They are divided into three types depending on how freely the bones can move. If we did not have joints no movement could occur.

Fixed or immoveable joints

The bones at an immoveable joint can't move at all. They interlock or overlap, and are held close together by tough fibre. The joints between the plates in the cranium are a good example. The fused joints in the sacrum are another example. We have this type of joint in areas requiring great strength.

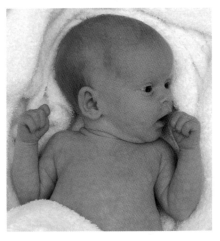

Gaps between plates in the cranium allow a baby's head to squash during birth. Twelve months later the gaps will have closed and fixed joints will have started to form. This strong joint will then almost completely protect the brain.

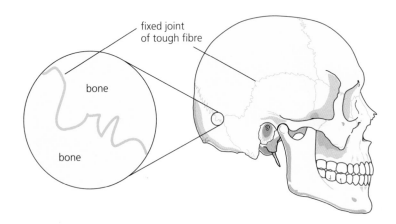

Slightly moveable joints

The bones at a slightly moveable joint can move only a little. They are held together by strong white cords or straps called ligaments and joined by **cartilage**. This is like a gristly cushion. It stops the bones from knocking together. It can squash a little to let them move.

The joints between most of your vertebrae are slightly moveable. The pads of cartilage between them act as shock absorbers so the bones won't jar when you run and jump.

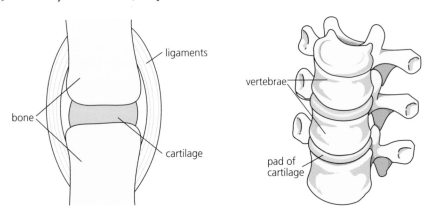

The joints between your ribs and sternum are also slightly moveable. They move a little when you breathe in and out.

Freely moveable joints

At a freely moveable joint the bones can move quite freely. The knee joint is a good example.

A freely moveable joint has these parts:
◉ an outer sleeve called the **joint capsule**. This holds the bones together and protects the joint. It is an extension of the skin or periosteum that covers each bone.
◉ a **synovial membrane**. This lines the capsule and oozes a slippery liquid called synovial fluid.
◉ a **joint cavity**. This is the small gap between the bones. It is filled with synovial fluid. This lubricates the joint so that the bones can move more easily.
◉ a covering of smooth slippery **cartilage** on the ends of the bones. It stops the bones knocking together.
◉ **ligaments** which hold the bones together and keep them in place. Freely moveable joints are also called **synovial joints**. (Why?)

Most of your joints are synovial. Otherwise you couldn't move so easily! The elbow, shoulder, hip and finger joints are examples.

Before we look at types of synovial joints (pages 34-35) we are going to look at types of movement (pages 32-33). Knowing about these will help you to understand what is possible at each type of joint.

Joints and injury

Joints can be damaged by general wear and tear or impact.
◉ Impact. Severe contact, e.g. falling from a horse onto your shoulder, could cause dislocation. This is where a bone is pulled out of its normal position at the joint. It would cause tearing of ligaments (sprain) and tendons. These would also tear with injuries such as going over on an ankle.
◉ Wear and tear. Exercise of a joint or an unusual use of it (perhaps due to another injury) could cause cartilage to be worn away. Just as in impact injuries, the joint would then swell causing it to stiffen – the body's way to tell you to stop moving it! In elderly people this wear and tear can cause arthritis. This makes the joint stiff and swollen.

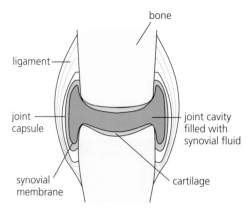

Knee joint from the back

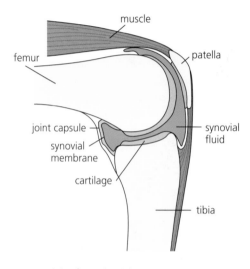

Knee joint from the side

QUESTIONS

1 What is a joint?

2 Describe: **a** a fixed joint **b** a slightly moveable joint. Give two examples of each.

3 Which type of joint is the most common in your body? Give four examples.

4 **a** Draw and label a synovial joint. **b** Explain what job each part does.

5 Why do we need joints?

6 Name two ways a joint could be injured.

7 Name two actual injuries.

8 Which type of joint is the most useful for sport?

9 What parts of a synovial joint **a** make it strong and stable **b** help it move easily.

10 How could an acute ankle injury lead to joint pains in your knee and hip?

11 What is the main purpose of the immoveable joints in our skull?

2.6 Movement

Flexion and extension

Extension means straightening a part of the body to its normal position. **Flexion** means bending it. (**Flexion** is nearly always **Forward**.)

*When you stand straight like this, your arms, legs, head, hands and feet are **extended** to their normal position.*

*Here the right arm is bent or flexed at the elbow joint. The left leg is **flexed** at the knee joint.*

When you run you repeatedly flex and extend your hip, knee, ankle, elbow and shoulder joints.

Some more examples of flexion:

arm at
shoulder joint

arm at elbow and
shoulder joint

leg at hip and
knee joint

back at
hip joints

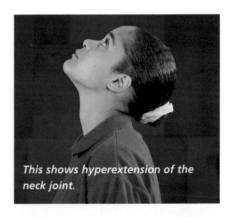

This shows hyperextension of the neck joint.

Abduction and adduction

Imagine a line drawn down the centre of your body. Abduction is a sideways movement of a limb, out from the centre line.

*Adduction is a sideways movement, like this, towards and even across the centre line. (A**dd**uction is towards the mi**dd**le!)*

This karate kick is an example of abduction. Can you think of another example from tennis? Or from gymnastics?

Rotation and circumduction

These are circular movements.

Rotation is a turning movement around an imaginary line, like a wheel turning on its axis. Turning your head is an example.

This backwards walkover is another example. The girl's body is rotating like a wheel on an imaginary axis.

In circumduction, the end of a bone moves in a circle. Swinging your arm in a circle is an example. Bowlers do it!

Joints, flexibility and health

All of the movements shown require a degree of flexibility. Risk of injury can be lessened if we make our joints more flexible and strong. The first step in this is a good healthy diet, which will give us strong bones, ligaments, tendons and cartilage. Regular exercise will strengthen them all and regular flexibility work will allow a greater range of movement due to increased elasticity. Look at the karate picture opposite. This person can balance and apply a high kick due to good hip flexibility. In some joints you may wish to only have limited flexibility to reduce injury, e.g. shoulders in a rugby player.

A lack of exercise leads to a decrease in flexibility. This is a big problem for the elderly who find it difficult to do everyday tasks, e.g. turning a steering wheel and picking up shopping. Gentle exercise will help to remedy this.

QUESTIONS

1 Sit straight in your chair, elbows by your sides, hands flat on your knees, feet flat on the floor. **a** Which joints are flexed? **b** Name two joints that are extended.

2 Stand up and show an example of: **a** adduction **b** abduction

3 In swimming front crawl what movements occur at your hips?

4 In breast stroke what movements occur at your hips?

5 Stretch your arm straight out palm up. Turn your palm over. What movement occurred?

6 For the photo above: **a** name each numbered joint **b** name the movement that has occured at it to bring it to this position.

7 When doing the Fosbury flop in high jump you arch your back over the bar. What is the movement at your hips and vertebrae?

2.7 Synovial joints

Most of your joints are freely moveable or synovial joints. They allow different kinds of movement, depending on the shape of the bones at the joint, and the ligaments that hold them together. The shoulder, hip and ankle are quite susceptible to injury due to the amount of movement possible at them. Sudden impact or over extension, etc. could cause dislocation or the tearing of ligaments and tendons.

These drawings show just the bones.

The ball-and-socket joint

This is the most moveable joint in the body. One bone has a bulge like a ball at the end. This fits into a socket in the other bone. It can turn in many directions.

Examples

◎ the hip joint. Cross over steps in badminton are caused by abduction and adduction, running comes from flexion and extension.
◎ the shoulder joint. Cricket bowling from circumduction, spin bowling in rounders from rotation.

The hinge joint

This works like a hinge on a door. The bone can swing backwards and forwards. The end of one bone is shaped like a cotton reel. It fits into a hollow in the other. The joint will open until it's straight, but no further.

Examples

◎ the elbow joint. Flexion and extension cause press-ups.
◎ the knee joint. Flexion and extension in horse riding cause rising trot.

The pivot joint

One bone has a bit that juts out, like a peg or a ridge. This fits into a ring or notch on the other bone. The joint allows only rotation.

Examples

◎ the joint between the atlas and axis. Rotation results in looking from side to side.
◎ the joint between the radius and ulna, below the elbow. Rotation here results in changing from backhand to forehand in table tennis, squash and badminton.

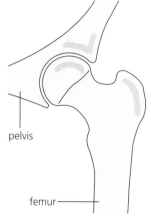

pelvis

femur

Hip joint

Types of movement: ALL

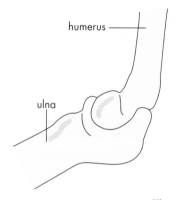

humerus

ulna

Elbow joint

Types of movement: FLEXION and EXTENSION

atlas

vertebrae

axis

Joint in neck

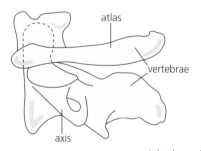

Types of movement: ROTATION

The gliding joint

Here the ends of the bones are flat enough to glide over each other. There is a little movement in all directions. Of all the synovial joints, this one gives least movement.

Examples

◉ the joints between carpals (hand) and tarsals (foot). Flexion and extension give final direction to a thrown object.

◉ the joints between most of the vertebrae. Rotation here helps to impart force in golf swings.

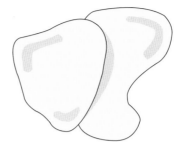

Types of movement:
FLEXION, EXTENSION, ABDUCTION AND ADDUCTION

Joint between two carpals.

Cartilage, ligaments and tendons

Cartilage protects bones and stops them knocking together. It forms a gristly cushion between the bones at slightly moveable joints. It forms a smooth slippery coat on the ends of bones at synovial joints.

Ligaments are the strong cords and straps that lash bones together and hold a joint in place. They are just a bit elastic – enough to let the bones move. (If bones moved too much they would tear your flesh.)

Tendons are the cords and straps that connect muscle to bone. The best known joins our calf muscle to our heel and is called the Achilles tendon.

Joints and movement: a summary

This is a summary of the different kinds of movement that different joints allow.

Type of joint	Movement allowed
ball-and-socket	flexion and extension
	abduction and adduction
	rotation and circumduction
hinge	flexion and extension
pivot	only rotation
gliding	a little gliding in all directions (no bending or circular movements)

QUESTIONS

1 Look at the shape of the ball-and-socket joint. Why do you think it is difficult to dislocate it?

2 What are the major joints (location and type) that are moving when you are running?

3 In what joint would a cricket bowler want to be very flexible?

4 Why would players of American football and rugby not want to be flexible in this particular joint?

5 In what joints would a batter in any sport want to be flexible?

6 Where in our body do we find **a** cartilage **b** ligaments **c** tendons? (In a joint is not enough.)

7 Name one tendon.

8 Why do you think that it is difficult to improve flexibility at a hinge joint?

9 Explain how **a** cartilage helps you when you land heavily **b** tendons help you to move.

Section I   The body

Questions on chapter 2

1

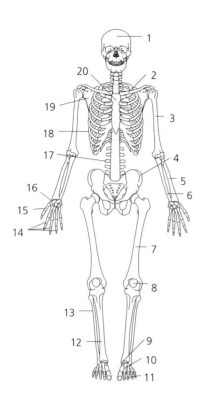

a Write the numbers 1 to 20 in a list, to match the numbers on the skeleton above.

b Beside each number write the correct scientific name for the bone.

2 Bones are long, short, irregular or flat. To which group do these bones belong?

a the bones of the cranium

b the humerus

c the carpals of the hand.

d the metatarsals

e the bones of the pelvis

f the vertebrae

3 The next diagram shows the vertebral column. Use it and the information to complete the table.

	Name	Number of vertebrae	Description
A			
B			
C			
D			
E			
F			
G			

a In the first empty column, fill in the correct name for the labelled part. Choose from this list:

   lumbar vertebrae, axis, cervical vertebrae, thoracic vertebrae, coccyx, atlas, sacrum

b In the second empty column, write the number of vertebrae in that part. Choose from this list:

   1   1   4   5   5   7   12

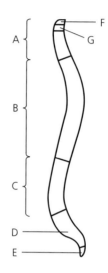

c In the third empty column, write the correct description. Choose from this list:

   allows the head to turn from side to side
   each vertebra connects with a pair of ribs
   forms a large triangular bone
   the largest and strongest vertebra
   the remnants of a tail
   vertebrae of the neck region allows the head to nod

4 Which two of these statements are correct?

The vertebral column is protected against damage by jarring because:

A its shape makes it act like a spring

B no movement between the vertebrae is allowed

C the discs of cartilage act as shock absorbers

D ligaments hold the vertebrae firmly in position

5 What bones are most likely to get damaged in football with impact injuries.

6 What safety item is worn to prevent this.

7 The most common impact injuries in netball and basketball are in the fingers and ankles. Why is this?

8 What damage could be done by dislocating a finger?

9 In sports involving running or jumping on a hard surface, ankle and knee joints can get worn out. Explain how this occurs.

10 How do the vertebrae help us with shape and support?

11 How do the ribs help protect us?

12 How can bones help us move?

13 The bones of a fit person produce more blood cells than those of unfit people. Why is this important to a sports person?

14 What three nutrients are essential for strong bones?

15 What mineral is most important?

16 Why shouldn't children and teenagers lift heavy weights in regular strength training?

17 The vertebral column can easily be damaged in many sports. What is it about its structure that makes it vulnerable to injury?

18 Give two examples from sports where the vertebral column could get damaged.

19 Which of your three types of joints are most useful in sport?

20 As young bones grow, bone replaces cartilage. What is this process called?

A ossification
B osteoarthritis
C osteopathy
D osteoporosis

21 Copy this table. Then complete it by filling in the everyday names of the bones.

Bone	Everyday name
cranium	skull
scapula	
sternum	
clavicle	
femur	
phalanges (foot)	
metatarsals	
tarsals	
tibia	
patella	
phalanges (hand)	
metacarpals	

22 The drawing below shows joints of the body:

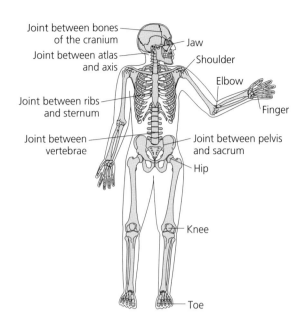

Joint between bones of the cranium
Jaw
Joint between atlas and axis
Shoulder
Elbow
Joint between ribs and sternum
Finger
Joint between vertebrae
Joint between pelvis and sacrum
Hip
Knee
Toe

a Make a table with five columns. Write these five headings on the columns:

Fixed   Slightly moveable   Ball-and-socket
Hinge   Pivot

b Now write each joint from the drawing in the correct column in the table.

23 Answer these questions about bones.

a Name a substance that is needed to form strong and healthy bones.

b Give two examples of foods which will provide this substance.

c What job does the cartilage on the ends of the bones do?

d Bones have spongy parts. How does this help you in playing sports?

e In which part of the bone are red blood cells made?

f Are red cells made in all bones?

g Around what age does the skeleton stop growing?

h How many vertebrae are there in the vertebral column?

24 a Draw and label an adult long bone

b Now write what each part of the bone does.

USE OF INFORMATION TECHNOLOGY

25 Typing the following phrases into a search engine on the internet will give you many sites to explore.

a skeleton, bones, -fossil, -prehistoric (note: the - sign means you will get rid of sites containing the words fossil and prehistoric)

b bone, marrow, ossification, calcium, -fossil, -prehistoric

c bone, joint, injury

3.1 Different kinds of muscle

You could not live without muscles. You couldn't breathe or digest food or even blink. They are involved in every movement of your body, inside and out.

All muscles work by shortening or **contracting**. When muscles between your mouth and jaw bones contract, you smile!

There are three different kinds of muscle in your body.

Voluntary muscle

This is attached to bones. It works when you want it to. Voluntary means *by your own free will*.

Suppose you decide to run or throw a ball. A signal races from your brain, along your nervous system, to the voluntary muscles needed for this job. The muscles contract, pulling on bones. This gives movement.

Voluntary muscle is also called:
◎ **skeletal muscle** because it is attached to bones
◎ **striped muscle** because when you look at it under a miscroscope you can see stripes across it.

Involuntary muscle

This is found in the walls of your internal organs: stomach, gut, bladder and blood vessels. It is called involuntary because it works on its own. You don't need to think about it.

When you digest food, the involuntary muscle in the walls of your gut contracts in waves, pushing the food along. In the same way, contractions in the walls of blood vessels help to keep blood flowing.

Involuntary muscle is also called **smooth muscle** because it looks smooth under a microscope, with no stripes.

Cardiac muscle

This is special involuntary muscle that forms the walls of your heart. It works non-stop without tiring. Like voluntary muscle, it is striped. When it contracts, it pumps blood out of your heart and round your body. Each contraction is a heartbeat.

More about voluntary muscle

Voluntary muscles form the red meat round your bones. They give shape to your body. Over 40% of your weight is voluntary muscle. So if you weigh 50 kilograms, over 20 kilograms of that is due to voluntary muscle.

With training we can adapt our muscles to help make us better at exercise. There is more on this later in the chapter.

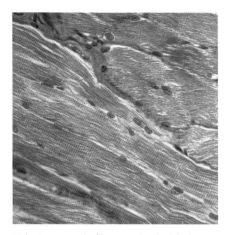

Voluntary muscle fibres, stained with dye to show up the stripes and magnified by 200. The fibres at the top left are in cross-section.

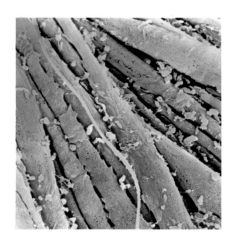

Smooth muscle fibres, magnified by 900. The wavy yellow line is a nerve.

Muscle fibres

Muscles are made up of cells called muscle fibres. Muscles contract (shorten) because the fibres do. But they don't all contract together. The number contracting at any one time depends on how much force is needed, e.g. more fibres in your biceps contract when you lift this book than when you lift a pencil.

There are two different kinds of muscle fibres, **slow twitch** and **fast twitch**.

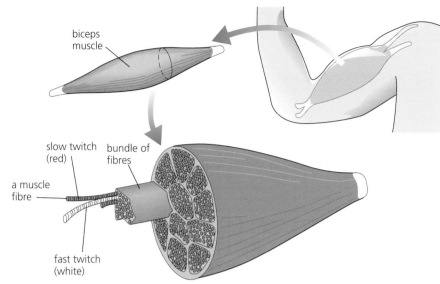

biceps muscle

slow twitch (red)

bundle of fibres

a muscle fibre

fast twitch (white)

Fast and slow twitch fibres

Which sports are you best at? It partly depends on the mixture of slow and fast twitch fibres in your muscles.

Slow twitch fibres contract slowly, and without much force. But they do not tire easily. So they are suited to activities that need endurance, e.g. jogging, long-distance running, and standing for long periods.

Fast twitch fibres contract much faster than slow twitch fibres, and with much more force. But they tire quickly. So they are suited to activities that need bursts of strength and power, e.g. sprinting and weightlifting.

Every muscle contains a mixture of these fibres. But:

the mixture is different in different muscles. For example your gastrocnemius contains a lot of fast twitch fibres. Standing on your toes gets tiring!

the mixture is different for different people. Some distance runners have 80% slow twitch fibres while some weight lifters have 80% fast twitch fibres.

Why the difference? It's all your parents' fault! You inherited the mixture from them and it's too late to change it now…

QUESTIONS

1 **a** Name the three kinds of muscle at work in your body as you answer this question. **b** Give examples of each of them.

2 What are the other names for voluntary muscle?

3 What is the proper name for muscle cells?

4 For the following activities say whether you would use mainly fast or slow twitch fibres: **a** walking to school. **b** hitting a ball in hockey, or a sliotar in hurling **c** a cross-Channel swim.

5 Name a muscle that usually has mainly fast twitch fibres.

3.2 The muscular system

	Muscle	Main action(s)
1	deltoid	Raises your arm sideways at the shoulder.
2	biceps	Bends your arm at the elbow.
3	abdominals (4 muscles)	Pull in your abdomen. Flex your trunk so you can bend forward.
4	quadriceps (4 muscles)	Straighten your leg at the knee and keep it straight when you stand.
5	pectorals	Raises your arm at the shoulder. Draws it across your chest.
6	latissimus dorsi	Pulls your arm down at the shoulder. Draws it behind your back.
7	trapezius	Holds and rotates your shoulders. Moves your head back and sideways.
8	triceps	Straightens your arm at the elbow joint.
9	gluteals (3 muscles)	Pull your leg back at the hip. Raise it sideways at the hip. Gluteus maximus is the biggest of these muscles.
10	hamstrings (3 muscles)	Bend your leg at the knee.
11	gastrocnemius	Straightens the ankle joint so you can stand on your tiptoes.

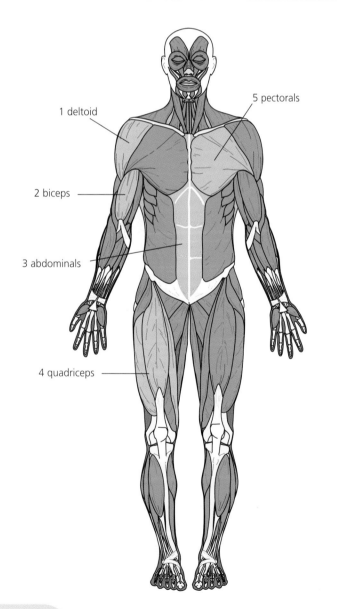

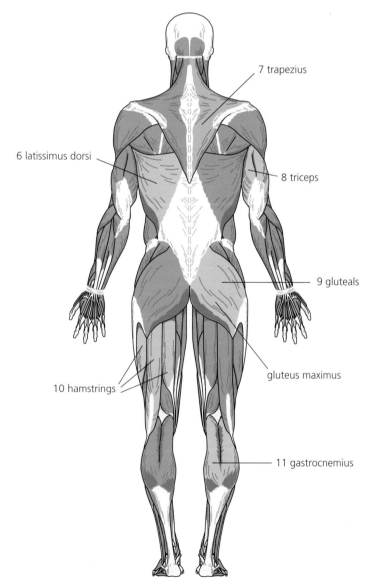

Muscles used in playing an overhead clear in badminton

Trapezius –
has pulled the head back to look at the shuttlecock.
Other examples: bringing head back as you arch over bar in Fosbury flop in high jump.

Deltoid –
has raised (or abducted) the arm at the shoulder.
Other examples: holding arms out to balance on the beam in gymnastics.

Biceps –
has bent (or flexed) the elbow.
Other examples: bending elbow for rowing.

Triceps –
is just going to start straightening the elbow (extension) to hit the shuttlecock.
Other examples: straighten elbow when rowing.

Latissimus dorsi (lower back) -
will pull arms down (adduct) after the shot has been played.
Other examples: pulling the arm down after throwing a javelin.

Gluteals –
have pulled this leg back at the hip slightly (extended it).
Other examples: pulling the leg back prior to kicking a ball in football AND pulling the leg out sideways at the hip (abduction), e.g. sidestepping.

Abdominals –
will soon have to work to straighten the spine again.
Other examples: pulling your upper body down as you go over a hurdle.

Hamstrings –
have bent (or flexed) the knee slightly.
Other examples: any jumping activity which requires you to bend your knees prior to take-off.

Quadriceps –
are just about to be used to straighten (or extend) the legs at the knee.
Other examples: straightening knees as you jump.

Gastrocnemius –
is being used to go up on tiptoes to push back to the ready position after striking the shuttlecock.
Other examples: Any running or jumping activity, or pointing toes in gymnastics.

QUESTIONS

1 Where are these muscles and what job do they do?
   a pectorals **b** biceps **c** triceps **d** deltoids **e** hamstrings **f** quadriceps.

2 Imagine performing a jump shot in basketball. What muscles are used to straighten your legs as you jump?

3 Which muscle contracts when you look upwards?

4 When running what muscles are used to: **a** bend/flex your knee? **b** pull your hip back after the step? **c** straighten, or extend, your knee?

3.3 Muscles and movement

How muscles work

A voluntary muscle usually works across a joint. It is attached to both the bones by strong cords called **tendons**.

When the muscle contracts, usually just one bone moves.

For example when the biceps in the arm contracts, the radius moves but the scapula does not.

Origin and insertion

When a muscle contracts, usually just one bone moves. The other is stationary. The **origin** is where the muscle joins the stationary bone (1 in the diagram above). The **insertion** is where it joins the moving bone (2). When a muscle contracts, **the insertion moves towards the origin**.

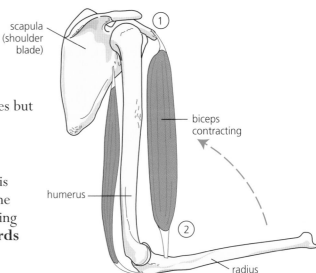

Muscles working in pairs

Muscles usually work in pairs or groups, e.g. the biceps flexes the elbow and the triceps extends it.

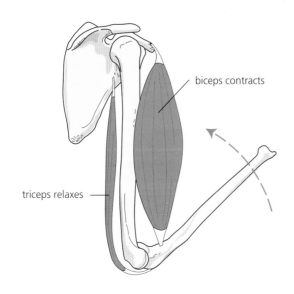

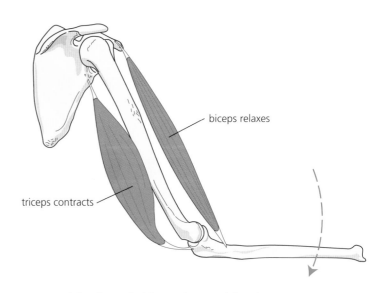

*To flex the elbow the biceps **contracts** (shortens) and the triceps **relaxes** (lengthens).*

To extend the elbow, the biceps relaxes and the triceps contracts.

This is called antagonistic muscle action. The working muscle is called the prime mover or agonist. (It's in agony!) The relaxing muscle is the antagonist. The other main pair of muscles that work together are the quadriceps and hamstrings. Imagine the picture above is a bent knee. Which muscle would be the agonist as the knee is bent (flexed) and then extended?

The prime mover is helped by other muscles called **synergists**. These contract at the same time as the prime mover. They hold the body in position so that the prime mover can work smoothly.

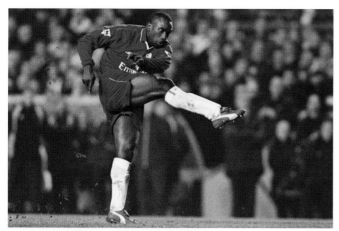

A network of muscles act as synergists to help hold her in position for this move.

Goal! To straighten the knee in the last stage of the kick, the quadriceps acted as agonist and the hamstrings as antagonist.

Tendons

As mentioned previously, tendons are the cords and straps that connect muscles to bones. At the bone, the fibres of the tendon are embedded in the periosteum of the bone. This anchors the tendon strongly and spreads the force of the contraction, so the tendon won't tear away easily.

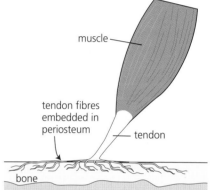

Muscle tone

Even when a muscle is relaxed, a small number of its fibres are contracted – enough to keep the muscle taut but not enough to cause movement. This state of partial contraction is called **muscle tone**. Without muscle tone you could not stand up straight!

Gravity tries to pull your head forward, as shown here. But partial contraction or muscle tone in the trapezius will keep it upright.

Muscle tone in the quadriceps balances the muscle tone in the hamstrings to keep your legs straight at the knee.

If the muscle tone in your abdominals is poor, your spine curves in too much. This leads to poor posture.

To maintain muscle tone without getting tired, groups of muscle fibres take it in turn to contract. They work in relays. Poor muscle tone leads to poor posture. But exercise improves muscle tone. It makes the muscle fibres thicker so they contract more strongly.

QUESTIONS

1 To jump we bend our legs and then straighten them.

   a What main pair of muscles help move the knee?

   b What is this working in pairs called?

2 Give an example from one of your chosen sports of antagonistic muscle action.

3 What are synergists?

4 What muscle is the prime mover when **a** doing a sit-up?

   b doing the upwards phase of a press-up?

5 **a** Draw a diagram to show how the biceps works.

   b Why doesn't the scapula move?

6 Explain how having poor muscle tone can cause bad posture.

3.4 Posture

The importance of good posture

Good posture means your body is in the position that puts **least** strain on your muscles, tendons, ligaments and bones. Good muscle tone is vital for this.

The benefits of good posture
◎ It helps to make you and your clothes look good, i.e. it develops self-esteem.
◎ It helps your heart, breathing and digestive system work properly.
◎ It helps prevent strain and injury in sport and other activities.
◎ It makes you less tired because you use less energy.

The penalties of poor posture

◎ You don't look as good as you could, no matter how great your clothes and hair are.
◎ Your muscles have to work harder so you get tired sooner.
◎ The strain on bones, tendons and ligaments can lead to injury, e.g. back strain and fallen arches.
◎ There's less space for your heart and lungs, which can interfere with their action. Round shoulders make it harder to breathe deeply.
◎ It can affect your digestion. Who wants that?
◎ Problems caused by poor posture can take years to put right.

Damage to the spine

The curves in your spine make it strong. But when they are out of shape, it is easily damaged, e.g. if you bend over to lift a heavy box, or twist violently, or develop poor posture. Pressure on vertebrae can squash the cartilage disk so much that it presses on the spinal cord. This is called a **slipped disk**. It is very painful.

Good posture means less strain on muscles, tendons, ligaments and bones.

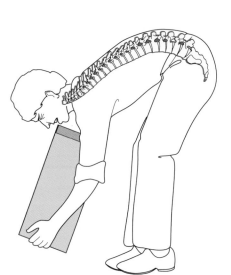

Lifting a heavy weight this way can damage your spine.

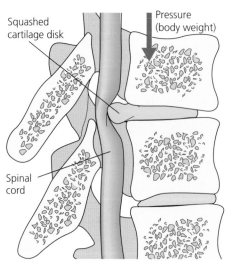

Squashed cartilage disk

Pressure (body weight)

Spinal cord

A section through two vertebrae showing a slipped disc.

High heels throw the body forward. Muscles work hard to straighten it again. That can be exhausting!

Practising good posture

Whether you are sitting, standing, walking or lifting something, the main rule is:

Keep your spine as upright as possible, with its normal curves.

Good standing posture

- Head up, neck lengthened.
- Chin tucked in just a little.
- Spine stretched upwards.
- Chest high and open, so that you breathe freely.
- Arms loosely by your sides.
- Knees relaxed.
- Feet about 15 cm apart, with your weight evenly balanced between your heels and the balls of your feet.

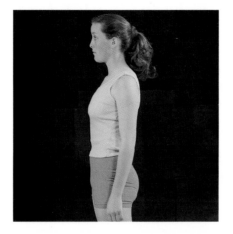

Good sitting posture

- Sit well back in your chair and let it support you.
- Spine and neck lengthened.
- Thighs straight in front of you.
- Feet flat on the floor in front of you (not under the chair).
- Arms relaxed.

When working at your desk:
- sit squarely in front of the desk
- bend forward from the hips instead of curving your spine.

Good lifting posture

- Stand directly in front of the object, close to it and with your feet apart.
- Bend your knees to reach it, keeping your spine straight.
- Use the full strength of your legs to help you lift it.

QUESTIONS

1 Give five reasons why poor posture is harmful.

2 Think of examples of sports where your spine is at most risk of injury.

3 What is the main rule of good posture?

4 Write posture instructions to tell someone: **a** how to lift a heavy suitcase **b** how to sit at the table to eat **c** how to walk upstairs.

3.5 Muscles and exercise

To recap so far, muscles cross joints and when they contract they shorten. This pulls the bones together. One bone tends to stay still and the other gets pulled towards it. The points of attachment are the **origin** and **insertion**, the insertion gets pulled towards the origin. Muscles usually work in pairs. You are expected to know the easy ones; biceps/triceps and hamstrings/quadriceps. This working in pairs is called **antagonistic** muscle action and the **agonist** is the muscle that shortens. Muscles are generally made to work quickly and powerfully (fast twitch) or for long periods of time (slow twitch).

How muscle speed affects performance

The more fast twitch fibres you have, the more suited you are to sports that need bursts of strength and power. When you play just for fun, the fibre mix does not matter. But at higher levels it can make the difference between winning and losing.

Suppose two sprinters X and Y are competing. They are the same age and weight and at the same level of fitness. But X has 75% fast twitch fibre in her leg muscles and Y has only 55%. So X should be able to start faster, accelerate faster and sprint faster than Y. She has a better chance of winning.

Muscles and fatigue

Fatigue is mental or physical exhaustion. When fast twitch fibres work maximally for too long they fatigue, e.g. the 400 metre sprint; any game activity where you sprint yourself to a standstill; the end of a floor routine in gym; canoe sprinting; downhill racing in skiing, etc.

The fatigue is caused by the build up of a poisonous substance – lactic acid. It causes pain and prevents any more energy from being supplied to the muscles.

When slow twitch fibres work for several hours they can also fatigue. If the exercise was gentle, the fatigue tends to be due to the body running out of glucose (stored as glycogen). The muscles literally run out of energy.

Muscles and training

Training and exercise have long-term effects on our muscles but if we stop exercising they return to their original state (reversibility).

Cardiac muscle. This grows bigger and stronger (this is called hypertrophy). This means more blood is pumped around the body which means more oxygen can reach the voluntary muscles.

Voluntary muscles. These also grow bigger and stronger. You would need to know whether your sport needs mainly fast twitch or slow twitch fibres, so you can train this area.

Top sprinters have a lot of fast twitch muscle fibres.

Running out of energy in long distance events, such as the marathon, can cause your muscles to completely give way.

Fast twitch fibres. With training these can contract more strongly. This would help improve your performance in maximum-effort activities, e.g. throwing events in athletics, jumping, sprinting, smashes in tennis and badminton, etc. You can also delay the build up of lactic acid for a few seconds. This doesn't sound much but if you can run the 100 metres in 14 seconds, you can cover about 20 metres in 3 seconds. Just think how useful this would be in many sports.

Slow twitch fibres. With the correct training and diet your body adapts to store more glycogen and you get used to using fat as an energy source. Most of us have plenty of that! Lots of energy can be obtained by the breakdown of fat but without training it takes a very long time before it begins to be used.

Training and everyday life

Gentle exercise combining strength work and stamina will help our hearts and muscles become stronger and fitter and help us with our general fitness for everyday tasks. After illness this must be done very gradually.

Muscle training is very important for older people. As mentioned in chapter 1, muscle strength is at its peak at about 25 years old, plateaus (keeps level) until 40 and then drops quite a lot. This loss of strength can impede everyday living – carrying groceries, etc. – so it is vital to keep training. Regular load-bearing exercise can also help prevent, or slow down, the weakening of bones (mentioned in chapter 2). Obviously huge weights are not necessary and it is better to concentrate on gentle endurance work as described in the next few pages.

All muscle changes are reversible:
IF YOU DO NOT USE IT YOU LOSE IT!

Muscle training and flexibility

Poor flexibility can cause poor performance, either due to injury or poor/inefficient technique. It can hinder both speed and endurance as the muscle has to work harder to overcome resistance. If you can combine strength work with flexibility then the muscle can contract more strongly along a full range of movement to provide maximum strength and power. Strength training without flexibility can cause individuals to become 'muscle-bound' and restricted in movement.

Flexibility training is very important for the elderly, as tendons and ligaments become less elastic. This could cause injury and prevent many movements, e.g. getting into a car or bath. For those very weak or suffering from arthritis this can be done in a pool where the warmth increases joint flexibility and body weight is supported.

Gentle endurance work is very important for older people.

QUESTIONS

1 Which of these training methods suit which fibres: **a** long distance cycling **b** sprint work **c** circuit training with bursts of 20-seconds' activity **d** walking fast for thirty minutes?

2 Explain, using a sport of your choice, why delaying the build up of lactic acid for a few seconds could be extremely useful to you.

3 Explain two important reasons why gentle training is important to older people.

4 If following a weights programme, why is it vital to work on flexibility?

5 Whilst racing a friend flat-out you have to stop due to the pain in your leg muscles. What is this caused by?

3.6 Testing muscle fitness

If you need to improve your overall muscular strength any sport/exercise is good. If you want to concentrate on a particular sport you need to decide if mainly fast twitch or slow twitch muscle fibres are used. Tests are often used to check your current level of fitness so you can measure improvement over a period of time. They can also help you to predict what sporting areas you may be good at, e.g. if you have good stamina it suggests that you may be good at long-distance events.

The grip dynanometer test

This tests the strength of your grip.

Equipment
◎ a hand-grip dynanometer

Method
1 Squeeze on the dynanometer as hard as you can with your preferred hand, for at least two seconds.
2 Repeat three times and record the highest reading of the three.

The sit-up test

This tests the strength and endurance of the abdominal muscles. Do you think the test relies mainly on fast or slow twitch fibres?

There are many tests like this but they can only test endurance (or slow twitch) if the person can actually do the exercise for a period of time. A similar test can be used for press-ups, burpees, etc.

Method
1 Lie on the floor with your hands touching your head above the ears, knees bent at 90°, and feet flat on the floor.
2 Get your partner to hold your feet down.
3 Raise your trunk until your elbows are past your knees. Then lower yourself to the floor again. This is one sit-up.
4 Do as many as you can in 30 seconds. Your partner keeps check of the time. Record your result.

Testing grip strength using a hand-grip dynanometer.

The sit-up test.

The vertical jump test

This tests the power or explosive strength of your muscles. You need good leg power for sports such as high jump, long jump, basketball and badminton.

Equipment
◎ a high wall
◎ talcum powder
◎ a vertical jump board if available

Method
1 Dip the palm of your preferred hand in talcum powder.
2 Stand sideways to the wall with your feet flat on the ground. Stretch your hand up as high as you can. Touch the wall or vertical board so that you leave a talc mark behind. (If using a board, arrange it so that you just touch the bottom of the scale.)
3 Dip your palm in talc again.
4 Now flex your knees and jump as high as you can, making a second mark as high up as possible.
5 Repeat three times. Work out how high you jumped each time. Record the best height of the three.

The sit-and-reach test

This tests hip flexibility. There are other tests for different joints. Remember the important link between strength and flexibility.

Equipment
◎ a gymnastics bench
◎ a metre ruler
◎ sellotape

Method
1 Turn a bench on its side. Sellotape the ruler on top so that it extends 15 cm over the edge, with the zero nearest you.
2 Get a partner to hold the bench steady.
3 Sit with your feet flat against the bench, legs straight.
4 Slowly reach forward as far as you can and hold.
5 Your partner notes where your fingertips reach on the ruler.
6 Subtract 15 to find how far they have stretched beyond your heels. Record your result.

The vertical jump test.

The sit-and-reach test.

QUESTIONS

1 Which of these tests would you expect an international netballer to excel in (be very good at) and why?

2 Which of the tests involve fast twitch fibres?

3 Explain why you would not use the vertical jump test on a long-distance runner?

4 If you scored very high in the strength test, does this mean you would be a good weightlifter? Explain your answer.

5 How could a fitness coach use tests to help him/her evaluate their coaching?

6 Why do you think that tests of flexibility should be included with muscle tests?

7 If you were doing the tests regularly to check improvement, why would it be important to have the same conditions, e.g. temperature, for all tests?

49

3.7 Methods of muscle training

In all sports you need strength. Once you have built up a basic level, then you need to concentrate on the important area for you.

Strength

This is the force you exert against a resistance. Here total strength or force is the all-important factor, e.g. weightlifting. It does not matter how quickly or slowly you lift it and it is only done once. You enter the competition near your maximum lift as you are not trained to keep on going for long periods of time. Despite being very strong, you may not necessarily be able to throw something a long way because speed of muscle contraction becomes important in throwing.

For strength you tend to train fast twitch fibres because they have to contract maximally. Strength training makes your muscles thicker. You can work on static strength or dynamic strength (see photos on the right). Static strength is where your muscles do not change length. Dynamic strength is where they do change length.

Power

This is the ability to do strength performances quickly. This explosive strength is important in nearly every sport – racket sports to give momentum to the ball, running and jumping actions for speed and height; gymnastics for height, lift and spring, etc. Power uses fast twitch fibres, and training for it makes the muscles thicker.

Muscular endurance

This is the ability to repeat and maintain contractions without getting tired. We use it in sports where you repeat the same movement, e.g. running, cycling, swimming, mountain walking, canoeing, etc.

Slow twitch fibres are used but endurance training does not make the muscles thicker. It does make them better at using oxygen and burning fat for energy. It makes more capillaries grow around the muscles so that more oxygen reaches the muscles and they can work for longer.

Strength or endurance?

All muscle training involves lifting or pulling or pushing a load or resistance. The load could be a dumb-bell or your own body weight. You can use the same exercise to improve strength or endurance. It depends on the load and how often you repeat the exercise:

◎ For endurance, use a lighter load and many repetitions.
◎ For strength, use a heavy load and a small number of repetitions.
◎ For power, use a medium load and repetitions, but do it fast.
◎ Holding a heavy load stationary will improve your static strength.
◎ Moving it will improve your dynamic strength.
◎ Moving it as fast as possible will improve your power.

Static strength is where your muscles do not change in length, e.g. pushing in a rugby scrum or holding a weight as above.

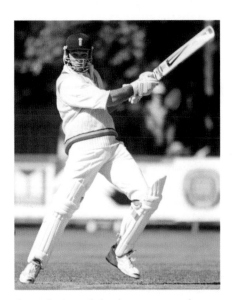

Dynamic strength is where your muscles change length, e.g. running. The cricketer above is using power.

STRENGTH

Heavy weight.
Few reps.

POWER

Medium weight.
Medium reps.
Done quickly.

ENDURANCE

Low weight.
Many reps.

What load should you lift during weight training? And how many repetitions should you do? It depends on what kind of fitness you're trying to improve.

Where to find the load

◎ You can use free weights such as dumb-bells, or weight training machines. This is usually called weight training.
◎ You can use your own body weight. For example in press-ups, sit-ups, dips and chins.
◎ For muscle training to have an effect, you need at least three sessions a week.

Weight training

Weight training is a popular way to exercise muscles.

◎ It is easy to tell what load you are using, since weights are clearly marked.
◎ It is easy to increase the load by the right amount.
◎ It is easy to work on different muscle groups, to suit your sport.
◎ But weight training is not suitable for people under sixteen. Your frame is still immature and you can get injured easily.

Body weight

You do not need special equipment for body weight training. That means you can do it anywhere.

◎ When you can do an exercise such as press-ups more than 10 times without stopping, you are moving into endurance work.
◎ There are several ways to overload. For example with press-ups:
 – ask a partner to press on your upper back to increase the load.
 – put your feet on a bench to increase the load on your arms.

Two ways of overloading using body weight. Which muscles are being overloaded?

QUESTIONS

1 What is: **a** strength? **b** endurance?
2 How does strength training change your muscles?
3 How does endurance training change them?
4 Which of the two is improved by:

 a high load, few reps? **b** low load, many reps?

5 There are three different kinds of strength. What are they? Say how you could improve each.
6 Give two advantages of weight training.
7 Think of two advantages of body weight training.
8 How can you overload in body weight training?

3.8 Muscle and flexibility training

Here are two different ways to train muscles, based on different kinds of muscle contraction. Both involve pulling or pushing or lifting a load.

Isotonic training

To bend your arm at the elbow, your biceps muscle shortens. This is called an **isotonic contraction**. All your body movements depend on isotonic contractions, when muscles shorten and pull on bones. Isotonic contractions can also be called **dynamic** contractions.

In **isotonic training** you use isotonic contractions to improve your muscle strength and endurance. Press-ups, sit-ups, chins and weightlifting are isotonic exercises. Can you think of others?

Advantages of isotonic training
◎ It strengthens a muscle through the full range of movement.
◎ You can choose isotonic exercises to suit your sport.

Disadvantages
◎ It can make muscles sore. This is caused by stress on muscles while they lengthen. For example, there is stress on your arm muscles when you lower your body during chins.
◎ You gain most muscle strength at the weakest point of the action. You don't gain it evenly throughout.

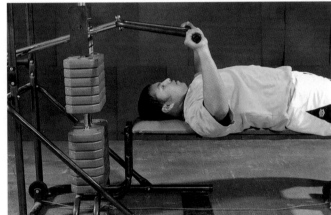

An isotonic exercise, since muscles are contracting. But which muscles? And what's the advantage of the machine over free weights?

Isometric training

When you push against a closed door, your arm muscles contract but stay the same length. This is called an **isometric contraction**.

Isometric contractions produce **static strength**. This is the strength you need to push or pull a very heavy object or hold up a heavy load. You need it in sumo wrestling, a rugby scrum, gymnastics and weightlifting. **Isometric training** uses isometric contractions to strengthen your muscles. It can help for these sports.

Advantages of isometric training
◎ It is quick to do and does not hurt.
◎ It does not need expensive equipment.
◎ You can do it anywhere.

Disadvantages
◎ A muscle gains strength only at the angle you use in the exercise. This might not help much in your sport.
◎ During isometric exercise, the blood flow to the muscle stops, blood pressure rises, and less blood flows back to the heart. This could be dangerous if you have heart problems.

Isometric training is best if you combine it with isotonic training.

A static exercise, as muscles are contracting but no movement is occuring.

Improving flexibility

Earlier in this chapter we looked at the importance of improving strength **and** flexibility. One developed without the other is not beneficial to your body and indeed could lead to injuries.

Flexibility is the range of movement at a joint. Good flexibility is important in many sports. For example:

◎ flexible shoulders help you play tennis better.
◎ flexible hip, knee and ankle joints help you sprint. Your stride is longer so you cover the ground faster.
◎ a flexible spine helps divers and gymnasts move more smoothly.

Stretching

You improve **flexibility** through **static stretching**.

In static stretching, a muscle is held in a stretched position for a number of seconds. This can be done actively or passively.

*In **active stretching**, you do the work. Don't jerk or bounce. Only stretch as far as is comfortable.*

*In **passive stretching** your partner does the work, holding you in a stretch for several seconds.*
Be careful. Too much force can injure you.

What happens at a joint when you stretch?

The joint capsule controls around half the movement at a joint. The rest depends mainly on muscles and tendons. When you stretch, your muscles and tendons get stretched. This makes them more flexible so the joint can move more freely. A flexible joint is at less risk of strain. So stretching is part of the warm up for every training session. Flexibility is also linked to **strength**. Muscles that are stretched well can contract more strongly.

QUESTIONS

1 What is an *isotonic* contraction?

2 What is an *isometric* contraction?

3 What kind of contraction do you use when you:
   a run? **b** pull on the rope in a tug-of-war?

4 Give two advantages of isotonic training.

5 Name two isotonic exercises *not* mentioned here.

6 Give two advantages of isometric training.

7 What is the difference between active and passive stretching?

8 Using rock climbing as an example, explain the use of isotonic and isometric contractions.

Questions on chapter 3

1 What three different types of muscle are there?

2 Which two of these are the most important with regards to sport.

3 Raj has been in hospital with a badly broken leg and has done no exercise for four months. Her doctor recommends a programme of slow walking with a gradual increase in speed and distance. What two muscular benefits will she gain?

4 Voluntary muscles can be mainly fast or slow twitch fibres. If you did a survey of the following world-class athletes, what would you expect to find in terms of these?

  a Shot-putter

  b Marathon runner

  c Rounders player

  d High-jumper

  e Channel swimmer

  f Rugby player

5 Matt wants to improve his muscles for javelin throwing by training. He decides to run three miles a day. Would this help him improve his distance? Explain.

6 What muscles cause the movement shown at joints 1, 2 and 4 and what movement occurs at them all?

7 Some sports need a mixture of slow and fast twitch muscle fibres. Why do you think a boxer would train his upper body for power (fast twitch) and his lower body for stamina (slow twitch).

8 While doing a biceps curl the prime mover is the biceps. Other muscles hold the body in position. What are they called?

9 Are the muscles below voluntary, involuntary or cardiac?

  a The heart muscle

  b The muscle in your stomach walls

  c The biceps

  d The trapezius

  e The muscle in your artery wall.

10 Give another name for voluntary and involuntary muscles.

11 Unless you are unconscious, your muscles are always partly contracted.

  a What is this condition called?

  b Explain how it helps you to hold your head up.

  c Explain how it helps you to look better.

  d Why do the muscles not get tired?

12 Each muscle in your body is a mixture of two types of muscle fibres, slow twitch and fast twitch.

  a Which gives the strongest contractions?

  b Which tires most easily?

  c Which can keep going for longer?

  d 'The more you exercise the more fast twitch fibres you have.' Is this statement true? Explain your answer.

13 Which type of muscle fibre do you depend on for:

  a jogging?

  b doing a back somersault?

  c lifting a really heavy weight?

  d carrying your books home from school?

  e shot-putting?

  f working behind the counter in a shop?

  g a 100 m swimming race?

  h playing golf?

  i pulling in a tug-of-war?

  j playing a tennis match?

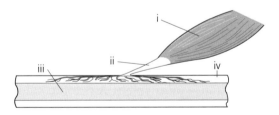

14 The above diagram shows where a muscle joins to a bone.

  a Name the numbered parts.

  b Part ii is deeply embedded in part iv Why?

15 A softball player decides to get really fit for their sport and starts weight training in the off-season (winter). They decide to build up their strength and then nearer the start of the season make it more specific.

a What sort of weights programme would you set for the winter and why?

b What area of strength would the player concentrate on nearer the start of the season and why?

c How would you change their programme at this point?

d If the player was under 16, what kinds of weights would you recommend and why?

e Should this person concentrate on isotonic or isometric work? Explain.

f By the start of the season this player has really improved their fitness, particularly the muscles of the trunk and shoulders. Unfortunately, because they were pushed for time when training in the evenings, they neglected any flexibility work. What problems can you foresee?

16 Usually two muscles work together to move a bone. For example to flex your hip joint as in A below, one muscle contracts and another relaxes.

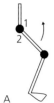 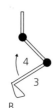

In drawing A:

a Which muscle must contract to raise the thigh?

b Which muscle must relax to allow this to happen?

c Which is the agonist?

d What other term is used for the agonist?

e Which number is the antagonist?

f What is this kind of muscle action called?

g What is the correct name for muscle 2?

In drawing B, the knee joint is being flexed.

h Which number is the agonist this time?

i Which is the antagonist?

j Give the correct name for muscle 4.

k Other muscles called synergists are also involved in these movements. What job do they do?

17 For actions a-d below, say which muscles you think are the agonists and which are the antagonists.

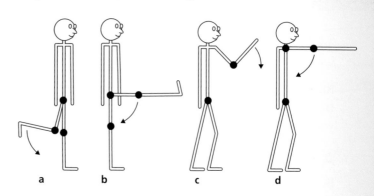

(The drawings on page 42 will help you.)

18 Give the anatomical name for the muscles listed below:

calf	stomach
chest	shoulder
front of thigh	bottom
back of thigh	lower back

19 Christine is the national under-15 javelin champion. After several months of flexibility training her performance improves. Why could this be?

USE OF INFORMATION TECHNOLOGY

20 Using a digital camera (or normal camera and scanner) take some pictures of your sport. Using the major muscles, label it as done for the badminton player on page 41. Make the best examples into posters for your PE classroom.

21 Collect data for your group for the sit-up and the vertical jump tests. Put the results into a spreadsheet and produce a scatter graph. Is there a relationship between the results of these tests? Explain your answer.

22 Repeat the data collection for the other tests and compare results to find any relationships. Use that information to say whether the following relationships are true for your group.

a A person who is good at the grip test is also good at the vertical jump test.

b People who are good in one test tend to be good in all the tests.

4.1 The heart

Your blood works non-stop, 24 hours a day. It carries food and oxygen to your body cells. It carries carbon dioxide and other waste away.

Blood is pumped round the body by the **heart**. It flows along tubes called **blood vessels**. The blood, heart and blood vessels together make up your **circulatory system**.

A first look at the circulatory system

Below is a simple plan of your circulatory system. It shows just the heart and four main blood vessels:

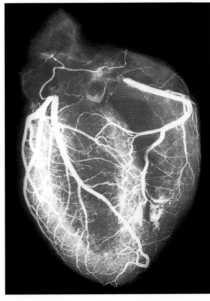

A heart treated with special dye to show up the arteries when x-rayed. This helps to spot heart disease and blockages.

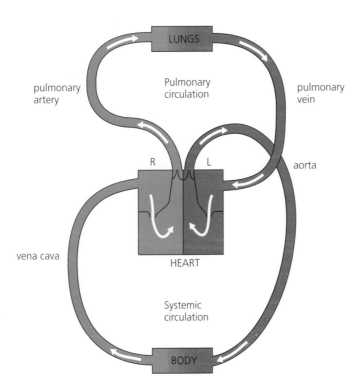

◎ Notice how the heart is divided down the middle. Each part is a pump so the heart is a double pump for a double circulation.
◎ The right side pumps blood to the lungs and then it returns to the heart. This is called the **pulmonary circulation**.
◎ The left side pumps blood to the body and then it returns to the heart. This is called the **systemic circulation**.
◎ Try to learn the vena cava and aorta first. Once you have done this it will help you with the rest. The **A**orta is an **A**rtery and **A**rteries go **A**way from the heart. The **V**ena cava is a **V**ein and veins go towards the heart.
◎ Look at the diagram. Oxygen is picked up in the lungs and then transported to the body, passing through the heart on the way. Carbon dioxide does the opposite.

The heart has four hollows or **chambers** inside. The two upper chambers are called **atria**. Each is an atrium.

The two lower chambers are called **ventricles**.

The walls of the heart are made of **cardiac muscle**.

The wall down the middle is called the **septum**. It divides the heart into two parts.

Valves prevent back flow of blood. The two between the atria and the ventricles are the tricuspid and bicuspid valves and the ones between the heart and the arteries are semi-lunar (half-moon) valves.

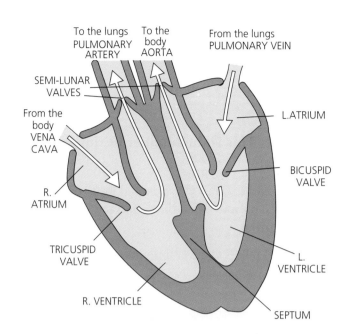

How the heart pumps blood

The heart pumps blood by contracting. It does this in two stages.

First the atria contract. Then about a tenth of a second later the ventricles contract. This shows what happens:

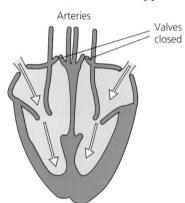

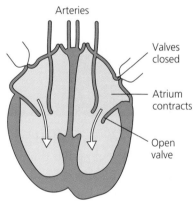

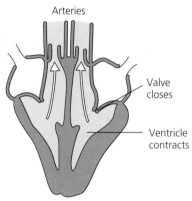

1 When the heart is relaxed, both sides fill with blood from the veins. (But no blood can flow in from the arteries. Can you see why?)

2 The atria contract. The veins contract where they join the atria. So blood from the atria is forced into the ventricles.

3 Then the ventricles contract. The valves between the ventricles and atria close. So the blood is forced out of the heart, into the arteries.

4 The heart muscle relaxes again and steps 1 – 3 are repeated.

QUESTIONS

1 What are the heart walls made of?

2 What are the two upper chambers called?

3 What are the two lower chambers called?

4 Where would you find **a** the bicuspid valve? **b** the tricuspid valve? **c** a semi-lunar valve?

5 Describe the route a molecule of blood would take from the vena cava to the aorta.

6 A 'hole in the heart' baby has a hole through the septum allowing blood from the left and right sides to mix. Why is this such a problem?

7 What are the names of the two circulations?

8 What is the function of each?

4.2 The heart and exercise

There are three very important definitions you must learn: heart rate, stroke volume, and cardiac output.

Heart rate. This is the number of times your heart beats per minute.

At each heart beat, blood is pumped into your arteries. It makes the artery walls expand. Then they contract. One expansion and contraction is called a **pulse**.

You can feel pulses at several points in your body. By counting the pulses you can tell your heart rate.

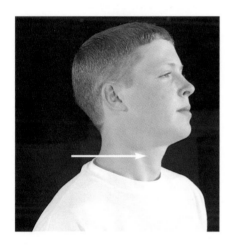

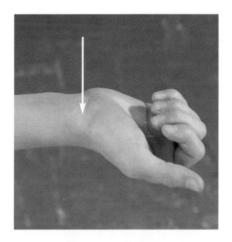

One **pulse point** is on the **carotid** artery in your neck, in the groove beside your windpipe. Either side will do! See if you can find it.

Another is on the **radial** artery at your wrist, below the thumb. To take your pulse, you need a watch with a seconds hand.

Press lightly on the pulse point with your first two fingers. Note the time. Start counting. Stop when a minute is up.

Heart rate. When we are at rest, the average heart rate is about 70 beats per minute (bpm). As soon as we start exercising, this rises. In extreme exercise it reaches its maximum (205 – at your age). This occurs because your body is desperate for oxygen and is trying to get rid of the poisonous carbon dioxide. This immediate rise is known as a short-term effect of exercise. A long-term effect is that your heart grows bigger and stronger (because it is a muscle). This is called hypertrophy. This means it can hold more blood and contract more strongly – in other words it has a bigger stroke volume.

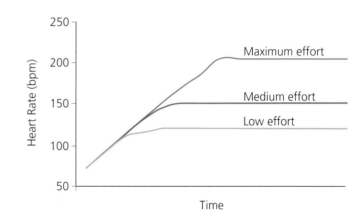

Stroke volume. This is the volume of blood pumped out of the heart by each ventricle during one contraction. At rest the heart chambers do not completely empty with every contraction. As soon as exercise starts, they fill more and empty more due to the heart contracting more strongly. As said on the previous page, a long-term effect of training causes hypertrophy and stroke volume increases.

This is how stroke volume increases during exercise:

◎ Contracting muscles squeeze on your veins, which causes more blood to squirt back into the heart.
◎ The heart gets fuller. That makes its fibres stretch more.
◎ Because its fibres are more stretched, the heart contracts more strongly – just like when you stretch an elastic band. A stronger contraction forces out more blood.

Cardiac output. This is the amount of blood ejected from the heart in one minute. This can be explained in an equation:

$$\text{heart rate} \times \text{stroke volume} = \text{cardiac output}$$
$$\text{e.g. 70 bpm} \times \text{70 ml} = 4.9 \text{ l}$$

In other words, at rest, nearly five litres of blood travels around your body. If we could get two identical people – one unfit and one fit – they would still need the same cardiac output at rest, i.e. 4.9 litres. However, remember the fit person will have a stronger stroke volume.

$$\text{Cardiac output} = \text{stroke volume} \times \text{heart rate}$$
$$\text{unfit } 4.9 \text{ l} = 70 \text{ ml} \times 70 \text{ bpm}$$
$$\text{fit } 4.9 \text{ l} = 90 \text{ ml} \times 55 \text{ bpm}$$

Look what happens – the fit person's heart does not have to beat as many times to supply the 4.9 litres. This means the fitter you are the slower your resting heart rate will be.

Now look what happens during maximum exercise for a fifteen-year-old:

$$\text{stroke volume} \times \text{heart rate} = \text{cardiac output}$$
$$\text{unfit} = 120 \text{ ml} \times 205 \text{ bpm} = 24.6 \text{ l}$$
$$\text{fit} = 150 \text{ ml} \times 205 \text{ bpm} = 30.8 \text{ l}$$

The fit person has more blood travelling round the body, and therefore, more oxygen. They can keep going for longer.

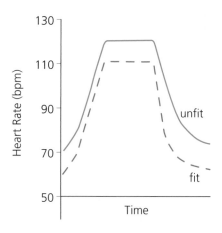

A graph of two people doing the same exercise at the same speed.
The fit person has:
- *a lower resting heart rate*
- *a lower heart rate during exercise*
- *recovers quicker, i.e. their heart rate returns to the resting level faster.*

AGE AND THE CARDIOVASCULAR SYSTEM

As you get older, your maximum heart rate drops, which means that your cardiac output is less. This means that intense exercise cannot be sustained for as long.

A good aerobic (endurance) based training programme can, up to the age of eighty, give the person an oxygen-transporting system similar to that of someone 20 years younger than themselves!

QUESTIONS

1 What short-term effect of exercise would you expect to experience with your heart rate?

2 What are the two reasons that this happens?

3 The long-term effect of exercise on the heart is hypertrophy. How does this effect your resting heart rate?

4 What is the definition of stroke volume?

5 What are the short- and long-term effects of exercise on it?

6 What is the cause of the long-term effect?

7 What is the link between cardiac output, stroke volume and heart rate (i.e. what is the equation)?

8 Write out (using figures) how you would find this person's cardiac output. Paul went for a jog. His heart rate went up to 130 bpm and his stroke volume to 110 ml.

4.3   Blood

We have three different types of blood vessel:

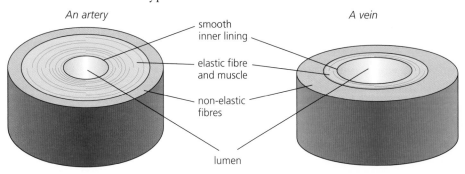

An artery

A vein

smooth
inner lining

elastic fibre
and muscle

non-elastic
fibres

lumen

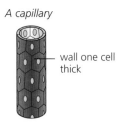

A capillary

wall one cell
thick

Arteries need a lot of elastic fibre and muscle to (a) cope with the surge of blood as it leaves the heart and (b) to change the lumen size when needed. Arteries and arterioles (see below) can become larger (**vasodilate**) or smaller (**vasoconstrict**). This means blood can be encouraged to enter some places and shut off from other places. During exercise little blood goes to the stomach but lots to the working muscles. This is called **vascular shunt**.

The valves in veins

By the time blood reaches the veins it is flowing more slowly, so at lower pressures veins have valves to make sure it can't flow backwards.

Many large veins are inside your leg and arm muscles. When the muscles contract, they squirt the blood towards your heart.

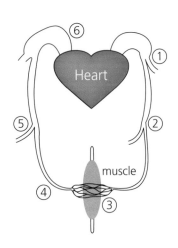

valves

contracting muscle

Blood vessels

1 The biggest artery – the aorta – swiftly divides into smaller arteries.
2 Arteries divide into smaller arterioles.
3 Arterioles divide into tiny capillaries that cover the muscle.
4 Capillaries join together to form the slightly larger venules (small veins).
5 Venules join together to form veins.
6 The largest vein enters the heart – the vena cava.

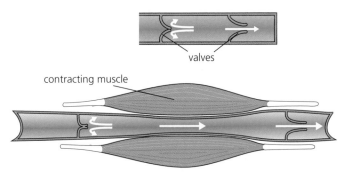

Heart

muscle

The differences between arteries and veins	
VEINS	ARTERIES
have valves	do not have valves
lead to the heart	go away from the heart
rarely pulsate	pulsate
blood flows under low pressure	blood flows under high pressure
have thin muscle and elastic tissue	have thick muscle and elastic tissue
mainly carry deoxygenated blood	mainly carry oxygenated blood

Control of temperature

Your body does not like change. Normally, your body temperature is 37 °C and your blood is about 50 % water. If you get too hot during exercise, or lose too much water in sweat, the body takes action to get back to normal.

If you get too hot

Exercise makes you warm. This is because cell respiration in the muscles increases, giving out heat. Blood carries the heat around your body. But when your temperature starts to rise, this is what happens:

1 Blood vessels under the skin expand. This is called **vasodilation**. Now more blood flows near the surface. It loses heat by **radiation**. Just like a radiator!
2 The sweat glands make more sweat. This is mainly **water**. Heat from your body makes it **evaporate**, which helps to cool you.

When you exercise on a hot dry day or in a sports hall you can lose a lot of water as sweat. If the air is hot and humid, sweat will not evaporate. Your temperature may rise out of control. This is called **heat stroke** and it can kill you.

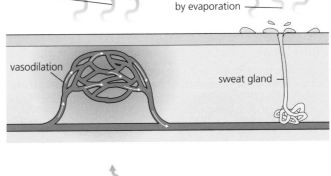

If you get too cool

If your body temperature drops below 37 °C, your body tries to stop it getting colder:

1 You stop sweating.
2 The blood vessels under the skin contract. This is called **vasoconstriction**. Now less blood flows near the surface so less heat is lost.
3 Your muscles may start to shiver. This produces heat.

But if you get cold enough, your reactions slow down. You lose control of your hands and you can't walk properly. You can't think straight. You are suffering from **hypothermia**. It can kill you.

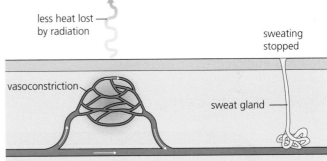

To be on top of our sporting performance we, therefore, need to control our temperature. Water intake is vital as we can lose up to three litres of sweat an hour. Lack of water can cause dehydration which makes you weak and dizzy.

QUESTIONS

1 Give two reasons why an artery has to have more elastic and muscle tissue than a vein.
2 What is meant by vasodilation?
3 Give an example of when we use it?
4 Why do veins have valves?

5 In the differences between veins and arteries it says veins 'rarely' pulsate and 'mainly' carry deoxygenated blood. One vein is different from the rest. Which one?
6 When doing mountain walking it is possible to get hypothermia. What is this?
7 What is dehydration?

4.4 What's in blood?

Blood is a liquid called plasma, with red cells, white cells and platelets floating in it. You have nearly 5 litres of it in your body – enough to fill 8 or 9 milk bottles!

Plasma

Plasma is a yellowish liquid. It is mostly water, with different things dissolved in it. The dissolved substances include:
◎ glucose and other nutrients from digested food
◎ hormones
◎ carbon dioxide and other waste from cells.

Red cells

Red cells are the body's oxygen carriers. They contain a red substance called haemoglobin which combines readily with oxygen. Haemoglobin gives the cells their red colour.

This blood sample has just been centrifuged. The yellow liquid is plasma. The red cells have collected at the bottom of the tube.

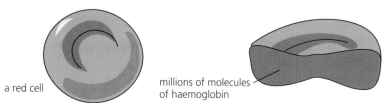

a red cell

millions of molecules of haemoglobin

The red cells are made in red marrow in some bones (mainly the ribs, vertebrae, humerus and femur). You have an enormous number of them: around 5 million *in each drop of blood*.

How red cells carry oxygen

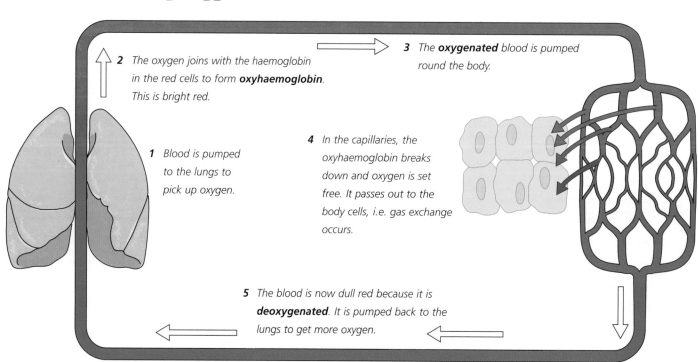

2 *The oxygen joins with the haemoglobin in the red cells to form* **oxyhaemoglobin**. *This is bright red.*

3 *The* **oxygenated** *blood is pumped round the body.*

1 *Blood is pumped to the lungs to pick up oxygen.*

4 *In the capillaries, the oxyhaemoglobin breaks down and oxygen is set free. It passes out to the body cells, i.e. gas exchange occurs.*

5 *The blood is now dull red because it is* **deoxygenated**. *It is pumped back to the lungs to get more oxygen.*

White cells

White cells defend your body against disease. They are larger than red cells, and have a nucleus. There are several different kinds of white cell, all doing different jobs. For example white cells called **phagocytes** eat up germs:

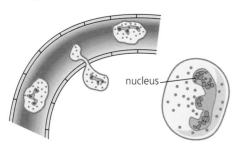

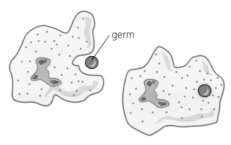

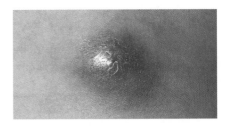

1 *The phagocytes pass out through capillary walls and into the infected tissue.*

2 *They change shape to surround the germs. They produce enzymes to kill and digest them.*

3 *Phagocytes live for only a short time. Dead phagocytes, dead germs and liquid form pus in the infected area.*

Other white cells make **antibodies**. These are chemicals that destroy germs. Different germs need different antibodies.

White cells are made in your red bone marrow, lymph nodes and spleen. Your blood has far fewer white cells than red ones. But when you are ill, more white cells are produced to help you fight infection.

Platelets

Platelets are fragments from special cells made in red bone marrow. They stick to each other easily. Their job is to stop your body losing blood. They do this by making the blood clot. This is how they work:

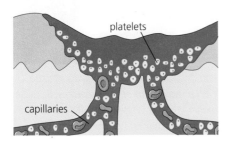

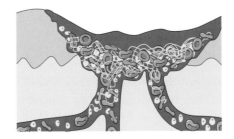

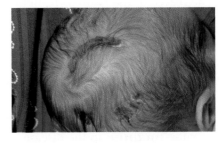

1 *When you cut your hand, platelets stick to the surface of the wound and to each other.*

2 *They produce a substance that makes tiny fibres grow. Red cells get trapped in these. A clot forms.*

3 *The clot hardens to a scab, like on this head wound. It will drop off when new skin grows.*

QUESTIONS

1 What is blood?

2 What is the main substance in plasma?

3 Name three other substances in plasma.

4 a What is the job of red cells? **b** What substance helps them do this job? **c** How does this substance work?

5 One kind of blood cell has a nucleus. Which one?

6 What is the job of white cells?

7 White cells called *phagocytes* eat up germs. Explain how they do this.

8 What are *antibodies*? What produces them?

9 Explain how platelets stop a cut bleeding.

4.5 What blood does

Your blood has two jobs: to carry things around the body and to protect you against infection.

What blood carries

Your blood is like a non-stop delivery service. It picks things up in one part of the body and carries them to another part.

Blood carries		How
1	oxygen from the lungs to all your body cells	in red cells
2	carbon dioxide from the cells to the lungs for excretion	mainly in plasma
3	other waste, and excess water, from cells to the kidneys for excretion	in plasma
4	glucose and other nutrients from the gut to the cells	in plasma
5	hormones from the hormone glands to the parts that use them	in plasma
6	white blood cells to infected places	floating in plasma
7	heat from warmer to cooler parts of the body and to the skin for removal	all parts of the blood

How blood protects you

Germs are **bacteria** and **viruses** that cause disease. They can enter your body through your lungs, through cuts, and in food and water. The platelets and white cells in blood protect you.

◎ Platelets cause blood to clot. This stops germs getting into cuts.
◎ If germs do get into your body, some white cells eat them up.
  Others make antibodies to destroy them.

If the germs are ones your white cells have not met before, it may take some time to make an antibody. But once they have done it, they can do it faster next time. If the germs return they are destroyed immediately. You become **immune** to the disease.

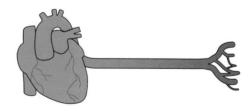

Immunization. The baby is being injected with a weak form of the bacteria that cause meningitis. Her white cells will develop antibodies, making her immune to the disease.

Blood pressure

When the tap is full on, and the nozzle nearly closed, the water pressure in a hose is very high. High enough to damage plants.

Now it is much lower. The pressure depends on how much water flows into the hose and how easily it can flow out.

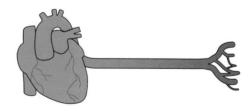

Blood pressure is the same. It depends on how much blood flows into a blood vessel and how easily it can flow out.

That's why blood pressure is different in different blood vessels.

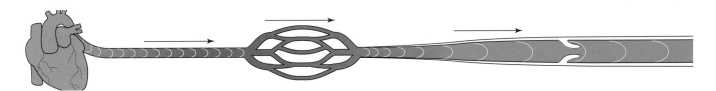

It is highest in the arteries. The blood pumps in fast, but it can't flow out through arterioles easily because they are so narrow.

It is lower in the capillaries, because the blood flows into them more slowly and then flows out to wider tubes.

It is lowest in the veins because the blood drains into them quite slowly and they are the widest blood vessels.

Measuring blood pressure

Blood pressure is always measured at an artery in your arm. It is measured using a rubber cuff attached to a thin tube of mercury.

The blood pressure in the artery rises when your heart contracts and falls when it relaxes. Both values are measured. Normal blood pressure is around 120/80. You say this as 120 over 80. It means that the pressure is 120 mm when the heart contracts and 80 mm when it relaxes. (120 mm and 80 mm are the height of the mercury in the tube.)

Blood and exercise

Short-term effects

When you exercise, your heart beats faster and pumps out more blood, so your blood pressure rises. If it rises too much it is dangerous. Your body takes action to prevent this. For example, the brain sends a message to the arterioles to open wider. This reduces blood pressure. But it also helps you in another way. Now more blood gets to your muscles faster, carrying oxygen for respiration.

Long-term effects

Training results in more blood cells being produced and more capillaries being made, i.e. *increased capillarisation*.

This means that more oxygen can be carried and gas exchange can happen quicker and more efficiently.

Measuring blood pressure. The doctor pumps up the cuff until the pressure inside it just equals the pressure in the artery. He can tell by listening through the stethoscope. As the cuff is pumped up, the mercury rises in the tube.

QUESTIONS

1 Why is blood pressure highest in arteries?

2 Explain why blood pressure is lowest in veins.

3 Where in the body is blood pressure measured?

4 If you cut an artery the blood pumps out in spurts. If you cut a vein it seeps out steadily. Try to explain this difference.

5 Blood does two jobs. What are they?

6 Name two things carried in blood: **a** which are gases (How does the blood carry them?) **b** which the body will get rid of (excrete).

7 What are germs?

8 Name two things in blood that protect you.

9 If you catch measles once, you won't catch it again. Explain why.

Questions on chapter 4

Question hints: the heart and circulation

To answer questions about the heart and circulation, start by scribbling a diagram like this.

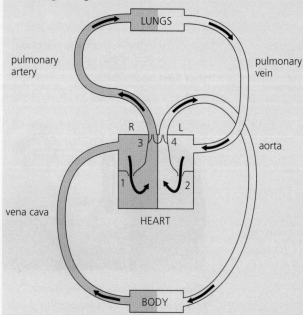

1   First draw a square box for the heart. Now draw a line down the middle to represent the septum. Mark the two halves **R** and **L** for right and left. (You are facing the drawing so **R** is on your left!)
2   Draw two more boxes, for the body and lungs.
3   Draw in the blood vessels and direction of blood flow. Remember, it flows out beside the septum.

    R → lungs → side of L (Ron loves London)

    L → body → side of R (Lessons bore Ron)

4   Label the blood vessels. Remember:
    • **arteries** carry blood away from the heart.
    • veins carry blood to it.
    • the main artery from the heart is the **aorta**.
    • the main vein to it is the **vena cava**.
    • **pulmonary** means to do with the lungs.

5   Now draw in the four valves in the heart.
    • 1 and 2 separate the upper and lower chambers of the heart. They are the **cuspid** valves.
        – 1 is called the **tri**cuspid valve.
        – 2 is called the **bicuspid** or **mitral** valve.
    • 3 and 4 lead out of the heart.
        – They are the **semi-lunar** valves.
6   The upper chambers of the heart are the **atria**. The lower chambers are the **ventricles**. Write these labels on.

7   Scribble a simple diagram of the heart and circulation by following the instructions on the left. Practise until you can do it in less than 2 minutes.

8   **a**   What is oxygenated blood?
    b   Name a blood vessel where you would find it.
    c   What is deoxygenated blood?
    d   Name a blood vessel where you would find it.
    e   Only one artery carries deoxygenated blood. Which one?
    f   Where does blood get oxygen?
    g   Only one vein carries oxygenated blood. Which one?
    h   A red substance in blood picks up the oxygen. What is the name of this substance?

9   On a scribble diagram from 7:
    a   shade the oxygenated blood red
    b   shade the deoxygenated blood blue.

10 When blood leaves the heart and travels around the body it passes through these blood vessels:

    1   veins
    2   arteries
    3   capillaries
    4   arterioles
    5   venules

    In which order does it pass through them?

    A 1, 5, 3, 4, 2
    B 1, 2, 4, 3, 5
    C 2, 4, 3, 1, 5
    D 2, 4, 3, 5, 1

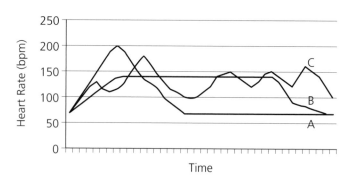

11 which of the above heart rates do you think belongs to:
    a   a 100 metre sprinter?
    b   a long-distance runner?
    c   a games player?
    Give reasons for your answers.

12 Anjou goes for a run at a gentle pace. What would be the immediate effects upon her heart? Use this equation to help you:

stroke volume x heart rate = cardiac output

If she trained regularly, what long-term effects would change the above equation at rest?

13 If Anjou trained regularly, her maximum cardiac output would be greater than before she started her training. Why?

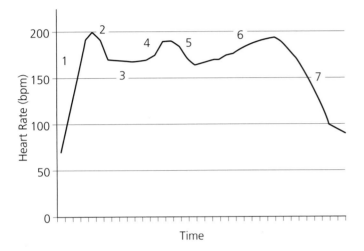

14 The above graph is the heart rate for a 10,000 metre runner. Match each statement to a correct number.
 a The race settled into a steady pace.
 b At the beginning of the race there was a sprint to gain position.
 c A sudden burst of speed left most of the other runners behind.
 d The pace increased during the last lap.

15 In many sports you see on TV you may have noticed people run on with drinks bottles during every stoppage. What do you think the effect of too little fluid would be?

16 List two sports, apart from mountain walking, where hypothermia could affect you.

17 What is the ideal body temperature?

18 Explain the two things that the body does to try to keep cool.

19 Explain the three things that the body does to try to keep warm.

20 What are the long term effects of training on:
 a the heart?
 b the blood and blood vessels?

21 Why do these effects help to improve a sportspersons performance?

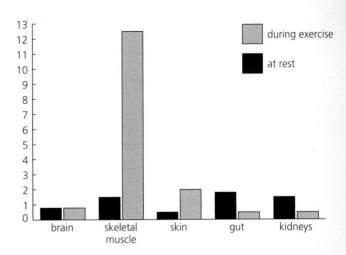

22 The above diagram shows how the blood flow to different parts of the body changes during exercise.
 a Explain how and why exercise affects blood flow to:
  i your skin
  ii your muscles
  iii your gut
  iv your kidneys
 b Blood flow to the brain is undisturbed by exercise. Why is this important?

23 Try taking your heart rate:
  i After laying down for 5 minutes
  ii After sitting down for 5 minutes
  iii After standing for 5 minutes
 a List your results.
 b Can you give an explanation for them?

THINGS TO DO

Using heart-rate monitors split your class into 3 groups. Each group needs to record their heart rates as they do 400 metres as follows:
i Group 1 will race the 400 metres as fast as possible.
ii Group 2 will do it at a pace comfortable to jog and talk.
iii Group 3 will repeatedly jog 50 metres and then sprint 50 metres.
 a What differences in the heart rates do you notice?
 b Were there any differences in the heart rates before you started running?
 c Which group's heart rates returned to normal the quickest?
 d Which group took the longest?
 e Can you tell from the heart rates if anyone 'cheated' and didn't run as asked?

5.1 The respiratory system

The respiratory system

Your cells obtain energy by aerobic respiration. That needs oxygen. Your body takes it from the air via the respiratory system.

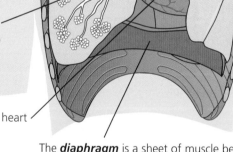

Air is drawn in through the nose, where it is filtered by tiny hairs and warmed and moistened by **mucus**.

The voice box or **larynx**, which makes sounds for speaking.

The windpipe or **trachea**. This is a flexible tube held open by rings of cartilage.

In the lungs, the trachea branches into two **bronchi**. Each is a bronchus.

The bronchi branch into smaller tubes called **bronchioles**.

The bronchioles end in bunches of tiny air sacs called **alveoli**. Their walls are so thin that gases can pass through them.

heart

A small flap of cartilage stops food going into the windpipe instead of the gullet. It is called the **epiglottis**.

The **lungs** are soft and spongy.

The lungs are in a space called the **thoracic cavity**.

The **pleural membrane** is a slippery skin lining the cavity. It protects the lungs as they rub against the ribs.

The **ribs** protect the lungs.

The **intercostal muscles** between the ribs help you breathe in and out.

The **diaphragm** is a sheet of muscle below the lungs. It helps you breathe in and out.

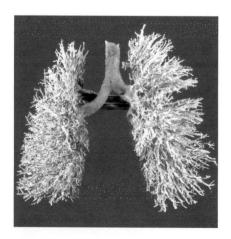

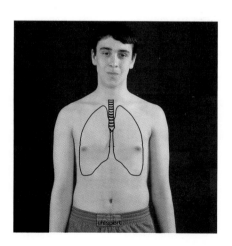

A resin cast of the lungs, and an outline of their position in the body. The green tubes in the resin cast are the ones that carry the blood supply.

The alveoli

Your lungs take in oxygen and give out carbon dioxide. This gas exchange takes place in the alveoli of the lungs (see below).

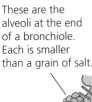
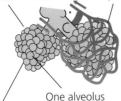

These are the alveoli at the end of a bronchiole. Each is smaller than a grain of salt.

The alveoli are covered with tiny blood vessels called **capillaries**. Gases can pass through the capillary walls.

One alveolus

The walls of the alveoli are thin and moist, which helps gases pass through.

Gas exchange in the alveoli

The diagram opposite shows what happens in the alveoli.

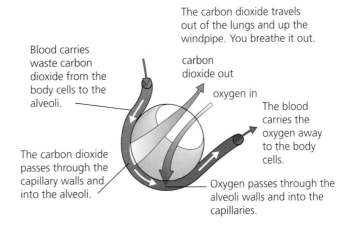

Blood carries waste carbon dioxide from the body cells to the alveoli.

The carbon dioxide passes through the capillary walls and into the alveoli.

The carbon dioxide travels out of the lungs and up the windpipe. You breathe it out.

carbon dioxide out

oxygen in

The blood carries the oxygen away to the body cells.

Oxygen passes through the alveoli walls and into the capillaries.

How air changes in your lungs

In the lungs, oxygen is taken from air and carbon dioxide added to it. So the air you breathe out is different from the air you breathe in.

This table shows the changes:

Substance	Amount in inhaled air (the air you breathe in)	Amount in exhaled air (the air you breathe out)
oxygen	21%	17%
carbon dioxide	a tiny amount	3%
nitrogen	79%	79%
water	little	more

Look at nitrogen. The amount does not change. Can you explain why?

QUESTIONS

1 What job does the hair in your nose do?

2 What's another name for your windpipe?

3 What stops food going into your windpipe?

4 What job does the pleural membrane do?

5 Which two gases are exchanged in the lungs?

6 Where in the lungs does gas exchange take place?

7 The alveoli have very thin walls. Why is this useful?

8 Do you use all the oxygen you breathe in?

9 You breathe out the same amount of nitrogen as you breathe in. Why is this?

5.2 Breathing and exercise

Breathing is also called **external respiration** or just **respiration**.
Don't confuse it with cell respiration (as described in the next unit)!
Breathing in is **inspiration**.
Breathing out is **expiration**.

When you breathe in

several changes take place.

1 The intercostal muscles contract. This
   pulls the rib cage upwards. So the chest
   expands.

2 The diaphragm contracts. This pulls it
   down and flattens it, making the chest
   even larger.

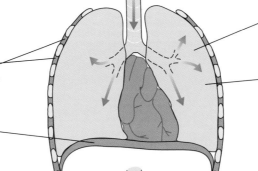

3 When the chest expands, the lungs
   expand too, because their moist surface
   clings to the chest lining.

4 When the lungs expand the pressure
   inside them falls. So more air is sucked
   down the windpipe and into the lungs.

When you breathe out

the opposite changes take place.

1 The intercostal muscles relax. This lowers
   the rib cage and makes the chest smaller.

2 The diaphragm relaxes so it bulges
   upwards again. This makes the chest
   even smaller.

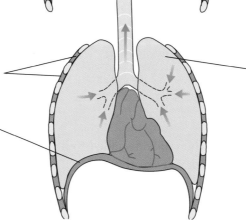

3 When the chest gets smaller the lungs are
   compressed. So air is pushed out of the
   lungs and up the windpipe.

How much air do you breathe?

◎ The **tidal volume** is the amount of air you breathe in or out with each
  breath. When you breathe deeply during exercise it increases. The
  main reason for this is to get rid of carbon dioxide.
◎ **Respiratory rate** is how many breaths you take in a minute. Once
  again this rises as a short-term effect of exercise.
◎ The **vital capacity** is the maximum amount of air you can breathe
  out, after breathing in as deeply as you can. It is usually around 4.5 or
  5 litres. It is very important to sports people as the more air you can
  get rid of in the first few seconds the less carbon dioxide is left in you.

**Tidal volume x respiratory rate =
minute volume**
ie the amount you breathe per minute

Effects of training

◎ Your breathing muscles grow stronger which allows deeper breaths, i.e.
  your vital capacity increases.
◎ More alveoli become surrounded with capillaries so gas exchange is
  more efficient.
◎ The joint effect of this is that aerobic/stamina work can continue
  longer before you tire.

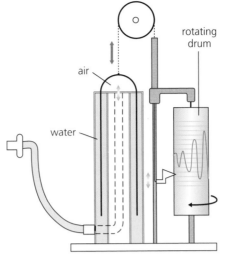

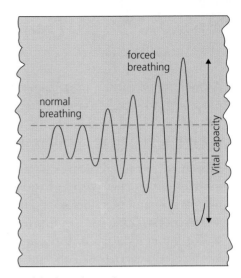

Tidal volume increasing

The volume of air you breathe in and out can be measured using a spirometer.
When you breathe into the mouthpiece, the dome rises so the pen falls, marking a trace on the paper.

Your lungs and exercise

Your lungs and heart work as a team to get oxygen round the body and clear carbon dioxide away. When you exercise, your heart and lungs have to work harder. This is what happens:

1 During exercise, cell respiration in your muscles increases, so the level of carbon dioxide in your blood rises.

2 Your brain detects this. It sends a signal to your lungs to breathe faster and deeper.

4 The brain also sends a signal to your heart to beat faster, so:
– more blood gets pumped to the lungs for gas exchange
– more blood gets pumped to the muscles, carrying oxygen and removing carbon dioxide.

3 Gas exchange in your lungs speeds up. More carbon dioxide passes out of the blood and more oxygen passes into it.

Look how breathing changes during exercise:

For an 18-year-old . . .	at rest	during exercise
tidal volume	0.5 litres	2.5 litres
respiratory rate	12 breaths a minute	30 breaths a minute
minute volume	6 litres a minute	75 litres a minute

QUESTIONS

1 What is: **a** inspiration? **b** expiration?

2 When you breathe in your chest expands. **a** Explain how this happens. **b** Explain why your lungs expand too.

3 Why does air leave the lungs when you breathe out?

4 What is: **a** tidal volume? **b** respiratory rate?

5 In the table above, how did exercise change: **a** the tidal volume? **b** the respiratory rate? **c** the minute volume?

6 Explain how these changes helped the person.

5.3 Cell respiration

As mentioned earlier, breathing in and out is known as **respiration**. Its purpose is to supply oxygen to the body cells and take away the poisonous by-product – carbon dioxide. In the body cells a different kind of respiration takes place – **cell respiration**.

Movement is caused by muscles contracting. This needs **energy**. Your muscles obtain energy from **food**. Food is a mixture of carbohydrates, fats, proteins, vitamins, minerals and fibre. When you eat, this is what happens:
◎ The food is broken down to a liquid in your gut. This is called **digestion**.
◎ The liquid food passes through the gut wall into your blood.
◎ The blood carries it to all your cells, including muscle fibres.
   The cells use it for energy, growth and repair.

How carbohydrates are digested

Your muscles use both carbohydrates and fats for energy. Here we look at just carbohydrates. They are first broken down into **glucose**.

blood stream

1 Starch is a carbohydrate found in foods like rice and pasta. It is a string of glucose molecules joined together.

2 In your gut, enzymes break the starch down into glucose.

3 The glucose passes through the walls of the gut, into your bloodstream.

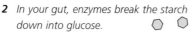
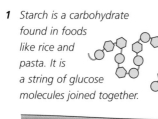

part of a starch molecule

glucose molecules

glucose to other body cells

6 The rest gets carried in the blood to all the other cells of the body.

glucose to muscle fibres

5 Some gets stored in your muscles as glycogen. This is changed back to glucose during exercise.

glucose to liver

4 Some gets stored in the liver as glycogen. It will be released again when the glucose level in your blood falls too low.

Aerobic and Anaerobic respiration

In muscle fibres (and other body cells), energy is obtained from glucose. When this process uses oxygen, it is call **aerobic respiration**. When it does not use oxygen, is called **anaerobic respiration**.

Aerobic respiration
glucose + oxygen → carbon dioxide + water + energy

produces heat, warming the body

used for muscle contraction, providing movement

Advantages	Disadvantages
The body has a plentiful supply of glucose stored, so it can supply energy for long periods of time. There are no dangerous by-products. The carbon dioxide is breathed out and the water is lost through sweat, urine and breathing, i.e. perspiration, excretion and expiration.	It takes 90 seconds after starting exercise for the aerobic system to get going. This is because we need to raise the heart and breathing rates in order to get oxygen into our muscles. Activities requiring all-out effort, e.g. sprinting, mean that we cannot get enough oxygen to our muscles in time. Therefore we cannot use this system.

Anaerobic respiration

During all-out effort, oxygen cannot reach the muscles fast enough: so we use anaerobic respiration.

Glucose → energy + lactic acid

The same amount of glucose will produce less energy, but it will be produced much faster.

Advantages	Disadvantages
Can be used immediately and for very powerful contractions, e.g. sprinting and jumping.	After approximately 60-90 seconds, lactic acid makes muscles tired and painful. All-out effort must cease or you will collapse. It creates an **oxygen debt**.

Oxygen debt

Muscles need extra oxygen to get rid of lactic acid. This extra oxygen is called the oxygen debt and **is the amount of oxygen needed to get the body back to its resting state**. Most of the lactic acid gets turned into carbon dioxide and water and a little back into glucose when enough oxygen is available.

Ways in which you create an oxygen debt:

◎ By taking part in any maximum-effort activities. As soon as the event is over, you repay the debt by breathing hard to take in extra oxygen.

◎ During long events (for example long-distance running and cycling, etc.) you create an oxygen debt at the beginning of the exercise while waiting for your heart rate and breathing to increase to get the extra oxygen to your muscles. This takes 2–3 minutes to happen. If your event is very gentle (for example a jog), you can then get enough oxygen to jog and repay the oxygen debt. If you are going faster (for example at $3/4$ speed), then you can only get enough oxygen for the exercise and will have to repay the debt at the end.

◎ In any sports that require a sudden burst of speed or maximum effort (for example: most team games, and long-distance running when you put in a small sprint to lose an opponent) you will use bursts of anaerobic energy. Depending on what you do between these bursts will decide on how easily your oxygen debt is repaid.

Tired but not out of breath after a gentle run.

Repaying oxygen debt after maximum effort.

QUESTIONS

1 Where do our muscles get energy from?

2 What is *digestion*?

3 Once glucose is broken down in the stomach where does it go?

4 The glucose gets stored in two places. How and where is it stored?

5 Give an equation of *aerobic respiration*.

6 What happens to the waste products?

7 Give an equation of *anaerobic respiration*.

8 What are the advantages and disadvantages of anaerobic respiration.

9 Name two ways in which you can create an oxygen debt.

10 Define *oxygen debt*.

5.4 Summary of training effects

In all the chapters so far we have looked at the changes that months of training can make to your body. We summarise them here.

The effects of aerobic training

1 On the heart and circulation. Over months of swimming or jogging or cycling these changes take place:

◉ Your heart grows bigger. It holds more blood and contracts more strongly. More blood gets pumped out with each heart beat. It becomes a more efficient pump.

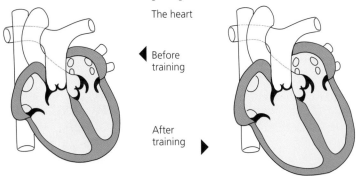

The heart

◀ Before training

After training ▶

This champion swimmer has a larger heart, more blood, more capillaries, and a greater lung capacity than he had when he started training.

◉ Your resting heart rate falls, because now you can supply the same amount of blood with fewer heart beats. The fitter you are, the lower your resting heart rate.
◉ After exercise, your heart rate returns to its normal resting rate faster than it did before.
◉ The volume of blood in your body increases. You produce more red cells and more haemoglobin to help with oxygen delivery.
◉ Arteries grow larger and more elastic so blood pressure falls.

2 On the respiratory system. Aerobic training also increases the fitness of your lungs and respiratory system.
◉ The rib muscles and diaphragm grow stronger. So the chest cavity gets bigger when you breathe in. This means the lungs can expand further, taking in more air with each breath.
◉ Since the lungs expand further, more alveoli are available for gas exchange. So more oxygen is picked up at each breath and carbon dioxide removed.
◉ More capillaries grow around the alveoli, which means more blood gets carried to them.

The combined effects of aerobic training on the heart, and the circulatory and respiratory systems is that your maximal oxygen consumption increases. This means that each kilogram of your body weight can process more oxygen which means exercise can continue for longer.

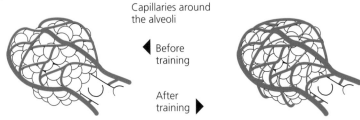

Capillaries around the alveoli

◀ Before training

After training ▶

◉ This means you can move oxygen to the muscles faster and get rid of carbon dioxide faster. So you don't get tired so quickly.

The effects of anaerobic training

Anaerobic training has these effects:

◎ Your heart walls get thicker to cope with the strain of all-out effort on your circulation system. Especially the left ventricle wall.
◎ Your muscles are able to tolerate lactic acid better and clear it away faster. So you can go all out for longer than before.

The effects of muscle training

Endurance training. Endurance training has these effects on muscles:

◎ They get better at using oxygen, so they can work harder for longer without fatigue.
◎ They get better at using fat for energy. This is good since your body has lots of stored fat. It gives more energy than glycogen per gram.
◎ More capillaries grow around the muscles so more blood reaches them, bringing oxygen and food and removing carbon dioxide.

Strength training. Strength training has these effects on muscles:

◎ They grow thicker, because the muscle fibres grow thicker. An increase in muscle size and strength is called **hypertrophy**.
◎ They contract more strongly and efficiently.
◎ The tendons get bigger and stronger.

The effect on bones

As you saw in chapter 2, bones are alive. Cells called **osteoblasts** build new bone while cells called osteoclasts break it down again. All training puts extra stress on your bones. This makes the osteoblasts work harder so your bones get stronger.

The effects on joints

◎ Exercise makes ligaments stronger.
◎ It also thickens the cartilage at joints, so bones are better at absorbing shock.
◎ Stretching increases the range of movement at a joint, and helps muscles contract more strongly.

The effects on body fat

◎ Training increases your basal metabolic rate. You burn up stored fat faster even when you are resting.
◎ Since your muscles get better at using fat for energy, more fat is burned up during exercise too. So you get slimmer.

Endurance training has no effect on the size of your muscles. It takes strength training with heavy weights to enlarge them like this.

> **ALTITUDE TRAINING**
>
> Training in a very high place, e.g. Mexico City causes a problem for distance runners. There is less oxygen in every breath. Training at altitude makes the aerobic changes on page 74 happen quicker.
>
> It is good for anaerobic events as there is less gas to push your way through. You can jump and throw further and sprint faster.

QUESTIONS

1 How would you expect these to change over months of jogging: **a** your resting heart rate **b** your lung volume **c** your rib muscles **d** your leg bones **e** the cartilage at your knee joints?

2 It takes all-out effort to lift heavy weights. So the muscles work anaerobically. What effect will this have on the weightlifter's heart?

3 Training reduces body fat in two ways. What are they?

Questions on chapter 5

1 Like other substances in food, carbohydrates are broken down during digestion. The substance that is produced can be used by your muscles for energy.

   a Name this substance.

   b Name the process by which energy is obtained from it.

   c Some of the substance is stored in your muscles. In what form is it stored?

   d Why is it stored in the muscles?

   e What happens to this store during exercise?

   f The substance is also stored in your liver. After a marathon run, your liver store of it will be low. Why do you think this is?

2 a Write down a sentence equation for aerobic respiration in your muscles using glucose.

   b Explain what happens to each substance that is produced.

3 a Write down a sentence equation for anaerobic respiration in your muscles using glucose.

   b Explain what happens to each substance produced.

4 Match each statement i - ix below to A, B, C or D. Choose the best match each time.

   A external respiration

   B cell respiration

   C inspiration

   D expiration

      i This process produces energy from glucose.

      ii The air moved in this process contains less oxygen than normal air.

      iii Oxygen is normally used for this process.

      iv This is another word for breathing.

      v During this you get rid of carbon dioxide.

      vi The air moved during this is called inhaled air.

      vii The air moved during this is called exhaled air.

      viii During this you take in oxygen.

      ix This can also take place without oxygen.

5 Explain what happens to a breakfast of muesli (a starch) from when you have eaten it, to when you have a PE lesson half way through the morning.

6 This diagram of the respiratory system has numbers but no labels.

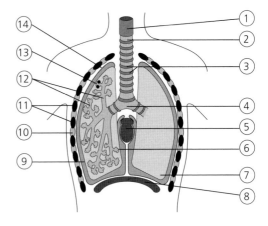

   a Write down the numbers 1 to 14 in a list.

   b Beside each number, write the correct label.

   c What is the purpose of the respiratory system?

7 Copy and complete the paragraph below, using words from this list. You may use a word more than once, or not at all.

   ribs   diaphragm   volume   decrease   exhaled
   relax   intercostal   lungs   expiration   heart

   During inspiration the _____ muscles contract and pull the _____ upwards and outwards. At the same time the _____ contracts, changing from a dome to a flatter shape. These movements cause the _____ to increase in _____. During _____ all these muscles _____, causing air to be _____.

8 Look at this table:

	% oxygen	% carbon dioxide
Inhaled air	21	0.03
Exhaled air during quiet breathing	17	3
Exhaled air during exercise	15	6

   a Why is there less oxygen in exhaled air than in inhaled air?

   b Why is there more carbon dioxide in exhaled air than in inhaled air?

   c Explain why the percentage of oxygen in exhaled air falls during exercise.

   d Explain why the percentage of carbon dioxide in exhaled air rises during exercise.

   e Exhaled air contains at least 15% oxygen. Explain why this makes the 'kiss-of-life' possible.

9 A spirometer was used to record an athlete's breathing at rest and after exercise. Each wave (from one trough to the next) represents one breath. From the height of the wave you can tell the volume of air breathed in.

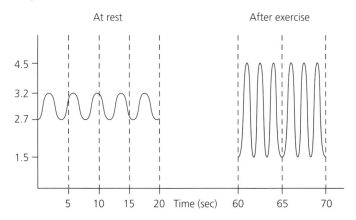

a What was the athlete's tidal volume at rest?
b What was her tidal volume during exercise?
c What was her respiratory rate:
   i at rest?
   ii during exercise?
10 Exhaled air during exercise still contains at least 15% oxygen. Why does our breathing rate and tidal volume increase when we obviously do not require more air?

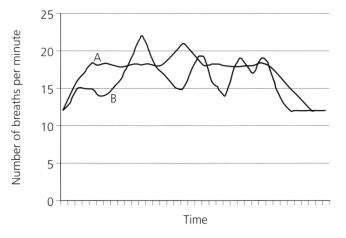

11 a Which of the above lines do you think is the long-distance runner and which the netball player? Give reasons for your answers.
b Can you explain why the runner might have had the sudden change in heart rate?

Answer **either** c or d below

c The netball player is a centre. Can you think of another position where the breathing rate would be very different and why?
d If the graph were for two football players what difference would you expect to see between a striker and a midfielder?

12 Jack started a game of basketball.
   a Is it aerobic, anaerobic or both? Explain your answer using specific examples from a game.
His breathing got deeper and faster during the first few minutes.
   b Explain the mechanics of how he breathes
   c What are the proper terms for
      i the number of breaths he takes per minute.
      ii the amount he breathes in and out in one breath.
   d Jack's vital capacity is 5 litres. He can breathe out 80% of this in the first second. His friend, David, has asthma and when affected by it his air passages swell. He can only breathe out 40% of his vital capacity in the first second. Why do you think that this could be a problem?

Below is a graph of Jack's exercise and an explanation of what he is doing. Once you have read it answer the question below the graph.

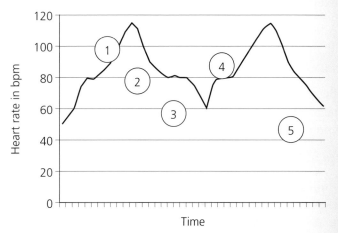

1: Twenty seconds of man-to-man defending, fast break and lay up.
2: Jogging while a team-mate has the ball.
3: Time out
4: Jogging then very hard defending for the last thirty seconds of the game.
5: Game over

13 Using the above graph and your information on oxygen debt, explain fully when one is created and when it can be partly or fully repaid.
14 What is produced in Jack's body that acts as a trigger for his brain to speed up his heart rate and breathing?
15 After several months of training Jack found that he could continue for longer before tiring. What long-term effects of training on his lungs would have helped to contribute to this?

6.1 Testing your cardiovascular system

As we did with muscles, we are going to look at how to measure current levels of fitness before moving on to how to improve them. In testing stamina remember it is a combination of heart, lungs and blood vessels, i.e. your whole cardiovascular system.

Testing aerobic fitness

(i.e. stamina or cardiovascular endurance).
The only foolproof method of doing this is in a sports lab with special equipment. The air you breathe out is collected and run through a special computer.

This measures your **maximal oxygen consumption** or $\dot{V}O_2$ **max**. This is the maximum volume of oxygen you are able to use when exercising. The larger the value, the fitter you are.

A large person will generally use more oxygen than a small one, because he or she has larger muscles. To get around this, $\dot{V}O_2$ max is usually expressed in *litres of oxygen per kilogram of body weight*.

Because the above test needs so much special equipment, other tests have been devised to do the same thing. They are not as accurate but do compare well.

The multistage fitness test

Equipment
◎ A distance of 20 metres marked out on the ground with sticky tape.
◎ A tape recorder and a tape with bleeps recorded on it. (The bleeps start slow but speed up each minute. The slowest are called level 1, the fastest are level 23.)

Method
1 Run 20-metre shuttles between the lines of sticky tape. Your foot should be on or across the sticky tape each time the bleep sounds.
2 When the bleep speeds up you must speed up too.
3 Stop when you cannot keep up with the bleep. The level and the number of shuttles you did at that level are recorded.
4 Your teacher will then work out your $\dot{V}O_2$ max from a table. The higher it is the fitter you are.

Although the multistage fitness test is good, it is a maximal test, i.e. you carry on until you cannot do any more. This is dangerous for the very unfit and also painful. The next test is sub-maximal, i.e. you stop before your maximum effort.

Sophisticated equipment is used to measure $\dot{V}O_2$ max in the lab. At school you can use the multistage fitness test (below) which is much simpler.

The multistage fitness test, or 'bleep test'.

The Cooper test

Equipment
◎ A measured running track, in the gym or outside.
◎ A stop watch and whistle.

Method
1 Jog on the spot to warm up.
2 When the whistle goes, start running round the track as fast as you can. Your laps will be counted.
3 The whistle will go again when twelve minutes are up. Stop running. The further you ran in the time, the fitter you are.

The Kasch-Boyer step test

Equipment
◎ One bench, 30 cm high.
◎ A stop watch.
◎ Paper and pen to record.

Method
1 Step onto the bench one foot at a time and then step down again at a pace of one every two seconds for three minutes.
2 Five seconds after finishing take your pulse for one minute.

The lower your heart rate at the end of this the higher your level of cardiovascular endurance. The results can be compared to a rating chart.

These three tests all look at a person's stamina. The last two are good indicators of general fitness. To be able to complete them they will also need muscular endurance. There is little point in testing strength as each muscle would require a different test. If you were going to set a programme to help general fitness it would involve activities using the whole body, e.g. swimming. This means overall strength would increase anyway.

The Cooper test.

The Kasch-Boyer step test.

QUESTIONS

1 What does $\dot{V}O_2$ max mean?
2 Why does it have to be expressed in litres of oxygen per kilogram of body weight?
3 Name two tests of aerobic fitness, one maximal and one sub-maximal.
4 Which of the two tests would you perform on someone just returning from injury?
5 If you did really well in the multistage fitness test does this mean that you could be a really good long-distance cyclist? Explain.

6 If your team did the 'bleep test' on a football pitch the first time and three months later repeated it but in a sports hall, the results could be said to be invalid. What do you think this means?
7 Very briefly state the changes to your cardiovascular system that should result in you doing better in any of these tests after several months of training.

6.2 Principles of training

Once you have worked out the areas you need to train, then the programme can be planned using the following principles:

1 The principle of progression

This means starting slowly and building up. Your body takes time to adapt to the increased demands on it. If you overdo exercise you could risk torn muscles and joint injuries.

You will notice the biggest changes early in your training programme. The fitter you get, the harder it is to gain further improvement. This shows you are getting close to your full potential. If you keep exercising at a constant level your fitness will stay at that level.

For aerobic effects you need to be doing a minimum of twenty minutes three times a week. It may take several weeks for an unfit person to build up to this. A good way to check if someone is ready to move onto harder work is to ask

a Did you feel really bad during the exercise?
b Did you have to stop?
c Were you sore or stiff the next day?
If the answer to these is 'no' then the sessions can be increased or **OVERLOADED**.

It is important to find out how someone feels after training.

2 The principle of specificity

By now you will have learnt what is meant by this. What energy systems do you want to improve – aerobic or anaerobic? This will also relate to whether you use fast or slow twitch fibres. Do you need general or specific fitness? What specific area, agility, coordination, etc.? When you have worked this out you will also know if you are going to need **pressure** training to test that you can apply these skills under competitive stress.

Specificity means just work on the areas you need, i.e. **BE SPECIFIC**.

> **PRESSURE TRAINING**
> - Pressure training is where you are put under pressure during training.
> - It usually means you have to complete a training task in a very short time, or train in a difficult situation.
> - For example, suppose you are doing skills training as a goalkeeper. Shots are taken very quickly, one after the other and from different directions, to put you under pressure.
> - Pressure training sharpens up your reactions.

Both students are exercising their muscles, but the end results will be different. Heavy loads will build strength, many repetitions of light loads will improve endurance.

3 The principle of overload

Fitness can only be improved by doing more than you normally do, i.e. overloading your body systems. For an unfit person any exercise could be more than normal! Remember that you must build up to the minimum of three lots of twenty minutes weekly. People can improve their fitness by basing their programme on **FITT**, i.e. increasing **F**requency, **I**ntensity, **T**ime they do it for and the **T**ype of exercise they do.

A training diary is very useful to help you plan future sessions. The person opposite is working on stamina. Their running work is fine but it looks like they need to break down the swimming into smaller parts, e.g. swim eight minutes, rest, swim eight minutes, rest and then do another one if they feel OK.

They could overload by using FITT, i.e. increasing the frequency to four sessions a week, increasing the intensity by running or swimming faster, increasing the time of some or all of the sessions.

> Week One
>
> Monday   Jogged 20 minutes. Felt ok.
> Tuesday   Rest day
> Wednesday   Tried to do 20 minutes swimming but
>   only did 12 minutes before needing a rest!
> Thursday   Rest. Felt really stiff in shoulders
> Friday   Still too sore to exercise
> Saturday   Jogged 7 minutes, speeded up for 7
>   minutes, jogged for 7 minutes. Felt good.
> Sunday   Rest

4 The principle of reversibility

This means any adaptations (changes) that occur due to training will be reversed when you stop. This is why you need to train every two to three days otherwise you would lose the effects before the next session started. If you had to rest for three to four weeks due to injury or illness you will need to start training at a lower level than when you last exercised.

Overtraining?

Training makes you fitter but overtraining can make you ill. Exercise must be done in **moderation** or you will suffer the ill effects of soreness, joint pains, sleeping problems, loss of appetite and feelings of anxiety and tiredness. You catch colds and flu more easily. These are signs that you should cut down, or take a break.

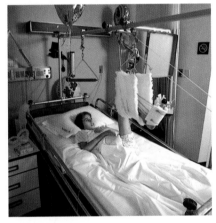

*Here today, gone tomorrow. Strength training enlarges your muscles. That's called **hypertrophy**. But if you're confined to bed they waste away. That's **atrophy**.*

QUESTIONS

1 List the four principles of training

2 What is meant by progression?

3 What is the danger of trying to progress too quickly?

4 What is the minimum weekly running training you should do to improve general fitness?

5 What areas of fitness should you concentrate on to get better at 100-metre sprinting?

6 What principle of training is question 5 refering to?

7 There is no gain without pain. Do you think this statement is true? Explain.

8 Draw up your last week's exercise in the form of a training diary.

9 Using the word FITT write down the ways in which you could overload ready for next week.

6.3 Training the energy systems

On pages 72 and 73 we learnt about energy systems:

Aerobic respiration – the production of energy using oxygen
Anaerobic respiration – the production of energy without using oxygen

Most sports are a mixture of aerobic and anaerobic work. You may use all-out effort during a tennis volley (anaerobic work) and then slow down again (aerobic work). Training makes both energy systems work better. But the training is different for each. So you must study your sport to see how much of each system you use. Then decide on the best mix of training.

Training and heart rate

The harder you exercise, the faster your heart beats. So heart rate shows how hard you are working and which energy system you are using.

The fastest your heart can beat is called your **maximum heart rate**. You can find it using this formula:

maximum heart rate = 220 – your age

At fifteen your maximum heart rate is 205 beats per minute (bpm). You can measure your *actual* rate by taking your pulse. If it is around 60% of the maximum (say 123 bpm) you are working aerobically. If it is around 90% (185 bpm) you are probably working anaerobically.

Heart rate and target zones

Depending on how fit you want to be (and how fit you are now) you need to work within a range of heart rates. This is your **target zone**.

To gain aerobic fitness:

◎ you must exercise **above** a minimum heart rate. This minimum rate depends on how fit you are. For an unfit fifteen-year-old it is about 60% of your maximum or about 123 bpm. Exercise below this will bring *no aerobic benefits*.
◎ you must also exercise below an upper limit. Once your heart rate rises above a certain point you are doing anaerobic work and lactic acid will build up and cause you pain. This point will vary depending upon your present fitness level and could be anywhere between 70-85% of your maximum. You must exercise below this point to gain aerobic benefits.

This means that for aerobic training you must work within a range of heart rates. This is called your **aerobic training zone**. You reach it, and stay in it, by adjusting the intensity of your exercise. The heart rates at the limits of the zone are called the **training thresholds**. The lower limit is the **aerobic threshold**. The upper limit is the **anaerobic threshold**.

When those leg muscles need energy for the really big push, anaerobic respiration takes over. Do you think they're working anaerobically here? What clues can you find?

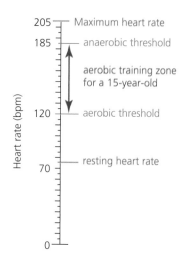

The aerobic training zone and the training thresholds. Where will the anaerobic training zone be?

The graph on the right shows that target zones are specific to you.

An unfit person should be working at 60-70% of their maximum heart rate, a fitter person at 65-75% and a fit person at 75-85%.

Keep this in mind when planning your personal exercise programme or PEP.

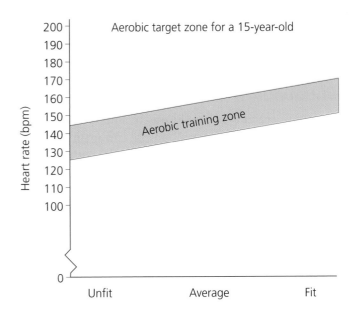

Aerobic target zone for a 15-year-old

Aerobic training

◎ Choose an activity which involves the large muscles of the body and where you can work rhythmically for a long time. For example walking, swimming, jogging, cycling or skipping.
◎ Work for *at least* 15 to 20 minutes a session.
◎ Your heart rate should be within your aerobic training zone. This means it should be *at least* 60% of your maximum heart rate. As you get fitter you can move up to 75% or so.
◎ Train *at least* three times a week otherwise it will not be effective.

Anaerobic training

Anaerobic exercise puts a lot of stress on your heart and circulatory system. This means it can be dangerous. If you are unfit, do several weeks of aerobic training *before* you start on anaerobic training.

For anaerobic training:

◎ Use all-out effort for any of the above activities (running, swimming, cycling and so on).
◎ Take turns using all-out effort and lighter effort or rest, so that your body has time to pay off the oxygen debt and remove lactic acid.

You can find out more about energy training methods in the next unit.

EFFECTS OF AEROBIC TRAINING
• heart grows larger
• blood volume increases
• more capillaries grow
• fat burned more readily
See page 74 for more details.

EFFECTS OF ANAEROBIC TRAINING
• heart walls grow thicker
• muscles tolerate lactic acid better
See page 75 for more details.

QUESTIONS

1 Name the two kinds of energy system your muscles use. What is the difference between them?

2 Describe how you could use both energy systems in a sport. (Not tennis!)

3 **a** What is *maximum heart rate*? **b** What is its value for a person aged 30?

4 **a** What does *aerobic training zone* mean?
b Roughly what is your aerobic training zone?

5 What is the *aerobic threshold*?

6 What is the *anaerobic threshold*?

7 For anaerobic training you must work above the aerobic training zone. Explain why.

6.4 Methods of energy training

Continuous training

Continuous training is a good way to improve your aerobic system. It is also a good way to burn body fat. You run, swim, cycle or walk for at least thirty minutes at the same pace, without rest. You overload by increasing the time, distance, speed or all three.

◎ Build up the time slowly, if you are unfit.
◎ Work in your aerobic training zone. Start at around 60% of your maximum heart rate and work up to 75%.
◎ If you are training for competitions, work up to distances that are 2 – 5 times the competition distance.

Continuous training has some disadvantages:
◎ It includes no skill work.
◎ It can get boring.
◎ If you are running to help improve your football game, for example, you will also need sprint sessions.

Continuous training improves your aerobic endurance – and tests your mental endurance. You need good motivation to keep going.

Fartlek training

Fartlek training was developed in Sweden. The word means *speed play*, and the method involves many changes of speed. You can use it to improve both aerobic and anaerobic energy systems. You can adapt it for running, cycling, skiing and other activities.

◎ Fartlek running sessions are very good for games players, since games have many changes of speed.
◎ Change the mix of fast and slow work to suit your sport and the energy system you want to work on.
◎ To overload, increase the time or speed for each activity or choose more difficult ground. For example run uphill or through sand.

Fartlek training has some disadvantages:
◎ The athlete decides on the speed. Coaches can't tell if athletes are working as hard as they should.
◎ It needs a lot of motivation to work at maximum speed, so it is easy to drop the effort.

A typical fartlek session	
Jog for warm up	8 min
Sprint every other lamp-post	8 posts
Jog recovery	5 min
Sprint 10 paces,	10 reps
Recovery	30 sec
3/4 pace for 30 sec	6 reps
Jog recovery	1 min
Jog to finish	10 min

Aerobics

Aerobics classes are a popular way to improve aerobic fitness. You do exercises for every part of the body. You work at a pace that keeps your heart rate in the aerobic training zone.
◎ You work in time to music, which makes it fun.
◎ Jumping and stamping can jar your bones and damage your joints. To avoid this, work on a sprung hardwood floor or soft mat. Or else choose low impact aerobics. What do you think these are?

Cross training

This is where you use other forms of exercise to help you get fitter for your sport, e.g. weight training to help rugby, or cycling to help running.

Aerobics classes make exercise fun. (But isn't it always?)

Interval training

In interval training you follow a fixed pattern of fast work followed by slow work or rest.

The jogging is to help remove lactic acid. The two-minute rest is to allow full recovery. You can tell by your heart rate if you have recovered. As you get fitter you can overload by:

◎ increasing the number of reps or sets or both
◎ reducing the time for slow work
◎ reducing the rest time between sets.

There is no point increasing the distance, since you are practising acceleration. By about 30 metres you are already at full running speed.

Note these things about interval training:

◎ You can use it for either anaerobic or aerobic work, depending on the distance and the number and length of the intervals.
◎ You can use it for other activities such as cycling and swimming.
◎ It does cause pain so you need high motivation to keep going.
◎ Since there is a set pattern it is easy to tell if someone is giving up.

Circuit training

This is a good way to organise your muscle or skill training. A circuit usually has 8 to 15 **stations**. You do a different exercise at each station, e.g. 1: step-ups, 2: sit-ups, 3: press-ups, 4: squats, 5: pull-ups, 6: ski-jumps, 7: dorsal raises, 8: short sprints.

You normally spend a set amount of time on each activity (from 20 to 30 seconds). You can overload by increasing the time spent on each exercise, try to do more repetitions in the time limit or by doing the circuit more times.

When designing a circuit make sure that you change muscle groups between each activity to delay fatigue.

Advantages:

◎ Can be adapted to use free weights or body weight.
◎ Can be adapted to shorter or longer bursts of work (aerobic or anaerobic).
◎ Can be adapted to concentrate on certain muscle groups.
◎ Can be adapted to work on skills.

> **A typical interval session to improve acceleration**
>
> A 30-metre sprint then 30 seconds of easy jogging.
> Repeat that 10 times.
>   (10 repetitions or reps.)
> This completes one set. (A set is made up of a number of reps.)
> Then take a two-minute rest.
> Do 3 sets altogether, with two-minute rests in between

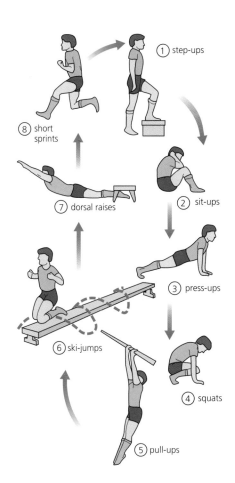

① step-ups
② sit-ups
③ press-ups
④ squats
⑤ pull-ups
⑥ ski-jumps
⑦ dorsal raises
⑧ short sprints

QUESTIONS

1 What is *continuous training*? What activities could you use?

2 Name one disadvantage of continuous training.

3 What is *fartlek* training?

4 Why is fartlek training good for games players?

5 Make up a fartlek training session for a cyclist.

6 What is *interval training*?

7 What is: **a** a rep? **b** a set?

8 Make up an interval training session for a swimmer who wants to do more anaerobic work.

9 Two of these training methods will *not* improve your anaerobic energy system. Which are they?

6.5　Skills testing and training

In chapter 1 we looked at specific fitness – power, agility, co-ordination, reaction time, timing and speed. These all involve our nervous system in some way and the more we practise the more the nerves and brain get used to what is required, i.e. we become more skilful.

With some areas such as power and speed, muscle training will help a lot but with others constant repetition of skills in isolation is needed, e.g. shooting in netball and basketball or a sequence in dance and gym. It is often very difficult to separate the different areas of fitness. Catching a ball in rugby and avoiding a tackle needs co-ordination to make hands and ball meet, timing to be in the right place to receive the pass, and to avoid the tackle you need agility, power, speed, timing and co-ordination.

On the following pages are several skill-related fitness tests which can:
◎ give an idea of whether a person has potential in an area
◎ help to test for improvements at a later date.

A balance test

This is a test of your balance when standing on one leg.

Equipment
◎ a gymnastics bench.
◎ a stop watch.

Method
1 Stand on one foot on the bar – whichever foot you prefer.
2 Hold the other foot high behind your back, using the nearest hand.
3 Stand for as long as you can. The attempt ends when you touch the floor or let go of the foot you are holding.
4 Keep trying until one minute is up. Record how many attempts you made.

A balance test.

The 5-metre shuttle

This tests your speed and agility. You need both of these for any sports involving you directly outwitting an opponent, e.g. invasion games, net and wall games, striking games and many water sports. Do you think the test relies mainly on fast or slow twitch fibres?

Equipment
◎ a running lane 5 metres long and 1.2 metres wide, marked out with sticky tape. It should be level and not slippery.
◎ a stop watch.

Method
1 Warm up by jogging on the spot. Then get ready at the start line.
2 At 'Go', sprint as hard as you can to the end line and back. Both feet must cross both lines. This is one cycle.
3 Do five cycles altogether, turning as fast as you can each time.
4 Your total time is recorded in seconds.

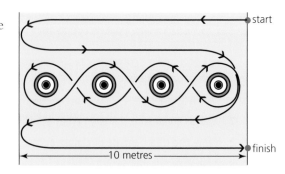

The 5-metre shuttle can be made more challenging with the help of plastic cones. Arrange the cones like this and run the route as fast as you can. A good test of agility!

A test of your 30-metres sprint speed

Do you think the test relies mainly on fast or slow twitch fibres?

Equipment
◎ a 30-metre distance marked out on a level non-slippery surface.
◎ a stop watch.

Method
1 Stand about 20 metres behind the start line.
2 At 'Go', sprint as fast as you can from there to the finish line.
3 Your partner will record your speed in seconds, from the moment you cross the start line to the finish line.

Reaction time test

This is a test of your reactions to a stimulus, in this case how quickly you can detect an object is falling and catch it.

Equipment
◎ a metre ruler.

Method
1 You rest your arm on the table with your hand over the edge.
2 Your partner holds the ruler vertically so that it passes between your thumb and fingers at the 50cm mark. Do not touch the ruler.
3 Without warning your partner drops the ruler and you have to catch it.
4 Record, by looking at the mark where you caught the ruler, how far it fell before you caught it. The faster you react the less it will have fallen.

The tests shown here are commonplace. It is possible to make up other tests to put certain skills under pressure, e.g. to test **co-ordination** you might try to bounce a ball in each hand at the same time for a set period like 30 seconds.

Each sport has a set of skills that need to be practised in isolation and then with degrees of pressure. In games like golf, a range can be used allowing you to repeat certain shots with the help of a coach. In many striking activities, a bowling machine can be set up to deliver a certain ball. In aesthetic sports such as dance and gym, the use of video equipment and mirrors can help fine-tune performance.

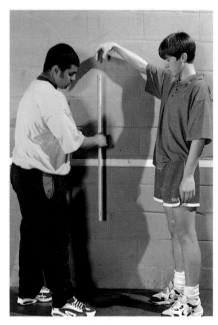

The ruler drop test to test speed of reactions. Fast reactions are needed in most sports

QUESTIONS

1 Define power, agility, co-ordination, reaction time, timing and speed.

2 Choose any three of the above and give specific examples from your sport of when they are used.

3 Which of the tests from this spread would it be useful to perform on a games player?

4 In two of your sports explain the need for good reactions.

5 What sort of weight-training programme would you set for someone who scored low in the 30-metre sprint test and wants to improve? (Use pages 50–51 to help you.)

6 Do you think the balance test or the 5-metre shuttle would be more useful in testing a netball player? Why?

7 List 3 skills in isolation to be practised from your sport.

Questions on chapter 6

1 What tests would you use to check the current level of fitness on the following people and why?
 a Sarah – a 15-year-old girl who is unfit but wants to be fitter. She enjoys most indoor sports.
 b Chloe – a sixteen-year-old girl who has just started ladies rugby. She plays other sports but really wants to excel in rugby. She plays as a forward.
 c Omar – an 18-year-old county basketball player preparing for county trials.
2 What is the word to use to help you devise a training programme.
3 List the four principles of training you should consider.
4 Using the answer to number two write a paragraph about what you would set Sarah to do during her first week and why?
5 How would you know if it was too hard or if you should start to increase it?
6 Look at the schedule below. It is what Chloe does at present. In what three ways could you overload her training schedule?

Monday –	25 minute gentle run
Tuesday –	Club training involving sprints, muscle work and skills.
Wednesday –	Rest
Thursday –	Netball match
Friday –	Weight training
Saturday –	Rugby match
Sunday –	Rest

7 Why would you not increase her schedule by all three ways in one go? (Refer to a principle of training.)
8 What specific areas of fitness would Omar want to train in?
9 What energy system would he use the most and want to improve?
10 Omar can reach level 14 in the multistage fitness test. Unfortunately he twists an ankle in a match and spends four weeks out of full training. When tested again he only reaches 12.5. Why could this be?
11 Which training methods would you include in your training for:
 a Running a marathon?
 b 100m swim race?
 c The rugby season?
 d Gymnastics?
 e The Tour de France?
 f Rock climbing?

You can choose more than one method if you wish. Explain your answers.

12 Match each statement below to the correct letter A, B C or D
 A progression
 B overload
 C reversibility
 D specificity.

 a Weight training will thicken your muscle fibres.
 b If you stop aerobic training your muscles quickly lose their improved ability to use oxygen.
 c Gradually increase the weights you lift, week by week.
 d You improve your fitness by increasing the demands you make on your body.
13 Is each statement below true or false?
 a Anaerobic training makes your lungs expand.
 b Running improves the endurance of your leg muscles.
 c You could use the fartlek method for weightlifting.
 d You must exercise at below 60% of your maximum heart rate to gain aerobic benefits.
 e You could use interval training for muscle strength
 f Your maximum heart rate is the highest rate it reaches during a training session.
 g Your heart rate is not affected by anaerobic exercise.
 h Cycling strengthens your diaphragm.
 i Continuous training is also called long slow distance training.
 j Endurance training does not make your muscles thicker.
14 Say whether the tasks below are isotonic, isometric or a mixture of the two.
 a Running
 b Holding a 50kg barbell steady at shoulder height
 c Doing a handstand and holding it
 d Cycling
 e Arm wrestling with a friend
 f Putting on your clothes in the morning.
 g Pushing a car that has run out of petrol
 h Rock climbing
 i Hanging from a beam.
15 Referring back to question (1), what heart rate would you expect Sarah to be working at and why?
16 After two weeks Sarah feels really good and goes for a run. Her heart rate goes up to 185 bpm after ten minutes and she has to stop because her muscles hurt so much. What has happened?
17 Omar needs anaerobic training and needs to pass his anaerobic threshold whilst doing interval training. What does this mean?

18 Continuous training
  Fartlek
  Interval
  Body weight circuit
  Which of the above would they need and why?
  a Sarah
  b Chloe
19 Chloe would need to do both isometric and isotonic work. Why? Would Omar need both? Explain.
20 Why is fartlek training so good for games players.
21 Give a disadvantage of fartlek training especially if you train alone.
22 Continuous training is sometimes a bit boring. What other fun method is there to improve aerobic fitness?
23 Omar weight trains three times a week
  a What kind of strength do you think he needs?
  b Which of the following do you think is his schedule and why?
    i Heavy weights, few repetitions,
    ii Light weights, many repetitions
    iii Medium weight, medium repetitions, fast.
24 If you could not get to a weight-training gym could you still do weight training? How?
25 Why should you not do weight training below the age of sixteen?
26 Devise an eight-station skill circuit that you could give either
  a a netball team
  b a basketball team
  c a rounders team
  d a cricket team
27 Give two benefits of good flexibility.
28 What actually happens at your joint when you stretch?
29 Would you set Sarah a weight-training programme? Explain your answer.
30 Chloe would need to improve her strength. Explain what type of weights session you would set in terms of repetitions and amount of weight.
31 Which type of muscle fibres would respond best to:
  a power work?
  b endurance work?
  (Remember your work from Chapter 3)

USE OF INFORMATION TECHNOLOGY

32 The table below shows the results of some fitness tests performed by students from Astor school.

Name	Weight (kg)	$\dot{V}O_2$ Max overall	$\dot{V}O_2$ Max per kg	vertical jump (cm)
Emily	47	33	0.70	30
James	50	45	0.90	34
Ryan	55	40	0.73	27
Beccy	56	47	0.84	27
Luke	64	45	0.70	15
Paul	53	50	0.94	20
Nic	75	32	0.43	10
Kayleigh	46	33	0.72	20
Richard	49	37	0.76	25
Hannah	60	33	0.55	23
Matt	54	54	1.00	21
Thom	40	32	0.80	26
Sarah	60	30	0.50	12

  a Plot a scatter graph to compare weight to vertical jump. Is there any relationship? Would you expect there to be one? Why?
  b Plot a scatter graph to compare $\dot{V}O_2$ max with the vertical jump. Is there any relationship? Would you expect there to be? Why?
    (If you are able to put these values into a spreadsheet the graph function will help you draw scatter graphs.)
  c If you have collected this data for your group could you say if your group is more, or less, fitter than the one above? What is the evidence?
  d Look at Emily and Beccy's vertical jump. Who jumped the highest? Does this mean that she is more powerful? Explain your answer supporting it with evidence from the table.

7.1 A training programme

We have now looked at the different parts of the body, their use in sport and briefly at the short- and long-term effects of exercise on them. We have looked at what principles to take into account when planning a programme of exercise and at the type of training methods possible. Using the next few pages you should now be able to plan your own fitness schedule. Here is one as an example. These are the steps to take.

1 Find out about the person it's for

Suppose it's for a female called Jane. It will work well only if it suits her needs. So find out these things about her:

◎ **Her age.** A programme that suits a a person of twenty could harm a person of fourteen.
◎ **Her current level of health.** If she has just recovered from a long illness, for example, you need to take that into account.
◎ **Her current level of fitness.** Does she exercise already? Is she generally fit? Is she overweight or overfat? Tests could help here.
◎ **Why she wants to get fitter.** Does she just want to feel healthier? Or to improve her skills in a sport?
◎ **What kind of exercise she enjoys.** If she likes your programme she is more likely to stick with it.

Use the information opposite to analyse Jane's needs.

2 Analyse the person's needs

An aerobic fitness programme is the best start for Jane, because:
◎ it will make her healthier as well as fitter.
◎ it will help her slim since aerobic exercise burns up body fat.
◎ it will help her when she takes up tennis. Aerobic fitness is a good basis for all sports.

3 Plan the programme (remember the word FITT)

Frequency. This is how often Jane should train. Training should be at least three times a week to take effect. Jane feels that's enough for her.

Intensity. It is important to start at the right intensity.
◎ If a programme is too demanding, muscles get sore and strained. This puts the person off. It is better to start too low than too high.
◎ Jane should start at around 60% of her maximum heart rate. Why?
◎ How Jane feels is also a good guide. If she feels it is easy, raise the intensity until she finds it difficult *but still manageable*.

Time. For training to take effect, a person needs to spend:
◎ at least twenty minutes for an aerobic training session
◎ at least fifteen minutes for a muscle training session
◎ at least four to six weeks to see real benefit.
(These times do not include the warm-up and cool-down. See page 92)

Hi, I'm Jane.

Jane - 16 years old.
No exercise for months.
Overfat. Wants to lose weight.
Has already started to eat less.
Likes swimming. Lives near a
    pool.
Hates jogging.
Later this year she would like to
    take up tennis.

Training activity or type of exercise. This is what you will ask Jane to do. It should be something:
◎ that will improve her aerobic fitness
◎ that will be safe and convenient for her, and that she will enjoy.

Swimming and cycling are good choices. They are safe for unfit and overweight people because the water or the bike supports the body and your bones do not jar.

Other things to think about
◎ Have an easy day after a hard one, e.g. gentle running after sprint work.
◎ Everyone needs a minimum of one rest day a week.
◎ A programme will need to run for several weeks before you make many changes due to the body taking time to adapt.

Let us look now at a programme for someone who is more active.
17-year-old male – Dale

Analysis of needs
He plays football twice a week for a club and once for school.
He wants to be fitter so his football improves.
He would like to be more skilful in the game.

Plan the programme
Frequency – He already does three times a week, but it is all football games. Dale could add running, circuits, fartlek or interval training up to an overall total of 5 times a week and then progress to 6 times.

Intensity – This person could cope with hard work. He needs aerobic and anaerobic work so bouts of maximum effort are needed.

Time – Thirty minutes for aerobic work. For circuit and interval work he will gradually add more repetitions or sets which will extend the time.

Type – During the football season he will need to maintain stamina (continuous work) but extend anaerobic fitness – interval, circuit or fartlek training. He could also weight train. Variety is important to prevent boredom. He would need to find a club that does skill training too.

Swimming does not jar the bones and is excellent for the unfit and elderly.

Dale already plays a lot of football. To improve his fitness he must use the principle of SPECIFICITY.

QUESTIONS

1 Why is aerobic exercise a good start for an unfit person? Think of as many reasons as you can.

2 What do the letters FITT stand for?

3 It helps if the person enjoys the training programme. Think of three reasons why.

4 Suppose a 15-year-old wants to improve his basketball skills. Would you give him Jane's programme? Explain why.

5 What is Jane's maximum heart rate?

6 At around what heart rate should she train? Why?

7.2 The training session

Having now decided on a programme of training, your actual training session should have three parts: **the warm-up, the activity** and **the cool-down**.

I The warm-up

The **warm-up** is light exercise to get you ready for the main activity. In cold weather wear a track suit and plenty of layers.

◎ Start with light jogging for 5 minutes or so. This warms your muscles. It makes them more flexible and lowers the risk of injury. It increases your heart rate and blood flow. It warms the synovial fluid and makes your joints more mobile.

◎ Next do some stretching. Work all the main joints. Stretching increases the range of movement at the joints. It helps to stop muscles, tendons and ligaments getting strained. Hold each stretch for at least 10–30 seconds, with no bouncing.

◎ Now do a specific warm-up for the activity. For example, a few tennis serves or some netball shooting practice. As well as working your muscles, this helps to prepare you mentally.

By the end of the warm-up you should be sweating lightly. Move on to the training activity as soon as possible.

Light jogging: a good start to the warm-up for any training session, and a good way to cool down.

2 The training activity

This is the body of the training session. It could be:
◎ continuous, fartlek, circuit, weights or interval training
◎ an actual practice game, for example netball or football
◎ a skills training activity, e.g. a typical session for a cricketer might be:

Activity		Time (minutes)
batting	working on the different shots, a few minutes on each – off-drives, on-drives, pulls and cuts	15
fielding	close catching, high catching, picking up and throwing	15

3 The cool-down

The cool-down is where you help your body to recover after vigorous exercise. It is just as important as the warm-up.

◎ Start with a few minutes of gentle exercise such as jogging. This helps to keep your circulation going. So more oxygen reaches your muscles and lactic acid is cleared away faster. This means less soreness.

◎ Finish with some stretching. This will help loosen your muscles and prevent stiffness. After heavy exercise muscles often get very tight.

Stretch those muscles. As part of the warm-up it helps to prevent injury. Do it in the cool-down to stop soreness.

Recovery rate

Your recovery rate is how quickly your body gets back to normal after exercise. These are some of the changes that take place.

Heart rate. This slows down to your normal resting rate. How long it takes depends on how hard you exercise and how fit you are. The fitter you are the faster it returns to normal. It may take just a few minutes.

Lactic acid. Lactic acid is removed by oxygen when you repay the oxygen debt (page 73). It is removed faster when you do a cool-down (active recovery), as the graph on the left below shows.

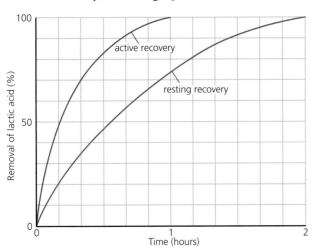

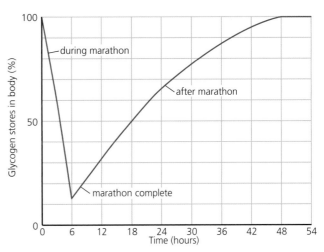

Glycogen stores. During exercise, muscle glycogen gets used up. It takes time to replace. After prolonged exercise such as marathon running, it can take 48 hours for glycogen stores to fully recover. Look at the graph on the right above.

Muscles. Your body has to repair any damage done to muscles during training. Stiffness and soreness take time to clear.

Recovery time

◎ Make sure you take enough time to recover between training sessions – 24 to 48 hours in the early stage of a training programme.
◎ If you train every day, follow a heavy session one day with a light session the next, to help recovery.
◎ Even during a heavy training period, take one rest day a week.

QUESTIONS

1 What are the three stages of a training session?
2 What should you do during a warm-up?
3 Describe all the ways a warm-up helps you.
4 What should you do during a cool-down?
5 Describe all the ways a cool-down helps you.
6 What is *recovery rate*?
7 If your heart rate returns to normal very quickly after hard exercise, what does that show?

8 Look at the first graph above. **a** What does it show?
   b How long does the process take:
   i without cool-down? **ii** with cool-down?
9 Now look at the second graph. **a** Why does the glycogen level fall at the start? **b** How long does it take to recover?
   c What could the athlete do to speed up recovery?

7.3 Your personal exercise programme

1 What are your needs?

Jot down in the first page of your training diary the answers to the following questions.
◎ Your age.
◎ Your level of health – any recent illness, asthma, etc.
◎ Your current level of fitness – write down what you do in an average week using FITT.
◎ Why you want to be fitter.
◎ Exercise (or things about it) you enjoy/dislike.

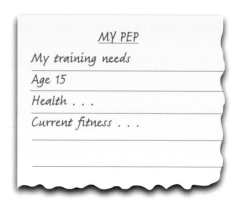

2 Analyse your needs

◎ What areas of fitness do you need to improve?
◎ What energy systems to you need to work on?

3 Plan the programme

Plan the programme using principles of training. Start by doing one week and filling in anything you do regularly. Below in red is Dale's from page 91.

Monday –	Rest day
Tuesday –	**Skills and sprint work at local club**
Wednesday –	School match
Thursday –	**fartlek, circuit or interval**
Friday –	Rest day
Saturday –	Match
Sunday –	Match

His new work is in black. Dale should keep to this for several weeks until his body adapts.

Aerobic or stamina work for games players is usually done out of season because once you have reached a good level you can maintain it by playing lots of matches and doing the training above.

A six-week programme

Once you have the basic plan of your week you can then sketch out a six-week programme. Try to vary it to prevent boredom. Remember if you are unfit you will improve rapidly. Very fit people only make marginal improvements despite a whole season of training. This is why in sports such as the 100m sprint, world records get broken by only 100ths of a second. Unfit people may improve their time by five whole seconds!

Jane's six-week programme

Week	Session	Activity (time in minutes)
1	1	Swim 10 easy pace, full recovery. Repeat three times.
	2	Cycle 20, easy pace.
	3	Walk fast to school/college/town/work – 20.
2	1	Swim over the next few weeks, try to extend swimming time and reduce the rest until able to do a full 20 minutes.
	2	Cycle easy pace 20.
	3	Walk 20 fast or do another swim or cycle.
3	1	Swim 15, full recovery, swim 10, easy pace.
	2	Cycle 8 easy, 8 faster, 8 easy.
	3	Aerobics.
4	1	Swim 7 easy, two lengths faster, two lengths easy. Repeat until 15 minutes completed. Easy swim 10.
	2	Find a cycle route that takes approx 25 minutes. Try to do it faster than this.
	3	30 minutes fast walk.
5	1	20 minutes easy swim. No rest!
	2	Repeat last week's cycle. Record time.
	3	Aerobics.
6	1	Swim 7 easy pace, 7 hard, 7 easy
	2	30 minutes cycle.
	3	Aerobics, walk, cycle or swim – minimum 20-30.

Remember Jane likes swimming. She is unfit and wants to lose weight. She *hates* jogging. Jane needs to do a minimum of three lots of 20 minutes weekly but at the moment she cannot do 20 minutes in one go. She needs to progress to this and exercise in moderation as too much causes pain and could put her off. In week one, Jane is really checking how much she can do and how she feels the next day. She did do 30 minutes of swimming but with rests in between.

Don't forget to keep a diary of how you feel. This will help you to know when to overload. Only work out detailed training for one week at a time as illness or other commitments may force a change.

QUESTIONS

1 Why do you think for a person like Jane it is better to increase time and intensity rather than frequency?

2 In week one Jane swims for ten minutes before resting. It takes her until week five before she has increased to twenty minutes. What is this principle of training called?

3 In Jane's cycling programme give examples of **a** how her intensity of training was overloaded. **b** how the timing of her sessions was increased.

4 If by week six Jane could complete that week's training comfortably, explain how you would overload her system for the following week.

7.4   Exercise you can do

Unfit performer

If, like Jane, you need to build up gradually you can do like she did with the swimming and apply the same principles to any other types of continuous training, e.g. cycling, rowing, or using aerobic machines in a gym. You will also gain benefits in muscular endurance, strength and provided you warm up correctly, also in flexibility. The aim is still the same – try to be out of breath for 20 continuous minutes then build up to 30.

Average performer

If you feel you are already quite fit (perhaps due to an active/busy lifestyle) and you want to be fitter you could do many different things. If your general fitness is OK (cardiovascular strength, flexibility, muscular endurance and strength) then you could do most other types of training without harm. You really need to be specific – why do you want to be fitter? If it is for general health, then continuous training methods – as above – are still very good. You should be able to train 5 times a week but may still need to build up to it. Include fun activities – if you are a social person – sports centres run aerobics and circuits. If you prefer working alone many have gyms where young people can use the aerobic machines, e.g. steppers and cross trainers. You can design a circuit based on body weight to do in your own home.

If you have decided that you want to be fitter for a certain sport then think about what areas of fitness your sport needs, e.g. water polo – requires strength, speed, agility, good reactions, flexibility, stamina, co-ordination – in other words EVERYTHING! Your training programme needs to reflect this. If you are playing water polo you probably belong to a club so train with them for skills at least once a week. A good circuit will help with strength, speed and agility and interval training will help your energy system and the necessary muscles for your sport.

Week 1   Session

1	Interval session in pool. Sprint half length swim to end. Repeat 10 times. Rest until heart rate is back to normal. This is one set. Do 3 sets if you feel ok.
2	Continuous training for 20-30 minutes.
3	Skill session with club.
4	Circuit session.
5	Match.

The good thing about the week's session above is that it is easily overloaded. The circuit will naturally overload as you get fitter and do more repetitions each week. The interval can have less or more repetitions, more sets or less rest. Vary to prevent boredom by changing the type of continuous training, or do aerobics instead occasionally. Try fartlek training occasionally – remember you can do it in a pool or by running and cycling. Remember to have an easy day following a hard one.

Continuous training.

Aerobic machines in a gym are fun and safe.

Water polo requires most areas of fitness – general and specific.

Fit performer

If you are very fit and seriously training then you should be able to put up with high heart rates. Do not be tempted to try to use weight training or long distance road running until you are fully grown.

The New Zealand netball team practising skills.

Your work is an extension of the programme shown on the previous page. With a high level of motivation you should be able to tolerate (put up with) high levels of lactic acid as top-level performance will require this. You must **always** have a weekly rest day and again try to have an easy day after a hard one. Here is an example based on netball:

Week 1	Session	Activity
	1	Sprint, circuit or interval session.
	2	Running – 20 minutes fast.
	3	Skills training with club.
	4	Rest.
	5	Fartlek training.
	6	Running – 30 to 40 minutes slowly.
	7	Match.

Progression, as with the last programme, should be obvious by applying overload.

Long-distance training

If your sport involves lots of different areas of fitness it is easier to prevent boredom. But what about if you are a long-distance sportsperson? For events like these you can either do shorter work with greater effort or longer than normal but easier. For example, here is a week's training for an adult, one month prior to a 10-kilometre race:

Week 6	Session	Activity
	1	40 minutes with 6 × 1 minute hard with 1 minute rest.
	2	75 minute run.
	3	Rest.
	4	40 minutes with 5 × 30 seconds hard with 30 seconds rest.
	5	45 minutes easy.
	6	Rest.
	7	50 minutes run.

QUESTIONS

1 Why do you think that people under the age of 16 can use aerobic machines in a gym but not weights?

2 If you were an unfit performer and were using cycling as a way of getting fit, describe 3 different sessions that you could do that all have the minimum requirement of 20 minutes of exercise.

3 If you were training for horse riding because you decided to take it up seriously, what areas of fitness would you concentrate upon?

4 Imagine that you have the opportunity to play a lot of golf because your parents work on a course. You play every day and are very good, but do no other sport. You decide that you are going to start fitness training. What areas do you think you should work on and why?

5 With your teacher's help it is now time to plan a PEP for yourself. Draw out your own six-week guide with a similar layout to Jane's.

7.5   The athlete's year

If you are a judo player, you can take part in judo events all year round. But many sports are **seasonal**. Cricket is an example. In the UK, cricket is played from May to September.

This shows how the year is divided for an athlete who plays a seasonal sport. The calendar is for a 'winter' sport such as netball or rugby. A cricket player will follow the same pattern but over different months, since cricket is a 'summer' sport. It is sometimes called **periodisation**.

June	July	Aug	Sept	Oct	Nov	Dec	Jan	Feb	Mar	April	May	June

1 PREPARATION   **2 COMPETITION**   **3 RECUPERATION**

(i) out-of-season   (i) pre-season

I Preparation

i Out-of-season Here the athletes build up to a high level of general fitness. They do continuous training over long distances to improve aerobic fitness. They have strength training for the major muscle groups. They are careful with diet: lots of carbohydrate, not much fat!

This shows a typical out-of-season training programme for the England netball team:

Weekly programme for June/July	
Monday	4 - 5 mile run
Tuesday	Strength training using weights
Wednesday	3 - 4 mile run
Thursday	Strength training using weights
Friday	3 mile run
Saturday	Rest
Sunday	Strength training using weights

ii Pre-season Here the athletes focus on fitness for the sport. They run short fast lengths to improve anaerobic fitness and speed. They continue strength training on the muscles needed for the sport but work faster to improve their power.

Skills training becomes important, with circuits designed to practise different skills. For example footwork, shooting and defending in netball. Now is the time to really sharpen up.

Weekly programme for August/September	
Monday	Skills training including jumping (plyometrics)
Tuesday	3 mile run (time it and aim to go faster next time)
Wednesday	Strength/power training using weights
Thursday	Skills training including intense anaerobic work
Friday	Strength/power training using weights
Saturday	Fast 3 mile run
Sunday	Rest

2 Competition

Here the athletes play at least two matches a week. The aim is to win! They still need training to maintain fitness, and to build up to their peak. The times of the season when you are at your fittest is called peaking. You aim to peak at the time of your biggest events. They need extra care to avoid injury at this time. It is easy to get injured through tiredness, or by overusing muscles.

Weekly programme for October	
Monday	Rest
Tuesday	Skills and weight training
Wednesday	Sprint or skills or plyometrics as necessary
Thursday	Fast 2 mile run, skills training
Friday	Strength/power training using weights
Saturday	Match
Sunday	Match

A happy and victorious Millwall women's football team after winning the women's FA Cup.

Many important events are overseas, in hotter weather or at higher altitude. The athletes will travel in advance so that they can train under the right conditions for the match.

3 Recuperation

Time for rest and relaxation. The aim is complete recovery from the competition season. But the athletes do not laze around. They play other sports for exercise and enjoyment. They are still careful with diet so as not to put on extra weight. Lots of carbohydrate, not much fat.

QUESTIONS

1 Give three examples of: **a** seasonal sports **b** sports which are played all year round.

2 For seasonal sports, the year has three main stages. **a** What are they? **b** What is the main purpose of each stage?

3 Look at the netballers' programme for June/July. What will be the effect of these activities?

4 The August/September programme includes some fast runs. Why?

5 What is a *skills training circuit*? Give an example.

Questions on chapter 7

1 If you were to devise a training programme what 3 steps do you need to take?

2 If you make the programme too hard what might happen?

3 In Jane's information it says 'is she overweight or overfat?' can you work out the difference between these? Explain.

4 Describe a warm-up you would do for either a rounders or a cricket game.

5 Why is an active recovery better than standing still?

6 Explain why you would be unable to run 2 marathons well if you were doing them on consecutive days.

7 This shows the first six weeks of a personal exercise programme designed for a woman aged 50. She hasn't done any exercise for months, but likes walking.

Week	1	2	3	4	5	6
Frequency	2	3	3	3	3	3
Time (min)	20	30	40	38	36	34
Distance (km)	1.5	2.3	3.1	3.1	3.1	3.1

   a What is the correct technical name for this training method?

   b Is it aerobic or anaerobic?

   c How often should the woman walk in week two?

   d From weeks three to six, the frequency and distance don't change. Does this mean there is no progression?

   e What is the woman's maximum heart rate?

   f About what should her *minimum* heart rate be, during the walk, to ensure she is gaining aerobic benefit?

8 Joel is an 18-year-old tennis player.

   a Why does he need to train regularly?

   b Is 'once a week' regular training? Explain your answer.

   c What would be the minimum weekly amount he would need to do to gain aerobic benefits?

   d What does 'aerobic' mean?

   e Name two sports that are mainly aerobic.

   f What two other benefits of exercise may Joel gain as well as physical benefits? (Remember the definition of health.)

   g Define the word 'fitness'.

   h David Beckham is fit but so is David Smith in Year 11 who plays basketball (very badly!) three times a week. How can this statement be true.

9 Use the graph below, showing Joel's heart rate during a game of tennis, to answer the following questions.

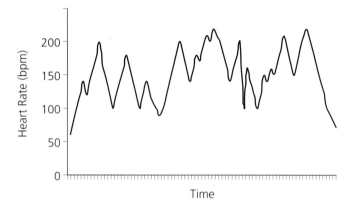

   a Using the work 'threshold' explain why you think both aerobic and anaerobic work took place.

   b What makes you think that Joel is fitter than the 'average' person?

   c What is Joel's resting heart rate?

   d What is the maximum it reaches?

   e How do you work out a person's maximum heart rate?

   f Joel has a quick recovery rate. What does this mean?

10 You are about to play a tennis match.

   a Name six muscles you will use a lot during the match.

   b What is the advantage of warming up these muscles before you start?

   c What will you do to warm up your muscles?

   d You should include stretching exercises in your warm-up session. Give two examples of how this will help you play a better game.

   e From your own experience of warm-ups, describe five stretching exercises you could do.

11 A very fit 16-year-old cross-country runner decides to overload their training and progresses to 6 miles a night around their local town. Is this a good training method?

12 A friend who is fairly unfit admires your level of fitness, why should you not encourage them to join in with your training schedule? Are there any parts of your schedule that would be suitable for them to do with you?

13

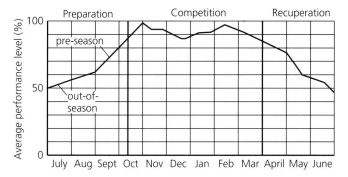

This graph shows how an athlete's level of performance changed through the year.

a Her performance level improved all through the preparation period. Explain why.

b It improved faster as she moved from out-of-season preparation to pre-season preparation. Why?

c The athlete **peaked** (hit her top performance level) twice in the competition season. When did this happen?

d There was a drop in performance in the second part of December. Why do you think this was?

e The athlete's main event took place at the end of March. Was she at her best then?

f Give reasons why an athlete's performance does not remain at its peak all through the competition season.

14 This shows a typical training programme for an 800 m male runner during pre-season preparation:

Monday	50 min road run.
Tuesday	800 m on grass x 4 times, with a 3-minute rest between runs.
Wednesday	8 km run followed by weight training for arms, shoulders and legs.
Thursday	400 m run on track in around 62 secs. Repeat x 11 with a 2-minute rest between runs.
Friday	45 minute fartlek training.
Saturday	10 km easy run followed by weight training for arms, shoulders and legs.
Sunday	Rest day.

a Give the correct name for the type of training he does:
  i On Mondays **ii** on Tuesdays and Thursdays

b What kind of fitness does the Monday session improve?

c What kind of fitness is improved on Thursdays?

d Give two examples of the type of activity he might do during fartlek training.

15 This shows a six-week PEP designed for an unfit and slightly overweight 15-year-old who wants to get fitter before the summer holidays. Her resting pulse rate is 76.

Week 1	Mon	Jogging 5 min + skipping 3 min
	Thurs	Jogging 10 min + skipping 5 min
Week 2	Mon	Jogging 15 mm + skipping 8 min
	Thurs	Jogging 20 min + skipping 10 min
Week 3	Mon	Jogging 25 min + skipping 12 min
	Wed	Jogging 30 min + skipping 14 min
	Fri	Jogging 35 min + skipping 16 mm
Week 4	Mon	jogging 40 min + skipping 18 min
	Wed	Jogging 45 min + skipping 20 mm
	Fri	Jogging 50 min + skipping 22 min
Week 5	Mon	Jogging 55 mm + skipping 24 min
	Wed	Jogging 60 min + skipping 26 min
	Fri	Jogging 65 mm + skipping 28 min
Week 6	Mon	Jogging 70 mm + skipping 30 min
	Tue	Jogging 70 min + skipping 32 min
	Thurs	Jogging 70 min + skipping 34 min
	Sat	Jogging 70 min + skipping 36 min

a What can you tell from her resting pulse rate?

b This a badly designed programme. Explain why. Give as many reasons as you can.

16 This graph shows time taken to clear lactic acid from the body after exercise.

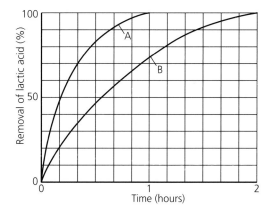

a Why is it good to clear away lactic acid quickly?

b One curve shows the time it takes to clear the lactic acid when the athlete does a cool-down. Which one?

c Name one other benefit of the cool-down. Describe what activities you would do for a cool-down, after a hard game of tennis.

USE OF INFORMATION TECHNOLOGY

17 Devise an initial questionnaire for use in a sports centre to assess the needs of visitors who wish to start training. This should be an A4 sheet of paper, word processed with clear instructions on how it is to be completed.

8.1   The foods your body needs

For energy, and to grow and repair itself, your body needs water and fibre and **nutrients**: carbohydrates, proteins, fats, vitamins and minerals.

Carbohydrates

Carbohydrates are used for energy. They are broken down to **glucose** in your gut and used as a fuel for cell respiration (page 72). Some glucose is stored as glycogen in the liver and muscles.

Carbohydrates are found in sweet and starchy foods. Examples are bananas and other fruits, bread, biscuits, breakfast cereals, rice, potatoes and spaghetti. People training every day should have a high energy intake with 60% carbohydrate. Starchy carbohydrate is longer lasting.

These are just some of the foods that are rich in carbohydrates.

Fats

Fats are also used for energy. Muscles use a mixture of fats and glycogen. The mixture depends on how intense the exercise is, how long it lasts and how fit you are. For example:
◎ on a long walk, muscles use mainly fat
◎ start jogging and they'll start using more glycogen
◎ switch to a sprint and they'll use glycogen only
◎ jog for a few hours and they'll switch increasingly to fat, as glycogen gets used up
◎ the fitter you are, the more your muscles will use fat not glycogen.

Butter, margarine, and cooking oils are fats. Hamburgers, red meats, sausages, bacon, cheese and cream contain a lot of fat. So do oily fish, nuts and avocado pears. Fats are used in making crisps, cakes and biscuits.

These are all rich in fats.

Protein

Your body needs proteins to build cells, to make blood, and to restore and repair muscle and other tissues. They are found in meat, liver, chicken, eggs, fish, beans, peas, lentils and nuts. Your body can also use proteins for energy. But it will do this only if it has run out of carbohydrates and fats.

Some people believe that a high protein intake will make your muscles bigger and help you recover after training. However in western societies we already eat twice as much protein as we need. Excess protein leads to kidney problems and makes joints more susceptible to injury.

Vitamins and minerals

Your body needs tiny amounts of vitamins. Vitamins A and D can be stored in your liver. Vitamin C can't be stored. If you eat more of it than you need, the extra is excreted. That means you must eat it regularly. Minerals are just as important as vitamins. There is enough iron inside you to make a large nail. Without iron your blood can't carry oxygen. Without calcium you'd have no bones, teeth or muscle contractions.

These are rich in protein.

Substance	Where you find it . . .	Why you need it . . .	A shortage leads to . . .
vitamin A	fish, liver, vegetables, eggs, milk	to see in dim light and for healthy skin	night blindness and flaking skin
vitamin C	oranges and other citrus fruits, vegetables	for healthy skin and gums and to help wounds heal	scurvy
vitamin D	made by skin in sunshine; found in milk, fish, liver and eggs	for strong bones and teeth (you can't absorb calcium without it)	rickets
calcium	milk, cheese, dried fish, sardines, green vegetables	for strong bones and teeth, and for muscle contractions	fragile bones
iron	liver, beans, lentils, green vegetables; added to bread	for the haemoglobin in red blood cells	tiredness and anaemia
iodine	seafood and vegetables grown near the sea	for thyroid hormones that control the rate at which you burn up food for energy	a swollen thyroid gland (goitre)

Water

Water does not give you energy. But around half your weight is water. Some is in your blood and other body fluids. Most is in your body cells, where it plays a vital part in reactions.

You could last for several weeks without food, but only 4 or 5 days without water. Once the level in your blood and body fluids falls too low, water is drawn out from the cells. You dehydrate and could die. You should drink at least eight glasses of water a day. If you play sports you may need to drink much more. Why?

Fibre

Fibre is a substance called **cellulose** from the cell walls of plants. You find it in fruit, vegetables, brown bread, bran and other cereals. You can't digest it. It passes straight through the gut and is excreted as faeces. But it is very important because:
◎ it makes a bulky mass which your gut muscles can grip and push along quickly. This prevents constipation and bowel cancer.
◎ it absorbs poisonous wastes from digested food.
◎ it makes you feel full, so you eat less.

These will provide you with plenty of fibre.

QUESTIONS

1 If you have a big match/race at midday what sort of things should you have for breakfast and why?

2 What energy source (what nutrient) would you mainly use for marathon running?

3 Why would a lack of the following affect your performance in sport **a** calcium **b** iron **c** iodine?

4 Why is vitamin C important if you are injured?

5 If you came from a country where the diet was mainly rice what might you need to eat more of to help in a heavy training programme?

6 Why don't we have to do this in most European countries?

8.2   A balanced diet

Your energy needs

Even when you are relaxed and resting you need energy.
You need it to keep you warm, to keep your heart beating and lungs breathing, and for all the reactions that go on in your cells.

◎ Your **basal metabolic rate** (BMR) is the amount of energy you need just to stay alive, awake and comfortably warm.

◎ To move around, digest food and do exercise, you need even more energy. This is called **working energy**. It depends on how active you are.

◎ **total energy needed = basal metabolic rate + working energy**

It can be measured in **kilojoules** (kJ) or in **kilocalories** (C).
1 kilocalorie = 4.18 kilojoules

Different people have different energy needs

Look at the table on the right. It shows how different people have different energy needs. It depends on:

◎ **your age.** You need more energy now than when you were little but as you get over the age of 40 your metabolism slows down and you need to eat less or you will gain weight.

◎ **your sex.** Males usually need more energy than females of the same age.

◎ **your lifestyle.** The more active you are, the more energy you need.

Total energy needed in a day (kJ)		
	male	female
child aged 8	8200	7300
teenager aged 15	11 500	8800
adult doing office work	10 500	9000
adult doing heavy work	14 000	10 500
a retired person of 75	9000	7000

How much energy do foods give?

Your body can use carbohydrates, fats and proteins for energy. Compare the energy each gives:

1 gram of carbohydrate	17.1 kJ
1 gram of protein	18.2 kJ
1 gram of fat	38.9 kJ

A gram of fat gives over twice as much energy as a gram of protein or carbohydrate. So it is very easy to eat much more fat than you need for energy. When this happens you put on weight!

Most foods are a mixture of carbohydrates, fats and proteins. Labels on tins and cartons often show what is in food and how much energy it will give you. Look at labels to find out what you are eating!

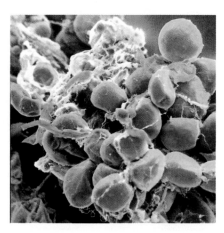

The yellow blobs are fat-storing cells, magnified by 150. Most of your fat-storing cells are laid down when you're a baby. When you eat more food than you need, they get bigger and you get fatter!

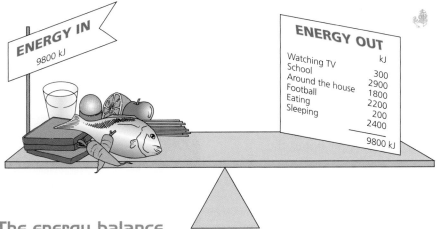

ENERGY IN
9800 kJ

ENERGY OUT	kJ
Watching TV	300
School	2900
Around the house	1800
Football	2200
Eating	200
Sleeping	2400
	9800 kJ

Energy in balance: if energy in = energy out you won't put on weight.

The energy balance

Suppose you need 10 000 kJ of energy a day. You eat enough food to give 15 000 kJ. This is much more than you need. But the extra food is not excreted. Instead it is stored as fat. Even carbohydrate and protein are changed into fat and stored.

◎ If energy in is greater than energy out, the extra food is stored as fat and you gain weight. If you gain too much you may become **obese**.

◎ If energy in = energy out, your weight will not change.

◎ If energy in is *less than* energy out, your body will use up stored body fat for the extra energy. You will grow slimmer. But if too much body fat gets used up you'll become **anorexic**.

A balanced diet

To be healthy you need a balanced diet. That means a diet that matches your energy needs and give the right mixture of nutrients and fibre. Here are some guidelines for you.

◎ If you have to lift your own body weight, for example jumping, you won't be building up a huge muscle mass in training so your build shouldn't require huge amounts of calories.

◎ If you are doing long-distance work then you need to have plenty of starchy carbohydrates.

◎ No athlete needs to eat fatty foods. Fat is made from excess carbohydrates.

◎ By eating a balanced diet you will get enough fat (for long distance/time sports) enough carbohydrate (for anaerobic work) enough protein (repairs) and enough vitamins, etc.

◎ Cut down on salt, sugar, fatty and processed (ready to cook) meals.

◎ Eat plenty of fresh fruit and vegetables.

A balanced diet: around 15% protein, 30% fat and 55% carbohydrate.
Not only are carbohydrates good for you, they are also comparatively cheap.

QUESTIONS

1 What is your *basal metabolic rate*?

2 Explain why a teenage male needs more energy than a retired female.

3 What two units are used to measure energy?

4 If you eat more food than you need for energy, what happens to the extra?

5 What is a balanced diet?

6 What is processed food? Why is fresh food better?

8.3 Weight control and fitness

Body weight

What weight are you? It will depend on:

◎ your height and frame size. The longer and thicker your bones the more you will weigh.
◎ how much muscle and fat you have. (Muscle weighs more than fat.)
◎ your gender. Males are usually heavier than females. Why?

Weight tables show what weight a person of your height should be. If you are more than this you are **overweight**. You have too much fat – or perhaps even too much muscle. More muscle than you need for your work or sport puts extra strain on the heart, joints and ligaments. (See page 18 for a reminder on body shapes)

Fitness and body composition

You could be the right weight but very unfit. For example, you could have lots of fat and only small weak muscles. So **body composition** is a better indicator of fitness. It shows how much fat you have compared with muscle, bone and other tissue.

◎ If you are male, no more than 13 – 15% of your weight should be fat. If it is more you are overfat. If it's over 20% you are obese.
◎ If you are female, no more than 18 – 20% of your weight should be fat. If it is more you are overfat. If it's over 30% you are obese.

You need a certain amount of fat. It forms a protective cushion around the kidneys and other organs. The layer of fat under your skin keeps you warm and acts as a store of energy. But **obesity** means you have an abnormal proportion of fat. If you are overfat or obese, the extra weight puts a strain on the heart, muscles, bones and ligaments. Exercise becomes difficult or even dangerous. Obesity causes joint and back injuries, and leads to heart attacks, strokes, liver disease and other problems.

Underweight?

You are **underweight** if you are below the normal weight range for your height. You could be underweight and overfat at the same time. Exercise will make you feel weak and tired.

Anorexia

Some people go on harsh diets to lose weight. This is very dangerous. It can lead to **anorexia**. You don't eat enough carbohydrate, so your body uses stored fat for energy. Then it runs out of fat and starts using proteins. It takes these proteins from your body tissues. So your organs stop working properly. You may die. Related to anorexia is **Bulimia**. Individuals will eat large amounts of food and then induce vomiting.

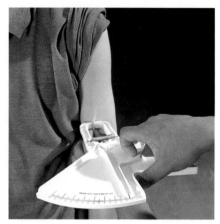

The skinfold test measures body fat. If you'd like to try it, ask your teacher.

If this young woman were anorexic, she'd see herself as horribly obese. People with anorexia have a distorted self-image. They need both medical and emotional help.

How to lose weight

The way to lose weight is by *combining* exercise and diet.

◎ Eat a healthy balanced diet and exercise more. Your body will use up stored fat to obtain the extra energy.
◎ Your muscles will grow when you exercise. Muscle weighs more than fat but takes up less space. So you won't lose much weight at the start but you will look slimmer.
◎ Regular exercise increases your basal metabolic rate. That means you use up more stored fat even when you are resting.
◎ Regular exercise reduces your appetite. You will find it easier to say no to food.

Eating for sport

The best food for sport is a healthy balanced diet.

◎ Don't eat more than you need. The extra will be stored as fat, and fat is a burden in sport.
◎ Carbohydrates will be your main source of energy. Remember, a balanced diet should contain at least 55% carbohydrate.
◎ You will also use fats for energy, depending on how intense the activity and how long it lasts. The more intense it is, the more you depend on carbohydrates. The longer it lasts, the more you depend on fats. But you don't need to eat extra fat. You have plenty stored.
◎ Intense exercise causes wear and tear to muscle and other tissue. Proteins are needed to repair the damage. But there's enough for that task in a normal diet. You don't need extra.
◎ Make sure you drink water during and after sport. Why?
◎ A balanced diet will give you enough vitamins and minerals. You do not need supplements. In fact an excess of vitamins A and D can be dangerous.

An athlete breakfasting before his big Olympic event. Plenty of carbohydrate!

Carboloading

For long events (two hours or more) athletes often use **carboloading**. First, cut down on carbohydrates and train hard. This uses up all your glycogen. Then eat lots of carbohydrates and train lightly in the days just before the event. Your muscles will now store more glycogen than usual.

By a combination of diet and exercise, some athletes have stored up to four times more glycogen than usual. But this can cause problems. Muscles may feel stiff and heavy. Kidneys may not function properly. The athlete may suffer chest pains. So a steady diet of at least 55% carbohydrate is a better solution.

QUESTIONS

1 How can you tell if you are overweight?

2 What does *overfat* mean?

3 What is *obesity*? What problems does it cause?

4 A person can be underweight *and* overfat. Explain.

5 Why are harsh diets dangerous?

6 List three ways exercise helps you lose weight.

7 What is *carboloading*? How does it help athletes?

8 What's the best mix of main nutrients to eat?

8.4 Drugs and sport (I)

Drugs and doping

A **drug** is any chemical substance you take that affects the way your body works. Most drugs were developed for medical purposes. They are dangerous when misused. **Doping** means taking drugs to improve sporting performance. It is a big problem in sports. Athletes take drugs for different reasons:

◎ to pep up their performance
◎ to kill pain so that they can keep going
◎ to build muscles faster than they can do by training
◎ to calm themselves before important events.

An athlete who dopes is cheating. The International Olympic Committee has drawn up a list of banned drugs. It includes the classes of drugs described below. International athletes can be tested for these drugs at any time, and face a ban of at least a year if the test is positive.

Stimulants

These stimulate the circulatory and nervous systems. They raise the heart rate and blood pressure, and speed up reactions. The person feels alert and confident, and can work hard for long periods without feeling pain or fatigue. Examples are:

◎ **amphetamines**, for example Dexedrine, Benzedrine, 'speed'.
◎ **caffeine**. This is a natural stimulant found in tea and coffee.

Stimulants are used in medicine to help patients with heart and lung problems. They are misused by athletes who want to improve their performance.

Dangers
◎ Pain and fatigue are the body's warning signals. If they are suppressed, the athlete carries on too long and risks cramps, strains, and overheating. Overheating can lead to heat stroke.
◎ When the stimulant has worn off the athlete feels really 'down'.
◎ Stimulants can cause violent and aggressive behaviour.
◎ Heavy use causes high blood pressure and liver and brain damage.

A dangerous drug? A caffeine level twenty times above 'normal' would get you banned from the Olympics.

Narcotic analgesics

These are pain-killers. **Narcotic** means causing drowsiness. **Analgesic** means killing pain. Narcotic analgesics act on the central nervous system and stop the body feeling pain. They give a feeling of well-being, relaxation and sleepiness. They include:

◎ **morphine** and **heroin**. These are used in hospitals to treat people in severe pain, for example cancer patients.
◎ **codeine**. This is a much milder drug. There is codeine in many of the pain killers and diarrhoea treatments on sale in chemist shops.

Some athletes use narcotic analgesics to kill the pain from injury, so that they can carry on competing in events.

Dangers

◉ Narcotic analgesics cause constipation and low blood pressure.
◉ They cause extreme apathy.
◉ They are addictive. (Even codeine has its addicts.) The withdrawal symptoms can be very unpleasant.
◉ Carrying on in spite of injury will make the injury worse.
◉ Morphine and heroin are illegal in most countries except for medical use. In some, the punishment for being caught is death.

Anabolic steroids

Anabolic steroids are hormones which help to build and repair muscle and bone. They occur naturally in the body. The male sex hormone **testosterone** is one example. They are also made artificially and used to treat people with wasting diseases. Some athletes and body builders take artificial steroids to increase the size and strength of their muscles and help them recover from training.

Dangers

If you take artificial anabolic steroids you stop the body making its own. This causes many problems, including:

◉ heart disease and high blood pressure
◉ weakened ligaments and tendons
◉ infertility and cancer
◉ aggressive behaviour
◉ the growth of facial hair, and deepening of the voice, in females.

Diuretics

These increase the amount of water excreted in urine. They are used to treat patients with heart disease who have excess fluid in their bodies. They are misused by boxers and wrestlers who want to lose weight quickly before the weigh-in for a match, so that they get into the right group. They are also misused by athletes who drink lots of water to flush out traces of other banned drugs.

Dangers

◉ Essential sodium and potassium salts get eliminated as well as water.
◉ Low levels of potassium lead to muscle weakness and heart damage.

Many athletes have recently tested positive for steroids, in particular nandrolone, e.g. Linford Christie, Edgar Davids, CJ Hunter, Merlene Ottey and Mark Richardson. Merlene Ottey and Mark Richardson were later aquitted.

QUESTIONS

1 What is a *drug*?
2 What does *doping* mean?
3 Athletes who dope are cheats. Explain why.
4 Explain why International footballers at a World Cup somewhere hot, e.g. Korea and Japan, might be tempted to use stimulants.
5 Describe three dangers in using stimulants.

6 Explain why a cyclist in the Tour de France might want to use a narcotic analgesic.
7 What are anabolic steroids? Give two reasons why throwers may use them.
8 What does a diuretic do?
9 Why might jockeys want to use diuretics?

8.5 Drugs and sport (II)

Drugs to reduce anxiety

Beta blockers. When you are anxious, the hormone adrenaline is released into your blood. It makes your heart beat faster and your palms sweat. It speeds up your breathing, and the conversion of glycogen to glucose in your muscles. You are ready for *fight or flight*.

Beta blockers block the effect of adrenaline. They slow down the heart and breathing. They are used in hospitals to treat patients with high blood pressure and heart disease. They are misused by athletes to calm their nerves before important events.

Beta blockers are banned in archery and shooting as well as some other sports. Can you explain why?

Dangers
◎ They can reduce blood pressure so much that the user faints.
◎ They lower performance during lengthy (endurance) events.
◎ They can cause sleeplessness, nightmares and depression.

Tranquillisers. These reduce anxiety and calm you down. Examples are Librium and Valium.

Dangers
◎ They make the person feel dull and lacking in energy.
◎ They are addictive and can be very hard to give up.

Blood doping

Oxygen is carried in red blood cells. The more red cells you have, the more oxygen reaches the muscles. This helps them work for longer.

In **blood doping**, an athlete withdraws blood a few weeks before an important event. The red cells are separated and frozen. Just before the event they are thawed and injected back into the athlete.

Dangers
◎ All blood transfusions and injections carry a risk of infection.
◎ Top athletes already have a high concentration of red cells. Adding more may block their capillaries.

Peptide hormones, mimetics and analogues

Peptide hormones are naturally-occuring substances in our body that control certain functions. Analogues and mimetics are man-made drugs that mimic the hormones resulting in similar effects. Amongst other functions these hormones and drugs:
◎ increase muscle size and strength
◎ help repair body tissue which promotes quicker recovery from injury and training
◎ improve the blood's ability to carry oxygen by increasing the red blood cell count

Andreea Raducan a Romanian gymnast whose doctor gave her a cold remedy containing banned drugs. Her gold medal was taken away from her at the Sydney Olympic Games 2000.

Dangers

◎ they can interfere with the normal hormone balance in the body
◎ allergic reactions
◎ high blood pressure
◎ diabetes
◎ abnormal growth of the hands, feet and face and enlarged internal organs
◎ an abnormal increase in red blood cells carries the same dangers as blood doping

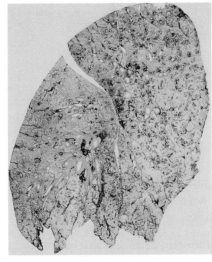

A section through a smoker's lung showing tar deposits. Imagine trying to breathe through that lot!

Socially acceptable drugs

Nicotine and alcohol are socially acceptable drugs. But that does not mean they are good for you! Both of them lower your fitness.

Smoking

This is what you get in a cigarette:

◎ **nicotine** which is a poison. It is addictive. It makes your heart rate and blood pressure rise. It makes new smokers dizzy. It causes heart disease.
◎ **tar**, which is treacly brown stuff that collects in your lungs and respiratory system. It contains thousands of different chemicals. It clogs the lungs and stops you breathing properly. It causes lung cancer and bronchitis. Because it fills the alveoli with tar your lung volume is also reduced. This means you tire quicker.
◎ **carbon monoxide**, which is a poisonous gas in the smoke. In your lungs, red blood cells pick it up in place of oxygen. Less oxygen reaches your muscles and the rest of your body.

There is no 'safe' level of smoking. Every cigarette is dangerous. In the UK around 111 000 people a year die from diseases caused by smoking and around 2000 have legs amputated.

Alcohol

All alcoholic drinks contain a chemical called **ethanol**. It is what makes people drunk. It doesn't do much harm in **small** quantities. But larger quantities are dangerous.

◎ Alcohol affects co-ordination, judgement, balance, speech and hearing.
◎ It can make people aggressive.
◎ It causes the blood vessels of the skin to dilate, so you rapidly lose body heat. This can be fatal outside in cold weather.
◎ It lowers the level of glycogen in your muscles. This means they can't work so long or so hard.
◎ Athletes who drink too much lose their drive to train and compete.
◎ Long-term alcohol abuse leads to kidney and liver damage.

After heavy drinking, there will still be alcohol in the blood next day. Drinking alcohol the day before an important event is a very bad idea.

QUESTIONS

1 What two drugs might a snooker player use and why?
2 In theory, blood doping should improve an athlete's performance. Explain why.
3 Name the substance in cigarettes that causes the heart rate to increase.
4 Why would smoking a cigarette just before an endurance race affect your performance?
5 It is not possible to be a heavy drinker *and* a top athlete. Explain why.

8.6 Hygiene and foot care

Sweating

You have about three million sweat glands in your skin. During hard exercise in hot weather you can lose up to 3 litres of sweat an hour.

Sweat is water containing salts, ammonia and other wastes. It does not smell to start with, but the bacteria that live on your skin feed on it and produce smelly substances. It is important to shower and change your underclothes often to get rid of these smelly substances, and especially after exercise.

Deodorants and **antiperspirants** help you avoid sweaty smells. Deodorants mask the smell of sweat with a nicer smell. Antiperspirants coat the sweat pores with a film so the sweat can't get out. Since sweat helps you during sport, using an antiperspirant before a game is not a good idea.

Choice of clothing

Sports clothing must let you move freely. It must also let you sweat freely since sweat is your body's normal way to cool. Light loose cotton or cotton-polyester clothing is good for hot weather. Shorts and short-sleeved tops expose plenty of skin for sweat to evaporate.

In cold weather it is a good idea to wear several layers. The layers trap heat between them. You can then peel off layers as you get warmer. Cover your head and hands if it's very cold.

Remember, you sweat during exercise even in cold weather. Sports clothing should be washed frequently to remove sweat and bacteria.

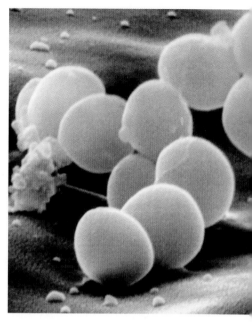

Some of the bacteria that live on your skin and feed on sweat (magnified by 30 000). These are usually harmless. But if they multiply inside blocked pores you'll get a boil or pimple.

Clothes like these are fine for summer sports – but white clothes are even cooler!

Foot infections

Athlete's foot This is a fungus that grows between your toes, making the skin cracked and itchy. It spreads from one person to another by direct contact, or you can pick it up from socks, towels and wet changing room floors.

To avoid athlete's foot, take care where you walk in your bare feet. Use flip-flops around swimming pools. Wash your feet often and dry them carefully between the toes. Avoid socks and shoes that make your feet sweaty. A fungus likes warm damp places!

Veruccas These are flat warts that grow on the soles of your feet. They usually grow where your weight falls, so they can be painful. They are caused by a virus and they spread in the same way as athlete's foot. Veruccas are very contagious. If you have them, wear flip-flops in the changing room to stop them spreading!

To treat athletes foot you'll find sprays, powder and ointment in the chemist's. For verrucas you'll find ointments and medicated pads.

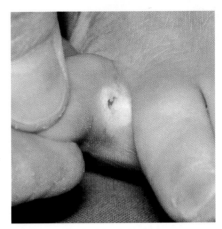

Watch out, there's athlete's foot about. It is highly contagious.

Corns, bunions and blisters

Shoes that are too tight can cause corns, bunions and blisters.

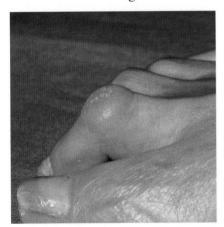

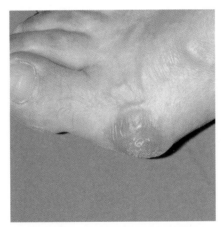

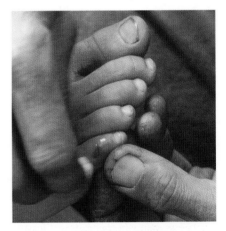

Corns are pads of thick hard skin that form on the toes and soles of feet. They can be very painful. Corn plasters may help, or go to a chiropodist.

At the joint of your big toe is a cushion of liquid called a **bursa**. If it gets inflamed the result is a **bunion**. If a bunion is very painful you will need surgery.

Friction causes skin to **blister**. Don't burst a blister. If it does burst keep it clean and dry and cover it with gauze. Don't pick off the scab that forms.

QUESTIONS

1 What makes sweat smell?

2 What does a deodorant do?

3 What does an antiperspirant do?

4 Why are shorts better than jogging bottoms for tennis on a hot day?

5 How would you know if you had athlete's foot?

6 Write down three things you can do to avoid catching athlete's foot.

7 What is a *verucca*? How would you treat it?

8 What is: **a** a corn? **b** a bunion?

9 Name three problems caused by wearing shoes that are too tight for you.

Questions on chapter 8

1 Which statement is not true?
   A Vitamin C is needed for healthy gums.
   B A gram of fat gives over twice as much energy as a gram of protein.
   C Vitamins give you energy.
   D Calcium, iodine and iron are minerals.

2 Match each substance i - v below to one of the statements A to E.
   A helps move food through your gut faster
   B your blood could not carry oxygen without it
   C the body's first choice for energy
   D is found in every cell in your body
   E needed for the hormones that control how fast you burn up food
      i water
      ii carbohydrates
      iii iodine
      iv fibre
      v iron

3 Name two foods you could eat to obtain each substance:
   a carbohydrate
   b vitamin C
   c protein
   d fibre
   e fat
   f vitamin A

4 **a** What is *basal metabolic rate*?
   b Why do you need energy even when you are lying down perfectly still?
   c The bigger you are, the bigger your basal metabolic rate is. See if you can explain why.

5 Arrange these in order of how much they need to eat. The person who needs to eat least should come first:
      a male student of 17
      a retired woman of 75
      a coal miner of 40
      a boy of 12
      a female student of 17

6 **a** What is a *healthy balanced diet*?
   b What proportion of carbohydrates, fats and proteins should you eat for a healthy balanced diet?
   c Write down six guidelines for a healthy balanced diet.
   d Grilling is a healthier way than frying to cook fish and meat. Explain why.
   e Give three examples of processed foods.
   f What are food additives?
   g A diet of only processed foods is unhealthy. Explain why.

7 Say whether each statement below is true or false.
   a You should take 55% of your carbohydrate in the form of sugar.
   b If you need more energy than your diet provides, the extra is obtained from stored fat.
   c Potatoes provide you with vitamin C.
   d You need more vitamins and minerals when you are training hard.
   e Lean meat is high in fibre.

8 1 kilogram of stored body fat = 32 000 kJ. Suppose your energy needs are 10 000 kJ per day, and you eat enough food to provide 14 000 kJ per day.
   a How much more energy do you take in per day than you need?
   b Are you eating too much food for your needs, or too little?
   c What happens to this extra food?
   d At this rate, how long would it take you to gain an extra kilogram in weight?

9 One can of orange barley Lucozade contains:

protein	a trace
fat	almost none
carbohydrate	63.03 g
energy	1089 kJ

   a Which nutrient provides the energy in Lucozade?
   b Suppose you need 10 000 kJ of energy a day. About how many cans of Lucozade would you need to drink to get this energy?
   c A diet that consisted only of Lucozade would be a bad idea. Give at least three reasons.
   d In Lucozade, the carbohydrate is in the form of glucose. You get energy faster from Lucozade than from eating spaghetti. Why do you think this is?

10 A small tin of baked beans contains:

protein	9.6 g
fat	0.4 g
carbohydrate	27.9 g
fibre	7.6 g
salt	2.5 g
energy	640 kJ

   a Baked beans are a good source of fibre. Why is fibre good for you?
   b You should eat around 18g of fibre a day. What could you eat with baked beans to provide more fibre?
   c You should eat no more than 1.6 g of salt a day. Why is too much salt harmful?
   d What advice would you give the makers of baked beans about the amount of salt they use?

11 A unit called the calorie is also used to measure the energy value of food. Labels will show both kilocalories and kilojoules. Copy and complete:

a 1 kilocalorie = _____ calories

b 1 kilocalorie = _____ kilojoules

c 50 kilocalories = _____ kilojoules

12 Copy and complete the paragraph correctly, by writing *carbohydrates* or *fats* in each space.

Your body uses both _____ and _____ for energy. _____ give more energy per gram. _____ are easier to digest. For intense exercise you use mainly _____, in the form of glycogen. For endurance events such as marathon running, you depend more on _____. The fitter you are, the more readily you can burn up _____.

13 Muscles can use both carbohydrate (glycogen) and fat for energy. As this bar graph shows, the extent to which your muscles depend on each source depends on the activity:

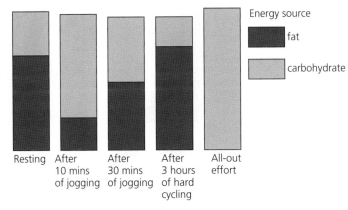

Energy source
■ fat
▨ carbohydrate

Resting | After 10 mins of jogging | After 30 mins of jogging | After 3 hours of hard cycling | All-out effort

Which is the main source of energy used in:

a the Tour de France?

b boxing (each round 3 minutes)?

c resting?

d a 20-minute jog?

e the 100m sprint?

14 **a** Write down all the reasons you can think of why sports people should not use drugs.

b Which reason do you think is the most important?

15 Write down two harmful effects of using:

a stimulants

b anabolic steroids

c pain killers during exercise

16 **a** Which substance in alcohol makes you drunk?

b Write down three ways in which alcohol will affect a competitor's performance during a sports event.

17 **a** Cigarettes contain an addictive substance which is poisonous. What is it called?

b Cigarette packets carry the message 'Smoking can kill'. Name three ways in which smoking is harmful.

THINGS TO DO

A calculator will help for some of these.

18 Before you do activities 19 – 21 you will need to:

a collect labels from at least one chocolate bar and one packet of crisps, showing how much energy they give.

b weigh yourself in kilograms.

19 This table shows the amount of energy burned up per kilogram of body weight per minute, for different levels of activity.

Energy used in . . .	kJ per kilogram per minute
resting	0.13
moderate exercise (e.g. jogging or swimming)	0.59
vigorous exercise (e.g. football or netball)	0.79

a Calculate much energy you burn up per minute when you are resting. (0.13 kJ × your weight)

b Calculate how much you burn up per minute during moderate exercise. (0.59 kJ × your weight)

c Calculate how much you burn up per minute during vigorous exercise. (0.79 kJ × your weight)

d Produce a spreadsheet using the above formulas where you can enter your weight and the number of minutes at each type of exercise and get a total energy usage.

20 A Picnic bar provides 960 kJ of energy. If you weigh 60 kg, you burn up 7.8 kJ of energy per minute when resting. So it will take you (960 ÷ 7.8) minutes to burn up the energy from the Picnic bar. That is 123 minutes, or 2 hours 3 minutes.

a Look at your chocolate bar label. How much energy does the bar provide?

b Work out how many minutes it would take you to use up this energy during vigorous exercise.

c Look at the crisps packet label. How much energy do the crisps provide?

d Work out how long it would take to work off this energy during moderate exercise.

21 1 gram of stored body fat = 3.2 kJ. If you do not burn off your chocolate bar, work out how much weight you will gain from it.

22 Keep a record of everything you eat for one week.

a Try to work out what proportion of carbohydrates, fats and proteins you ate. (Labels on food packets will help you.)

b Try to estimate how much energy this food has provided. Then work out your average daily energy intake.

c Assume your energy needs are 11 000 kJ if you are male and 9000 kJ if you are female. Did you eat too much? Or too little?

d Did you eat a healthy balanced diet? Explain.

9.1　Preventing injuries

Sports injuries can be very painful. They can ruin an athlete's career. Some can take years to heal properly. So avoid them if you can!

Two kinds of sports injuries

All sports injuries fall into two groups:

◎ injuries caused by a sudden stress on the body. For example a violent collision during football. Such injuries are common in contact sports like rugby and football.
◎ injuries which develop through overuse. Tennis players may suffer from tennis elbow and runners from an inflamed Achilles tendon. Overuse injuries can be brought on by heavy training programmes, insufficient rest between events, poor technique, or badly designed footwear or equipment.

How you can avoid injury

Follow these ten rules to prevent injury to yourself and others.

1　*Make sure you are fit for the activity.*
  The best way to prevent injury is be fit for your sport. If you are feeling ill, weak or in pain you should not take part in an event. If you do get injured, make sure you are fully recovered before you compete again.

2　*Make sure you develop the right techniques, using a qualified coach.*
  A good coach with recognised qualifications is needed to prevent poor technique and long-term injury that could otherwise be caused.

3　*Play at the right level.*
  Choose a team which matches your physique and your level of skill. It would be dangerous for a fifteen-year-old rugby player to play scrum half with a senior team.

4　*Know the rules for your sport and obey them.*
  Rules were developed to protect players as well to as test skills.
  In football, for example, you may not slide into tackles with studs up.

5　*Make sure you are wearing the right kit.*
  If your sport requires protective gear such as mouth guards or shin guards, make sure you wear it. The correct footwear is especially important. Many injuries are due to poor footwear as the weight going through your feet can be at least three times your body weight. Well-cushioned shoes protect your knees and back as they absorb impact. Good sports footwear is built to prevent long-term effects such as fallen arches.
  If you have long hair, tie it back. Do not wear a watch or jewellery that could catch in equipment or clothing. For sports such as wrestling and netball you must keep your fingernails short.

*A football injury. Injury like this, due to a collision or other sudden stress, is often described as **acute**. Injury due to overuse is described as **chronic**.*

If you're a goal keeper in ice hockey, getting ready can take some time!

6 Make sure the equipment you use is in good repair.

For example make sure that rugby boots have no loose studs, that bouyancy aids have all their ties in place, and that gymnastics mats are in good condition.

7 Lift and carry equipment with care.

If you lift equipment the wrong way – for example windsurfing equipment or trampoline wings – you may find yourself injured before you even start! See page 45 for the correct way to lift things.

8 Watch out for hazards in the playing area.

For example broken glass on pitches, wet patches on floors, or rakes left lying in long jump pits. The weather can also be a hazard. Frost can make ground too hard. High winds and fog are hazards for canoeists, windsurfers and sailors.

9 Warm up correctly.

Many injuries such as sprains and pulled muscles can be avoided by warming up correctly. See page 92 for the right way to warm up.

In any sport involving throwing, good technique is vital to avoid injury to the arm or shoulder. In the javelin, it's also necessary to follow strict safety guidelines.

Warming up before a training session. As well as improving your performance it helps to protect you from injury.

10 Cool down correctly.

The cool-down helps to prevent stiffness and soreness. That means you are better prepared for the next event. See page 92 for more.

QUESTIONS

1 Give two examples of sports where: **a** people are grouped according to age **b** people are grouped according to weight. Why is this done?

2 Why is it better to join a team that matches your skill level? Give as many reasons as you can.

3 What protective gear is used in these sports: **a** windsurfing? **b** boxing? **c** baseball?

4 What steps could you take to reduce the risk of injury in: **a** canoeing? **b** swimming? **c** dance? **d** tennis?

9.2 Emergency action (I)

DRABC

What do you do if an ill or injured person collapses in front of you? Following the **DRABC** routine could save a life. The aim of DRABC is to keep the person breathing until an ambulance arrives. Because, without oxygen, the brain is damaged within just three or four minutes and dead within ten.

D is for Danger

◎ First, stop and check for danger before you rush to help a casualty (injured person). There could be danger from equipment, falling masonry, electricity, gas, fire or fumes.
◎ If there is danger, do not put yourself at risk. **Your own safety comes first**. Shout or phone for help.
◎ If there is no danger, clear the area around the casualty. This could mean stopping a game.

R is for Response

◎ Shake the casualty gently by the shoulders and shout 'Can you hear me?'
◎ If the casualty shows any response, he or she is **conscious**. You can tell from the response how weak the casualty is.
◎ If the casualty can speak, find out if and where he or she has pain. Do what you can to stop the casualty's condition from getting worse. For example stop severe bleeding and support broken bones (pages 122–125). Send for an ambulance, if necessary, as soon as possible.
◎ If there is no response the casualty is **unconscious**. This is very serious. Move on to **resuscitation** (A, B and C).

A is for Airway

When a person is unconscious, the tongue can block the airway. Preventing this is the most important thing you can do.

◎ Loosen any tight clothing.
◎ Raise the chin and tilt the head back to open the airway fully.
◎ Remove any obvious obstruction such as a gum shield. Use a tissue round your fingers to scrape away any vomit.

> **REASSURING THE CASUALTY**
> * The casualty is probably scared as well as in pain.
> * So reassure the casualty. Explain what you are doing. Say that help is on the way.
> * Do this even if he or she is unconscious.
> * Speak calmly and quietly.
> * Do not pass your anxiety onto the casualty.

Tongue blocking the airway in an unconscious person.

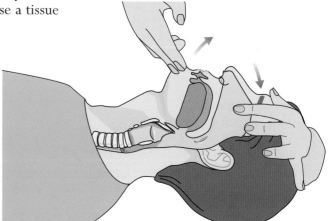

Raise chin and tilt head back to unblock the airway.

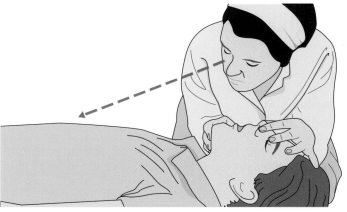

Looking, listening and feeling for breathing.

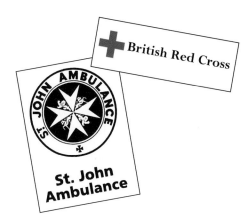

The best preparation you can make for dealing with an emergency is to take a First Aid course with the British Red Cross or St John Ambulance.

B is for Breathing

Is the casualty breathing?

◎ Look for the chest rising and falling. Listen for breathing sounds. Feel for breath on your cheek. Moistening the cheek will help.
◎ If the casualty is breathing, do what you can to stop severe bleeding and support broken bones (pages 122-125).
◎ Then place the casualty in the recovery position (page 121) while you get help.
◎ But if the casualty shows no signs of breathing, move on to C.

C is for Circulation

◎ Feel for the carotid pulse, below the ear, at either side of the Adam's apple (page 58).
◎ A pulse shows the heart is beating and the blood circulating. So you need to give mouth-to-mouth ventilation (the kiss of life) to restore breathing.
◎ If there is no pulse you need to give both cardiac massage and mouth-to-mouth ventilation, to restore circulation and breathing. You can find out about these on pages 120-121.

Calling for help

◎ Dial 999. The emergency operator will ask you:
　– which service you want (police, fire or ambulance)
　– what your phone number is, in case you get cut off.
◎ You may have to wait to get through to the ambulance service. Do not hang up!
◎ When you get through, be ready to explain:
　– exactly where the casualty is. Clear directions save vital time.
　– the nature of the injuries, as far as you can tell.
　This information will help the ambulance staff to prepare.

In an emergency, if you're on your own, it may be wiser to phone for help before you try to help the casualty. You need to stay calm and decide how urgently help is needed.

QUESTIONS

1 What does DRABC stand for?
2 Why is it important to check for danger before you rush to help a casualty?
3 How can you tell if a person is unconscious?
4 How do you ensure an airway is open?
5 How should you check for breathing?
6 Why do you think it is better to check the carotid pulse than the radial pulse, in a casualty?

9.3 Emergency action (II)

Mouth-to-mouth ventilation

In **mouth-to-mouth ventilation**, you force air from your lungs into the casualty's lungs. The oxygen in this air can keep the casualty alive.

1 Make sure the casualty's airway is fully open (page 118).
2 Pinch the casualty's nostrils closed with your thumb and first finger.
3 Take a deep breath. Then seal your lips firmly around the casualty's open mouth. Breathe out smoothly and firmly until you see the casualty's chest rise, as shown below.

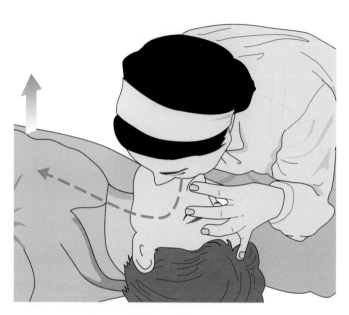
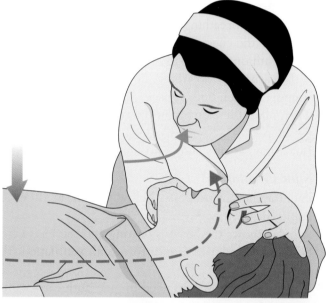

4 Take your mouth away and breathe in. The chest will fall.
5 Repeat with 1 breath every 6 seconds, for one minute.
6 If breathing has not returned within a minute, phone 999 for an ambulance. Get back to the casualty as quickly as you can.
7 Continue mouth-to-mouth ventilation until breathing returns or help arrives. Check the pulse at the end of each minute. Be prepared to do cardiac massage if the pulse disappears.
8 If breathing returns to normal, place the casualty in the recovery position.

Cardiac massage

Cardiac arrest is when your heart stops beating, for example during a heart attack. When it stops the circulation and pulse stop too.

Cardiac massage or **external chest compression** is a way of squeezing the heart so that blood is forced out of it and round the body. It must be combined with mouth-to-mouth ventilation so that the blood gets oxygen too. Cardiac massage probably won't start the heart beating properly. A special machine called a **fibrillator** is usually needed for that. But it can keep the casualty alive until the machine arrives.

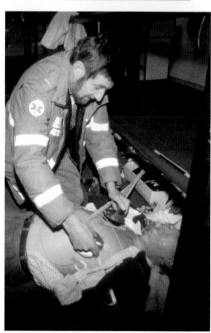

An ambulance man using a fibrillator on a heart-attack victim.

How to do cardiac massage

X2

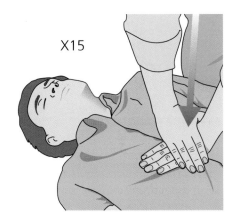

X15

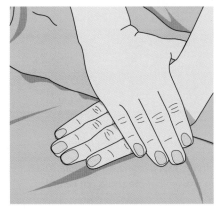

Note how the hands are positioned.

1 Dial 999 for an ambulance.
2 Make sure the casualty's airway is open.
3 Start with 2 breaths of mouth-to-mouth ventilation.
4 Now use your weight to compress the chest 15 times as shown. Do it smoothly and quickly, a bit faster than once per second.
5 Next give 2 more mouth-to-mouth ventilations.
6 Repeat the pattern of 15 compressions and 2 ventilations until help arrives. Don't stop unless the casualty's condition improves. (Skin colour may improve or the casualty may move.) Check the pulse.
7 Continue with mouth-to-mouth ventilation if necessary. Check the pulse every minute.
8 If breathing also restarts, place the casualty in the recovery position. Check the breathing and pulse every three minutes.

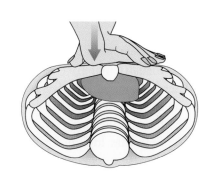

The recovery position

It is the safest position for an unconscious breathing person.

The head is tilted so that the tongue can't block the throat. Since the head is a little lower than the rest of the body, vomit will drain from the mouth and not choke the person.

You can safely leave an unconscious person in this position while you get help.

The recovery position.

QUESTIONS

1 Give another name for mouth-to-mouth ventilation.
2 How does mouth-to-mouth ventilation work?
3 What does *cardiac arrest* mean?
4 How does cardiac massage work?

5 Explain why mouth-to-mouth ventilation is always combined with cardiac massage.
6 Explain why the recovery position is a safe position for an unconscious breathing person.

9.4 Bone and joint injuries

Fractures

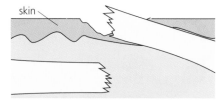

This is a simple or closed fracture. The bone is cracked but the skin is not damaged.

This is an open or compound fracture. The skin is damaged and the bone may stick out.

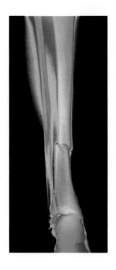

An X-ray showing a closed fracture of the tibia or shinbone. (Colour has been added to show up the fracture more clearly.)

A **fracture** is a break or crack in a bone. Since bones contain nerves and blood vessels, a fracture brings pain and bleeding. Bleeding leads to **swelling** and **bruising** when the blood leaks into the surrounding tissue.

Signs and symptoms
◎ The casualty may have heard or felt a snap.
◎ There is pain and tenderness around the injury. Moving makes it worse.
◎ The casualty will not be able to move the part normally.
◎ The bleeding leads to swelling. Bruising develops later.
◎ The limb may look deformed. For example a foot may be twisted backwards. To check, compare the two limbs.
◎ There may be a grating noise when the parts of the cracked bone rub against each other. But don't try to test for this!

What you can do
◎ Dial 999 for an ambulance.
◎ Do *not* move the casualty and do not try to straighten the fractured limb, since this will make the damage worse.
◎ Support the limb *above and below the fracture* using towels, cushions or folded clothing.
◎ If the fracture is in an arm bone, a sling made of a towel, bandage or T-shirt can be used for support. But be very careful!

Dislocation

This is where a bone is pulled out of its normal position at a joint. It is usually caused by violent twisting. It usually happens at the shoulder, elbow, finger, thumb and ankle joints. Dislocation and fracture often go together. If in doubt, treat as a fracture.

Signs and symptoms
◎ There is severe pain at or near the joint.
◎ The joint appears deformed and the casualty can't move it.
◎ There is swelling, and bruising appears later.

What you can do
◎ Dial 999 for an ambulance.
◎ Support the injured part using clothing, towels or cushions.
◎ Support injured elbow or finger joints with slings or bandages.

OTHER TYPES OF FRACTURE

Stress fractures
High impact sports where a bone is repeatedly used on a hard surface, e.g. running, can lead to stress fractures – cracks in the bone.

Greenstick fractures
Usually associated with young bone which is still pliable, this type of fracture is where the bone is not broken completely from one side to the other.

Spiral fractures
Created when the bone is being twisted as it breaks.

The more common type of fracture in sport is the contact injury, as shown below.

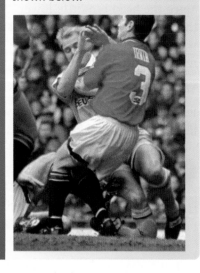

Contact can lead to many injuries as shown above with Dave Busst's broken leg.

Sprain

A **sprain** occurs when a ligament at a joint gets stretched and torn. Twisting your foot when running can give you a sprained ankle. Some sprains are minor. But in a severe sprain the ligament is badly torn and the injury looks like a fracture. If in doubt, treat it as a fracture.

Signs and symptoms
◎ There is pain and tenderness around the joint, and movement makes it worse.
◎ Swelling appears around the joint, followed later by bruising.

What you can do
◎ If in doubt, follow the instructions for a fracture.
◎ For minor sprains follow the **RICE** routine below.

RICE

When bones, joints, ligaments, muscles or tendons get damaged, the blood vessels around them get damaged too. Blood leaks into the surrounding tissue. This causes swelling, pain and bruising, and slows down healing. So the aim of RICE is to stop the blood leaking.

◎ **R**est. Movement keeps the blood leaking. So stay still.
◎ **I**ce. Place an icepack around the injured part for 30 minutes or so. Cold makes blood vessels constrict and this reduces bleeding.
◎ **C**ompression. Bandage the injured part firmly but not tightly, using a crepe bandage. This reduces bleeding.
◎ **E**levate the injured limb. This reduces blood flow to the limb because the blood has to flow against gravity.

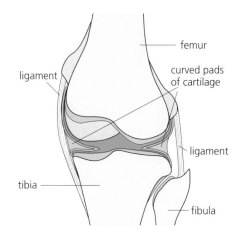

RICE treatment under way. To elevate the injured limb use whatever support is available.

Torn knee cartilage

Your knee joint has two special curved pads of cartilage. These may tear when the knee is twisted violently. This is called torn cartilage.

Signs and symptoms
◎ There is pain on one side of the knee joint.
◎ The joint may 'lock' and not straighten fully for a time.
◎ It may swell later that day or next morning.

What you can do
◎ Use an icepack to reduce the swelling.
◎ Get the athlete to the doctor.

Torn cartilage cannot be properly repaired. The athlete must drop out of sport, or have surgery to replace the cartilage with artificial material. Surgery cannot make the joint as good as it was before the injury.

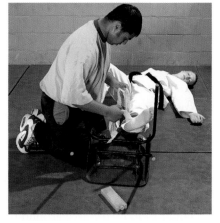

The cartilage pads in the knee.

QUESTIONS

1 Describe two different kinds of fracture.

2 Give four signs and symptoms of a fracture.

3 What is **a** a dislocation? **b** a sprain?

4 a What is RICE? **b** What is it used for, and why?

9.5 Muscle and skin damage

Strained or pulled muscles

A **strain** or **pull** is a tear in a muscle or its tendon, caused by violent over-stretching. It often happens with hamstrings and calf muscles, especially if you don't warm up properly. The Achilles tendon of the calf muscle (gastrocnemius) can tear completely. That is very painful.

Signs and symptoms
◎ A sudden sharp pain at the site of the injury.
◎ This is followed by swelling, stiffness and sometimes cramp.
◎ A casualty with a torn Achilles tendon will collapse to the ground and be unable to get up again.

What you can do
◎ For minor strains follow the RICE routine (page 123).
◎ A casualty with a serious sprain must be brought to hospital.

Tennis and golfer's elbow

These are muscle injuries caused by overuse of muscles in the lower arm. In tennis elbow the area around the outer bony bump on the elbow is inflamed, tender and painful. This injury can occur in fishing as well as racket sports. In golfer's elbow the area around the inner bony bump is affected.

What you can do
◎ If the injury is very painful, an icepack will help.
◎ The elbow must be rested until it recovers, which could take weeks.
◎ The usual treatment is physiotherapy and injection of a steroid into the muscle.

Powerful repetitious movements in any sport can lead to overuse injury. For golfers, it's golfer's elbow!

Cramp

Cramp occurs when muscle fibres fail to relax and their blood supply is cut off. This causes pain. It usually happens when muscles are tired, or when you have lost a lot of salt through sweating.

What you can do
◎ Stretch the muscle slowly and gently. Hold the stretch.
◎ When the muscle has relaxed, massage it very gently.

Stitch

This is a small sharp pain in your side or upper abdomen. You get it during vigorous exercise. It may be caused by exercising too soon after eating. Stop exercising for a short time and it will go.

Winded

A blow to the abdomen from a ball, elbow or knee can leave you 'winded'. You can't breathe in or out because your diaphragm has stopped working.

What you can do
◎ Relax. You will normally recover within a few minutes.

Cuts

The secret of treating a cut is to stop the bleeding and let the blood clot as quickly as possible.

◉ Cover the cut with a clean pad or cloth and press down firmly on it to stop the bleeding. Use plastic or rubber gloves if you can. (Why?)
◉ Lie the casualty down and raise the injured part, to reduce blood flow to it.
◉ Continue to apply pressure until bleeding stops. For a bad cut this could take 15 minutes or more.
◉ If blood seeps through the pad, do not remove it. (Why?) Just put another one on top.
◉ When bleeding stops, tie the pad firmly but not tightly in place using a bandage, scarf or tie.
◉ If bleeding is severe, dial 999 for an ambulance. The casualty will probably need stitches.

Bruises

If you fall hard during a game, or crash into an opponent, you'll probably get bruised. Bruises are caused by blood leaking from damaged blood vessels under the skin.

Signs and symptoms
◉ First there is pain and swelling in the bruised area.
◉ Then the skin discolours. It goes mottled blue and yellow.

What you can do
The treatment is part of the RICE routine.
◉ Apply an icepack or cold compress to the bruised area to reduce the blood leakage.
◉ For serious bruising, compression with a crepe bandage will help.

Abrasions

Abrasions or grazes occur when skin is scraped off your body. For example during a sliding tackle on a hard pitch, or a fall on gravel.

What you can do
◉ If the wound is dirty, clean it gently with tepid water.
◉ If it is bleeding a little, just let the blood clot.
◉ Allow the wound to dry naturally if possible. But if there is danger of infection, cover it with a plaster.

Blisters
Blisters are caused by friction repeatedly occurring on the same bit of skin. To prevent it make sure that clothes/socks fit well. Resist the urge to pop them and allow them to dry naturally.

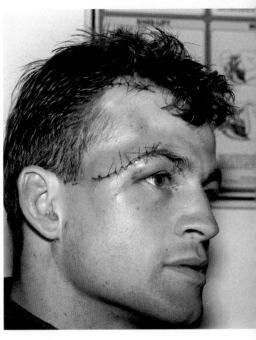

The England player Jon Callard needed 20 stitches after an opponent stamped on his face during a rugby international.

QUESTIONS

1 What is a *strain*? How could you prevent it?
2 Explain how to treat a strain.
3 How would you treat cramp in your calf muscle?
4 What is *tennis elbow*? What is the treatment for it?
5 Describe the steps to take in treating a bad cut.
6 Explain why bruises form when you get hit or fall.

9.6 Some dangerous conditions

Concussion

Concussion results from injury to the brain. It is caused by a knock on the head which shakes the brain around.

Signs and symptoms
The casualty may:
◎ become unconscious. This could last from seconds to hours.
◎ feel sick, dizzy or drowsy.
◎ get confused, stare and suffer memory loss.
These signs may not appear until hours after the injury.

What to do
◎ Place an unconscious casualty in the recovery position. Dial 999.
◎ A player who's been knocked unconscious, even briefly, should be kept under medical observation for at least twenty four hours.

Shock

Shock is when there is not enough blood circulating round your body. It may be caused by:
◎ fluid loss. For example from severe bleeding or burns, vomiting, diarrhoea, or heavy sweating.
◎ severe pain, when blood is diverted to the painful part.

Signs and symptoms
◎ The skin is cold, grey and clammy. The lips may be blue.
◎ The pulse is rapid and weak, and breathing rapid and shallow.
◎ The casualty feels dizzy, thirsty, and may try to vomit.
◎ The casualty feels anxious and panicky.
◎ If fluid loss continues the casualty becomes unconscious and dies.

What to do
◎ Dial 999 for an ambulance.
◎ If the casualty is bleeding do what you can to stop it (page 125).
◎ Place the casualty in the recovery position.
◎ Reassure the casualty. Shock is very frightening.

Hypothermia (freezing)

Hypothermia means your core body temperature has fallen below about 35 °C. Your body is too cold to work properly. This could happen if you have been out in the cold, wet and wind for too long and you are very tired. For example when sailing or climbing.

Signs and symptoms
◎ The casualty starts to act strangely. For example he or she may become aggressive, dreamy or apathetic.
◎ The casualty's skin is cold and pale, and breathing shallow.
◎ The casualty is weak, stumbles a lot, and has an overwhelming urge to lie down and rest.
◎ He or she may collapse, become unconscious and die if not treated.

A sea rescue. Sea-rescue teams have plenty of experience in detecting and treating hypothermia.

Treatment

◎ If possible bring the casualty indoors or to a shelter. Replace damp clothes by warm dry ones and let the casualty rest.
◎ A conscious recovering casualty can be put in a hot bath.
◎ Give hot sweet drinks if available, but no alcohol.
◎ If shelter is not possible, protect the casualty by covering damp clothes with dry clothes or sleeping bags, and a polythene sheet.
◎ Lie the casualty down on blankets or other insulation.
◎ If the casualty's condition gets worse, send for help.

Hyperthermia (overheating)

Hyperthermia means your body temperature has risen above 39 °C. This can lead to several different conditions.

Heat exhaustion. When your temperature rises you sweat a lot. If you lose too much water and salts by sweating, you get heat exhaustion.

Signs and symptoms
◎ The skin is pale, grey and clammy.
◎ The pulse is weak and rapid.
◎ The person may feel weak and dizzy and get cramps and headache.
◎ If water loss is severe, shock may develop.

What you should do
◎ Lie the casualty down in a cool place, with legs raised.
◎ Give him or her frequent sips of a weak solution of salt in water.
◎ Call a doctor for further advice.

Dehydration. This is like heat exhaustion but less severe. The casualty feels weak and dizzy. Give plenty of water to drink.

Heat stroke. This is when your body suddenly loses its ability to sweat and your temperature rises out of control. It usually happens during long, vigorous exercise on a hot and humid day.

Signs and symptoms
◎ The casualty suddenly lapses into confusion or delirium.
◎ The casualty is flushed, with a rapid strong pulse and hot dry skin.
◎ He or she may become unconscious and die if not treated quickly.

What to do
◎ Lie the casualty down in a cool breezy place. Remove outer clothing and wrap the casualty in a cold wet sheet. Keep the sheet saturated with cold water and fan it as much as possible.
◎ Continue until the casualty has cooled down.
◎ Call a doctor for further advice.

In hot weather, players need plenty of liquid to avoid dehydration.

QUESTIONS

1 What causes concussion? How should you treat it?

2 What is shock? List four signs of shock.

3 How would you treat hypothermia?

4 Explain what heat stroke is and how to treat it.

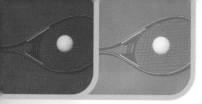
Questions on chapter 9

1 Two kinds of injuries occur in sport.
   a Which are they?
   b Give two examples of each, and say how they might occur.

2 Explain why these are important in preventing injury:
   a the warm-up
   b the cool-down

3 Give as many reasons as you can why it is essential to keep to the rules in sport, and obey the umpire or referee.

4 Match each condition i - x with a treatment A - I. You may choose more than one treatment if necessary.
   A RICE
   B support around injured part, move as little as possible
   C rest, shelter and insulation
   D wrap in wet sheet in breezy area
   E hot sweet drink
   F elevation and direct pressure using a clean pad or cloth
   G recovery position and reassurance until help arrives
   H ice pack
   I DRABC
   i   someone about to drown
   ii   hypothermia
   ii   heat stroke
   iv   a large gash on the leg
   v   bruising above the eye from a blow
   vi   sprained ankle
   vii shock
   viii fracture of the collar bone
   ix   heart attack
   x   tear in a calf muscle

5 **a** Which features of this rugby boot help the player to play safely?

   b Which feature(s) could be a danger to both the player and his opponent? How?
   c Can you see anything about the shape that leaves the player open to injury?
   d How would you improve the design of rugby boots?
   e Studs require a British Standards kitemark. This confirms that they have passed tests with regard to how they get worn down. Why do you think this is?

6 The tennis shoe below on the left is too big. The one on the right is too small.
   a Say what problems each could cause the player. Think of as many as you can.
   b One of the shoes is badly cushioned. What problems can this lead to?

7 Below is a list of common injuries for some different sports. See if you can match the injury to the sport.
   A blisters on hands and buttocks
   B dislocation of finger joints
   C permanently slurred speech and memory loss
   D 'grass' burns
   E sprains of the wrist
   F an inflamed Achilles tendon
   G inflammation around the elbow joint
   i   soccer
   ii   boxing
   iii tennis
   iv   rowing
   v   basketball
   vi   distance running
   vii shot-putting

8 This list shows the parts of the body injured in rugby:

	% of all rugby injuries
lower limb and ankle	33.1
head and neck	24.0
shoulder	13.0
trunk	11.0
knee	9.9
arms	9.0

Find out what steps are taken (if any) to protect these different parts of the body in rugby.

9 You are in the middle of a hockey match. The centre forward and goal keeper have just collided at speed. The centre forward is lying still with her eyes closed.
   a Explain how you would deal with this situation using the DRABC principle.
   b Once she comes to, for what else might the centre forward need treatment?

10 Match each condition i - vii with a letter A - H.
You may need to use a letter more than once.

A sprain
B strain
C fracture
D cramp
E abrasion
F pain and swelling
G bruising
H dislocation

  i muscle 'stuck' in contraction
  ii damaged skin
  iii tear in muscle or tendon
  iv bone out of position at a joint
  v torn ligament at a joint
  vi crack in a bone
  vii blood leaking from damaged blood vessels

11 Explain the reason for each of these rules.

  a No jewellery can be worn during a match, apart from a wedding ring taped to the finger. (Netball)
  b In certain weather conditions, the length of a match can be decided by the country concerned. (Netball)
  c After taking a corner, if the attacking team's first shot is a hit it must be no higher than the backboard. (Hockey)
  d As soon as a scrum collapses, play must stop. (Rugby)
  e Shin pads must be worn. (Football)
  f One bouncer per batsman per over. (Cricket)
  g If you commit five fouls you will be sent off. (Basketball)
  h If the umpire sees you bleeding, you will be sent off to cover or stop the bleeding. (Netball, rugby and other sports)

12 Below is a list of activity specific safety considerations.

Games activities
- Wear protective equipment:
- Shin pads, face mask, batting helmets, shoulder pads, scrum cap, gum shield, goggles, etc.
- Check free standing equipment such as goals, posts and nets.
- Check the safety of the playing area.

Gymnastics activities
- Check condition of floor, mats, fixed and portable equipment.
- Know how to carry equipment.
- Use of supporters/spotters. Check ceiling height.

Dance activities
- Wear correct footwear and clothing.
- Check condition of floor and ceiling height.

Athletic activities
- Safety of throwing areas, roping off and throwing sirens.
- Check conditions of jumping pits and mats.
- Safe placement of rakes, shovels and throwing equipment.
- Have throwing rules.
- Check spikes on running shoes are tight and kept in boot bag when not in use.

Swimming activities
- Check depth of water before jumping, diving.
- Be aware of depth particularly if non/poor swimmer.
- No running on pool side.

Outdoor/adventurous activities
- Weather hazards, pre-plan activities, inform people of plans and return time.
- Carry emergency gear, e.g. food, clothing, first aid, whistles, survival bag, a phone, etc. Risk and risk control.

Analyse the risks in *your* sport. Briefly list:

a the parts of the body most likely to be injured and how to prevent injury.
b hazards that could arise from equipment – large or small.
c hazards that could arise from surroundings.
d possible dangers to onlookers.
e Now look at a rules book for your sport. What rules are designed to prevent injury?
f What protective kit or materials do they suggest, or insist, you use?

THINGS TO DO

13 Using the internet, find information on sports injuries related to equipment and their prevention. (One site at the time of writing was www.ipsm.org) Typing "sport" and "injury" into a search engine will produce many results.

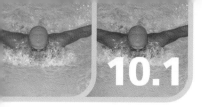

10.1 Skill in sport

How do you succeed at a sport? The main ingredients you need are **skill** and **ability**.

Skill

Skill is the learned ability to bring about a pre-determined result with maximum certainty and efficiency. In other words, skill means you can perform an activity or movement to get exactly the result you intended, without wasting energy or time. It is also something you must learn.

Think about these phrases:

◎ **learned ability.** Skill is something you learn. You are not born with it. You improve with practice.
◎ **pre-determined result.** This means you have an aim you set out to achieve. For example breaking a serve in tennis.
◎ **maximum certainty.** You are very likely to be successful. A skilful athlete can perform a movement successfully time after time. Getting it right once by chance is not skill.
◎ **maximum efficiency.** You perform the movement smoothly, without wasting any energy or time.

Skill at tennis means you have full control of your body, the racket and the ball. You place your shots exactly where you want, at the speed you want. You are **skilful**.

Ability

It is impossible to become skilful if you do not already have **ability**. This is something that we are all born with but some of us have more of it than others! Abilities are qualities like speed, agility, coordination, flexibility, balance and reaction time and you have already come across them on pages 14 and 15.

If you want to be a good sprinter like Maurice Green then you need to have been born with a very good potential for speed and a fast reaction time. Top gymnasts such as Andreea Raducan need a lot of flexibility, balance, agility and coordination amongst their abilities.

If you have these basic abilities it is then up to you to train so that you make the most of them. Someone with good coordination could learn how to perform an advanced skill like a tennis serve.

Open and closed skills

An **open skill** is one where your movements vary, depending on what is going on around you. It depends on your **environment**. For example on where your opponent is (netball) or the wind direction (sailing).

A **closed skill** is one where the movements are always exactly the same. They do not depend on the environment.

What abilities are required to perform this skill?

*A goalkeeper saving a goal. This is an **open skill**. His move depends on where the ball is coming from. So next time it will be different.*

*A gymnast performing a backflip. This is a **closed skill**. She will repeat it exactly next time. Her environment is stable and does not affect her.*

Look at this tennis serve. Next time the player will repeat the moves but change the timing and placing of the shot. So is the skill closed or open?

For the tennis serve, the sequence of movements is closed. But the timing and placing of the shot depend on the position of the player and his opponent. In that respect the serve is open. You can place it between closed and open on a continuous scale or **continuum**.

closed   open

forward roll   tennis serve   rugby hook   saving a goal

Most motor skills, and sports, lie somewhere between closed and open. Hooking the ball in a rugby scrum is another example.

What is a skilful performer?

In your next PE lesson try and look at two people performing the same skill, one of whom is a beginner, the other a skilful performer. What do you imagine the differences will be between the two?

As a beginner or a novice you will make a lot of mistakes as you learn. Your performance will, therefore, be inconsistent. You may waste a lot of energy and you may take a long time to perform the skill. As a skilful performer, however, you will have learned the skill and so you will be able to repeat it frequently, you will be efficient with energy and time (remember the definition of skill?). Being skilful also means that you will be able to adapt within your game. A novice often does not fully understand the game situation and whilst they may be able to perform individual skills, they do not do as well when they are in a game and have to think and play. As a skilled performer you will be able to adapt your game as you go and select the right skills to suit the situation.

QUESTIONS

1 Ben Ainslie is skilful at sailing. What do we mean by this?

2 Take one of your practical activities. List the abilities required to become skilful in this activity.

3 Explain why swimming is a closed skill.

4 Why is making a pass in football an open skill?

5 List four qualities you would expect to see in a skilled performance.

10.2 Information processing

Whether you're playing tennis or throwing the discus or washing the dishes, your brain is in control. It processes information from your eyes, ears, skin and muscles, then tells your muscles what to do.

The information processing system

This diagram shows the stages in processing information:

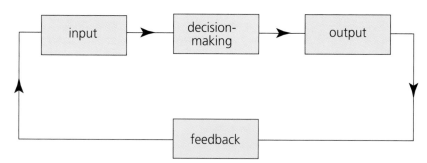

The information processing system.

Input

Input means the information you receive. In sport you take information in through your **eyes** and **ears**. For example, in tennis you see your opponent hitting the ball and hear the thwack.

But that's not all. You also **feel** a lot of information within your body. You feel how hard your hand is grasping the racket, and the position of your limbs, and how ready your muscles are to respond.

This awareness of your own body is called **proprioception**. It is made up of information from your skin, your muscles, and the tiny organs inside your ears whose job is to detect balance.

Decision-making

Next your brain must decide how to respond to the input. The decision will have a big effect on the quality of your performance. Decision-making involves **perception** and **memory**.

Perception. This is the process of **interpreting** information. Suppose your opponent lobs the ball towards you. From what you hear and see and feel, your brain will judge:

◎ how hard the ball was struck
◎ how fast it is moving
◎ where and when it will arrive
◎ where your opponent will be standing by then
◎ how prepared you are.

Then it decides how you should respond. But it can't do any of this without memory.

If you've never seen a shuttlecock before, you won't know how hard to hit it. There's nothing stored in your memory to help your brain make decisions.

Memory. Your memory has two parts: short-term and long-term.

Short-term memory is your 'work space'. All the information you receive goes in there. It stays only a short time – about two minutes at most. If you ignore it, it fades very quickly. Paying attention holds it for longer. By concentrating you can transfer it to your long-term memory.

Long-term memory is your 'library'. It holds images, tastes, sounds, smells, feelings and actions you are familiar with, and all the sports skills you have learned and practised. It can hold a limitless amount of information, and store it for a lifetime.

How perception depends on memory. A great deal of information arrives in your short-term memory at any one time. Your brain ignores most of it, and focuses on what seems important. (This is called **selective attention**.) It interprets information by scanning your long-term memory for similar information from before. Then it decides on suitable action.

If you have learned your tennis well and practised a lot, your long-term memory will have all you need for interpreting the information you receive during a tennis match, plus programmes of instructions for action.

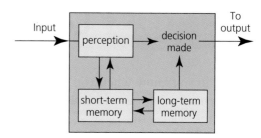

Decision-making

Output

This is the action you take as a result of your brain's decision. For example you might play a drop shot. If your information processing is working well, and your long-term memory is well stocked with skills, your output is likely to be successful.

Feedback

Feedback is the response you receive to your output. It tells you whether the output was successful or not. For example:

◎ you can usually *feel* whether a shot was good or bad
◎ the score changes
◎ your opponent misses the shot
◎ if it's a practice match, your coach may say something to you.

Note that an arrow goes from **feedback** to **input**, completing the loop. Feedback becomes part of input. It will affect your next decision. Feedback from your coach helps you learn and improve. You will find out more about this on pages 136–137.

A figure skater waits nervously for her marks – feedback – from the judges to see if she's a medal winner.

QUESTIONS

1 Draw a simple diagram to show how you process information when playing your sport.

2 What is *proprioception*? Give two examples from your own sport.

3 Describe how a skill is performed using the information processing model.

4 If you are just starting tennis, you probably won't play very well. Why?

5 What is: **a** output? **b** feedback? Give two examples of each from your sport.

6 What is *perception*? How is it linked to memory?

10.3 Learning a new skill

How do you know when you've learned a new skill? When your performances of it are **consistently correct**.

How to learn a new skill

You use your information processing system to learn a skill as well as perform it. So what's the best way to learn? These ideas will help you.

◎ Your information processing system can process only a limited amount of information at a time. It has **limited channel** capacity.
◎ If you try to process too much information at a time, the system gets **overloaded**. You feel confused.
◎ This means you learn best when there are no distractions. Noise and chatter use up some of your limited channel capacity.
◎ It also means you shouldn't try to learn too much at once. If you do you'll suffer from overload. If you tried to learn the tennis serve all at once you probably wouldn't succeed. The best way is to break it into parts and learn each separately.
◎ To help avoid overload, instructions from your coach should be clear, simple and to the point.
◎ The instructions should concentrate on the most important aspects of the skill at first. Your brain will focus on these through selective attention.
◎ When your coach demonstrates a new skill, it goes into your short-term memory. Learning it means moving it into your long-term memory. You do this by **practice**.
◎ Your long-term memory can hold an almost limitless amount of information, and it is permanent. Once you have learned to swim or ride a bike you do not forget, although you may feel 'rusty'.

*. . . then shift **all** your weight to your left foot, bend your left knee, swing your right leg through a hundred and eighty degrees, flex your left elbow, take a deep breath and . . .*

HELP!

Types of practice

You have to practise a new skill many times before you've really learned it. The best way to practise depends on the skill.

◎ If it's a basic skill such as catching a netball, you can practise the whole skill. This is called **whole practice**. Then you can move on to practise it within a netball game.
◎ If it's a complex skill, you should watch someone perform it first, and perhaps even try it out, to get a feeling for it. Then break it down and practise it in parts. This is called **part practice**. For example with a tennis serve you could practise the toss, then the swing and so on. Then put the parts together and practise the whole skill. And finally, try it in a game of tennis.

The lay-up shot in basketball is a complex skill that lends itself to part practice.

◎ When you're practising an open skill, for example dribbling a basketball, you should practise it in lots of different situations. This is called **variable practice**. It is important because your movements in an open skill will vary, depending on the environment.

◎ When you're practising a closed skill, keep repeating it under the same conditions. This is called **fixed practice**.

◎ When you are practising a skill within a game, it is usually best to work in small groups to begin with. This way you won't have to pay attention to too many other players, which might confuse you.

Types of guidance

When you are learning and practising a skill, you usually need help or **guidance** from a teacher, coach or friend. This becomes **input** for your information processing system.

There are three types of guidance: **visual**, **verbal** and **manual**. A good coach will use more than one kind.

Visual guidance. This is guidance you can *look* at: demonstrations, video, posters and wall charts. Visual guidance is especially useful when you are just starting to learn a new skill.

Verbal guidance. This is guidance you can *listen* to. The coach explains in words what you should do. It is useful because he or she can explain on the spot, repeat the instructions as often as needed, and tailor them to suit you.

Manual guidance. This is guidance you can *feel*, where:

◎ the coach takes hold of you and guides you through the movement, for example a difficult dance routine

◎ or a device is used to restrict your movement and keep you safe, for example a swimming float or a climbing tight rope.

Manual guidance is useful where a skill is very complex, or dangerous, or you are scared. It gets you used to the movements for the skill before you try them out on your own.

A mixture of verbal and manual guidance.

QUESTIONS

1 Your information processing system has *limited channel capacity*. What does that mean?

2 Why should you not try to learn too much at once?

3 When a coach is giving you instructions, he or she should stick to the point and not ramble. Why?

4 How does a skill get transferred into your long-term memory?

5 What is *part practice*? When is it useful?

6 After part practice, it is important to put the parts together and do whole practice. Why?

7 Why is variable practice important for open skills?

8 Name and describe the three types of guidance.

9 For each type of guidance, try to think of: **a** two advantages **b** two disadvantages

10.4 Types of feedback

There are several types of **feedback** used in sport and skill learning: intrinsic, extrinsic, knowledge of performance and knowledge of results.

Intrinsic feedback

Intrinsic means it is internal. In other words it comes from proprioception. Information from your muscles, joints, skin and the organs that control balance tell you about the performance you have just made. Sometimes when you hit a ball you can tell from the feel of it that it was a really good shot. This is proprioception at work and this is the basis of intrinsic feedback. The opposite is also true. Sometimes you can feel if you have made a mistake or need to adjust something. Again the intrinsic feedback is telling you about your performance.

If you try to stand on one leg you will notice that you probably make minor adjustments with your muscles to try and hold your balance. You are receiving intrinsic feedback and using it to alter your position and prevent yourself from falling over. Have a go!

A lot of intrinsic feedback is ignored by a novice as they often do not recognise it and do not yet understand how to use it.

Extrinsic feedback

Extrinsic means external. In other words this feedback comes from outside sources. You can often *see* the results of your performance, e.g. when the ball goes into the basket or misses. If you do score, the crowd and your team-mates may congratulate you and you will *hear* this. If you are in a practice session with your coach, he or she may give you information about how well you are doing or offer advice on how to improve. All of this is extrinsic feedback.

Try and teach a friend a simple skill. You will probably try to help them by telling them what they have done right, what was wrong with their performance and how to improve it. All of this is extrinsic feedback.

Knowledge of performance

Knowledge of performance (KP) tells you how well, or badly, you performed. For example how smooth your serve was, or your somersault.

◎ Some KP comes from proprioception – your own body awareness. You can feel how hard you hit a shot or kick a ball.
◎ Your coach and friends will provide KP.
◎ Recording your performance on video, and watching it later with your coach, is a good way to obtain KP.

Note that feedback from proprioception is called internal feedback. Why? Feedback from outside you is external feedback.

The only way that this gymnast knows that her leg is straight is through proprioception.

If you're a racing driver like Eddie Irvine, technical data will provide knowledge of performance.

Sven-Goran Eriksson providing knowledge of performance during an England squad training session.

Knowledge of results (KR)

Knowledge of results (KR) tells you the outcome of your actions.

◎ You obtain KR when you watch the football fly into the net, or see how far you've thrown the javelin.

◎ The announcement of the score, or a cheer from your supporters, also provides KR.

◎ You can sometimes get KR from proprioception. At the end of a somersault on the trampoline, you can tell if you've landed correctly.

Both KP and KR will help you improve your performance. For example KR tells you that you've landed badly from a somersault. But you don't know the reason. Your coach can give you KP and suggest what to do next time.

The importance of feedback

Now that you have seen what feedback is and how the information processing system works, you will begin to realise the importance of feedback. Whether you are working on your own or with a coach the feedback you receive can help you to evaluate your performance, analyse it and plan for improvement. The more skilled you are the more use you will be able to make of the feedback, as you will understand it better.

The feedback given or received can tell you what you have done, what needs to change and even how you can make those changes.

QUESTIONS

1 What is *feedback*? Give three examples.

2 Name four types of feedback in sport.

3 **a** Give three examples of ways to obtain KP.

   b Which of these do you think is best? Why?

4 KR alone will not help you improve much. Explain why.

5 Imagine you are learning a new and difficult skill. Give three reasons why feedback will help you.

6 What is meant by *intrinsic* feedback? Give an example.

7 What is meant by *extrinsic* feedback? Give an example.

10.5 Learning, refining and adapting skills

Whether you are learning a new skill from scratch or you are changing a previously learned skill, the basic principles of how this is done are the same.

Copying

One way that we learn skills is to copy someone else. Teachers often use demonstrations in PE lessons so that you can see what has to be done and try and copy it. Four things are important here:

◎ Pay **attention**. You cannot copy someone if you are not watching.
◎ **Remember** what you have seen or you won't know what to do.
◎ You must have the **ability** to copy what you have seen. You cannot perform the splits if you do not have the flexibility to do it yourself.
◎ You must want to learn. Without motovation it won't happen.

Trial and error

We can often learn by trial and error. We try something and if it works we do it again, if it doesn't we change it and try again. This is usually how we learn if we are teaching ourselves but coaches and teachers can help. If you are to learn skills correctly by trial and error, your coach or teacher must give appropriate feedback when you perform. If they see you do a correct move, they should praise you and point out what you have done correctly so that you learn to do it again. Alternatively, they may point out mistakes so that you do not repeat them.

Role models

We can learn skills (and often behaviours) from role models. These are important people in our lives like a good friend, parent, teacher, coach or any other person we admire. A young footballer might have David Beckham as a role model and so he looks up to him and tries to copy skills he sees him use. The best role models for learning skills from are:

◎ similar in age and ability to ourselves,
◎ skilful performers
◎ someone we can identify with.

Refining and adapting learned skills

Once a skill is learned it is very difficult to change it. This is a problem if we have learned a skill incorrectly. We must go back to the beginning and try to relearn the skill but without the error. This takes a lot of time, patience and practice and even then we may not be successful.

These students seem to be paying attention so they may well learn from this demonstration.

QUESTIONS

1 a When learning by copying someone else, what four factors are important? **b** Why is this so?

2 How do we learn by trial and error?

3 Why is it difficult to change an error once you have learned it?

10.6 Technological developments

From the best possible diet and training methods to high-tech facilities and equipment, improvements in technology are helping athletes push their performances higher and higher.

Equipment and facilities

Sports governing bodies are careful to watch the technical developments happening in their sport. Scientists and technologists have developed swimsuits to help swimmers move faster in the water, and football boots that give players better grip. If the governing body decides equipment is allowed, top performers use it and performances improve. Sometimes, however, governing bodies decide the equipment is not allowed, as it requires less skill from the athlete.

Technological advances are also evident in helping judges to make decisions. Races in athletics and swimming can now be timed to within hundredths of a second due to accurate sensors in starting blocks and at the finish. In cricket, action replays are used to help the umpire make decisions. In football and rugby, video is often used after the game to review discipline issues.

A ski jumper testing special equipment and clothes in a wind tunnel.

Training and physical factors

Athletes in all sports are using technology to help them improve their technique. Videoing performance allows them and their coach to scrutinise technique and make changes. Computers are also used to analyse every move in the hope of improving performance. As we have already seen this is not as easy as it sounds!

As we learn more about sports and the way our bodies work, so scientists and coaches can use this information to help athletes improve. Even an athlete's diet is carefully planned and monitored thanks to new information learned.

Technology and participation

Technology has helped everyone. New equipment and improvements in facilities and safety factors have made some sports more accessible to everyone. Computer technology allows people to enjoy interactive games on DVD. More people can now enjoy the thrills of skydiving and bungee jumping as technology has made them safer.

QUESTIONS

1 Name three ways in which technology has made measuring performance more accurate.

2 How has technology helped top athletes maximise their performance?

3 How many different ways does technology, including computers, affect you and your sport? List as many as you can.

4 Sometimes a governing body may ban technological advancements. Why?

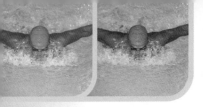

Questions on chapter 10

1 Skill is the **learned ability** to bring about **pre-determined results** with **maximum certainty** and **maximum efficiency**. Explain each of the terms in bold using examples from your sport to help you.

2 What differences would you expect to see between a novice and a skilled performer if you were watching them perform the same skill?

3 Many sports fall between closed and open on a continuum, like this:

a What is a *continuum*?

b Draw a continuum and mark these sports on it: swimming, rugby, badminton, gymnastics, canoeing

c Draw a continuum and mark these skills on it:
   • a free throw in basketball
   • the front crawl
   • tacking (windsurfing)
   • putting (golf)

4 Think of your chosen practical activities.

a Describe two skills from each activity.

b Put these skills on the open and closed continuum.

c Try to say why you have put them there.

5 Draw a diagram of the information processing system, and label the parts.

6 In processing information, what is meant by:

a input?

b decision making?

c output?

d feedback?

e overload?

f selective attention?

Give one example of each.

7 a What is ability?

b Think of these skills:
   • mountain walking
   • throwing the discus
   • saving a penalty
   • the splits

Name two abilities needed to perform these skills well and, in each case, say why they are important.

8 When teaching the front crawl to a friend which kind(s) of guidance would you use? Explain why your task is likely to be more difficult and less successful if you rely on:

a visual guidance only

b verbal guidance only

c manual guidance only.

9 Explain why it is better to break some skills down into parts to learn them.

a Give one example of a skill from your sport which could be learned in parts.

b Which of these skills would not be suitable to learn in parts? See if you can explain why.
   • running
   • the backhand in tennis
   • the breast stroke
   • bouncing a ball
   • a somersault
   • throwing a javelin

c Give one disadvantage of learning a skill in parts. How would you overcome this disadvantage?

10 Think of your chosen practical activities and list 5 skills from each one. For each skill, say whether you think fixed or variable practice is best. Now try to say why you think this is the case.

11 Name three types of guidance and give an example of each. (Find an example you have not used before)

12 Explain the difference between intrinsic and extrinsic feedback. It will often depend on whether you are a novice or a skilled performer as to how much use you can make of these types of feedback. Why is this?

13 You are practising the lay-up in basketball, where you dribble in and jump to shoot the ball off the backboard and into the basket.

a How would you obtain KR?

b How would you obtain KP?

c Why do you need KP as well as KR?

14 Whether we are learning skills or behaviours, role models are important to us.

a What is a role model?

b What makes someone a good role model to learn skills from?

15 If a skilled performer has an error in their technique, what must they do to try to correct it?

16 With reference to at least one of your chosen activities, list

a Three ways in which technology has improved equipment.

b Three other ways in which technology has improved performance.

17 Computers have changed the way we live our lives. How have they affected sport?

THINGS TO DO

Investigating proprioception

Stand with your arms stretched out straight and level in front of you. Close your eyes. Swing one arm up and the other down. Now return them to their original position. When you think they're back where they started, open your eyes and check.

With your eyes closed, you depend on proprioception to know the position of your arms. If they were level when you checked, it shows good proprioception.

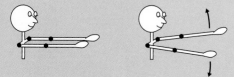

Investigating feedback

The class should divide into three groups. Each group has the same task: to draw ten 5-cm lines while blindfolded.

Group A will receive no feedback, group B will receive knowledge of results (KR) only, and group C will receive knowledge of performance (KP). Those in group A can work alone. Those in B and C will work in pairs. One person in each pair measures the lines and provides the feedback.

When you measure a line write the measurement beside it, to help you compare the results.

Group A: put on the blindfold and draw the ten lines. Now measure them to see how you did.

Group B: after each attempt, the person providing feedback measures the line and calls out 'Yes' or 'No'. He or she says nothing more.

Group C: after each attempt the person providing feedback describes how close the attempt was to success, and gives a little encouragement. For example, 'Good, just half a centimetre short'.

Compare the results for the three groups. Which group gave the best performance? What does that teach you about feedback?

Investigating guidance

For this experiment we will not use manual guidance, as some people do not like to be touched.

Think of a new skill that can easily be taught to your class and think of a way to test/measure people's performance in it. Divide the class into three even-ability groups and get one person from each group to volunteer to be the teacher.

GROUP 1 will be taught the skill using visual guidance only. The teacher will only show the group what to do. He or she cannot speak to the group at all.

GROUP 2 will be taught the skill using verbal guidance only. The teacher cannot use any kind of demonstration or other visual guidance.

GROUP 3 will be taught the skill using a combination of both types of guidance.

At the end of the experiment, test each group's performance in the skill.
1 Which group performed the skill best in the test?
2 Which group seemed to learn fastest?
3 Why do you think this was the case?
4 What did you learn about guidance by doing this experiment?

Investigating practice

Think of a new skill that can be easily broken down into parts. Divide your class into two even-ability groups and get two volunteers who will teach the skill to each group.

GROUP 1 will be taught the skill in parts. They will then put the parts together and perform the whole skill.

GROUP 2 will be taught the skill as a whole. The teacher can refer to the parts but every time the group practise the skill, they must practise the whole skill.

1 Which group seemed to learn the skill fastest?
2 Why do you think that this was the case?
3 Do you think it would be the same if we used a skill that was not easily broken down into parts?

Think of your own experiment to investigate fixed/variable practice.

11.1 Motivation and goal setting

What makes you put effort into your sport? How can you stay motivated? This unit will give you some ideas.

Motivation

Motivation is the driving force that makes you do what you do, and determines how much effort you put in. The more motivated you are about something the harder you will work at it, and the more likely you are to succeed. Your motivation may be **intrinsic** or **extrinsic** or a mixture of the two.

Intrinsic motivation means you do something because you get satisfaction from it. The drive comes from the activity itself. (Intrinsic means built in.) If you play a sport because you enjoy it and feel proud of your skill at it, you are intrinsically motivated.

Extrinsic motivation means you do something in order to earn money from it, or win a prize, or please another person. It is called extrinsic because it comes from outside.

Extrinsic motivators such as trophies and medals are used a great deal to encourage athletes. The Ryder Cup for golf and the FA Cup for football are examples. Money is an important motivator in some sports. The winner of the men's singles at Wimbledon gets a cheque for around £500 000! There are many award schemes to attract young people to sport, set up by companies and sports bodies. Extrinsic motivators are useful. But they don't always work.

◎ Not everyone feels rewards are important. (Do you?)
◎ If a reward is too difficult to obtain, or too easy, it may put you off.
◎ Competition for prizes may put you under too much pressure.
◎ A reward may lower your motivation because you feel someone has 'bought' you.
◎ Athletes may lose interest in their sport if they fail to get a prize.

But if you are intrinsically motivated, you will stick with your sport regardless of rewards. So coaches must ensure that their athletes enjoy the sport. Then when the rewards stop, the athlete doesn't.

Motivation and goals

One good way to stay motivated is to have a goal to work towards. For example your goal could be to perform the forward roll with your legs fully stretched, at your next attempt.

◎ A goal motivates you to work hard.
◎ It helps you to prepare mentally for a performance, since you know exactly what you are aiming for.
◎ It is like a signpost in your training, giving you direction.
◎ It also gives you something to check your progress against.
◎ Having a goal makes you feel less anxious, and more in control.
◎ Meeting your goal increases your confidence.

It's only a piece of metal . . . but it's a very powerful motivator.

What makes a good goal?

Think SMARTER!

S **is for specific.** A goal such as 'I must run faster' is far too vague. 'I must run 30 metres in under 4 seconds at my next attempt' is much more specific. It gives you something definite to aim for.

M **is for measurable.** '30 metres in under 4 seconds' is a measurable goal. You can easily check whether you've been successful.

A **is for agreed.** You and your coach should discuss and agree about your goals. If you're not happy with them, they won't motivate you.

R **is for realistic.** A realistic goal is one you are capable of achieving. '30 metres in under 2 seconds' is unrealistic. If a goal is too difficult it will put you off. But if it's too easy you'll get bored.

T **is for time-phased.** Your goals should be mapped out in advance to give you direction, and get increasingly difficult. A short-term goal for a tennis beginner could be: 'Serve the ball over the net three times in this training session'. A long-term goal could be: 'Get 80% of my first serves in rather than out, by the end of the season.'

E **is for exciting.** Exciting and challenging goals help to keep you motivated and stop you getting bored.

R **is for recorded.** Your goals should be written down. Then you can see clearly where you are going and keep check on your progress. You will feel more confident when you see that your training is well planned and monitored. You will feel better prepared for competitions.

Have a specific goal in mind every time you practise your sport. You'll find it makes a lot of difference.

Motivation and arousal

Motivation is linked with arousal. Arousal is a state of readiness or alertness. All athletes need to be aroused if they are to perform at their best but this is an individual thing. Whereas some athletes need to increase their arousal, others need to control it. Athletes can learn to control their arousal levels by using several techniques:

◎ **Relaxation.** Techniques include slow deep breathing and relaxing different muscles in turn.

◎ **Mental rehearsal.** This is where you imagine yourself performing your event. You 'see' yourself performing well and staying calm and confident.

◎ **Focusing.** You concentrate completely on the activity you are about to perform. You do not allow any distractions to affect your concentration.

QUESTIONS

1 What is *motivation*?

2 Explain the difference between *intrinsic* and *extrinsic* motivation.

3 What motivates you to play your sport? There may be several factors.

4 Give three examples of extrinsic motivators.

5 Name one extrinsic motivator connected with your sport.

6 Give four reasons why goals help an athlete.

7 List the seven characteristics of a good goal.

8 Map out some sports goals for yourself for the next six months. Discuss them with your teacher.

9 How do athletes control arousal?

11.2 Aggression in sport

Aggression in sport can mean two different things:

◎ acting with intent to injure someone
◎ acting forcefully within the rules of the sport to achieve your aim.

This unit deals with just the second meaning.

Are all athletes aggressive?

All athletes show aggressive behaviour. But it's not always obvious!
The more physical contact there is between players, the more obvious the
aggression will be. Look at this diagram:

swimming gymnastics	golf javelin	tennis cricket	netball basketball	boxing rugby
little obvious aggression	aggression against an object	indirect aggression	non-contact aggression	direct aggression

increasing aggression →

◎ Contact sports like boxing and rugby rely on physical contact. Boxers
punch their opponents hard, and rugby players push hard in the scrum.
This kind of aggression aimed directly at other players is called **direct
aggression.**
◎ In sports like netball and basketball there is little physical contact. But
players can still act aggressively within the rules, for example when
blocking an opponent in netball.
◎ In other sports there is no physical contact, but opponents throw
objects at each other in an attempt to make the other person lose. This
is called **indirect aggression.** A bowler may hurl a hard fast ball
straight at the batter in order to intimidate him or her.
◎ In some sports the aggression is towards an object. A golfer may hit the
ball very hard. But he is hitting it towards the next green, and not at
his opponent.
◎ In sports like swimming and gymnastics there is no physical contact.
But even here, an athlete needs an aggressive attitude in order to
succeed. It takes a huge amount of determination to keep on training
and competing, especially if you are losing.

Aggressive behaviour can cause injury, even within the rules. In many
sports players must wear protective gear. It is often hard to tell whether
an injury was caused by accident or on purpose. So coaches must ensure
that their players obey the rules. They should not encourage dirty play, or
the attitude that you must win at all costs.

The kit suggests that American football scores high on aggression.

QUESTIONS

1 What does aggression in sport mean here?
2 Give two examples of: **a** direct aggression **b** indirect aggression.

3 How might this person show aggressive behaviour within the rules: **a** a tennis player **b** a shot-putter **c** a batsman **d** a dancer **e** a snooker player?

11.3 Sport and personality

Your **personality** is the set of characteristics that makes you you.
Are you the shy, quiet type? Or lively and outgoing? Does it affect your
performance in sport? What do you think?

Extrovert or introvert?

There are many ways to classify personality. One way is to classify people
as introverts or extroverts. **Introverts** tend to be calm, shy, thoughtful,
quiet and careful. **Extroverts** are the opposite. They tend to be lively,
sociable, optimistic, outgoing and talkative.

But beware. You can't label someone as extrovert or introvert until you
have observed that person closely, in different situations. For example in a
room full of strangers you may feel quiet and shy even though you are
usually very talkative.

Personality and sport

There has been a lot of research into links between sport and personality.
This table compares the findings about introverts and extroverts. But
remember, these are generalisations, not facts. A lot more research is
needed.

Introverts tend to . . .	Extroverts tend to . . .
• prefer individual sports	• prefer team sports
• prefer a low level of excitement	• prefer a high level of excitement
• work hard in training	• get bored in training
• get nervous before important competitions	• enjoy important competitions
• perform intricate skills well	• get impatient with intricate skills
• enjoy sports with more restricted movements	• enjoy sports with lots of action
• dislike contact sports	• enjoy contact sports
• have lower tolerance for pain	• have higher tolerance for pain

Do you think you are introvert or extrovert?
Do the descriptions in the table fit you?

*Marathon running is a solitary activity in
many respects. Suitable for introverts?*

QUESTIONS

1 What is an *introvert*?

2 What is an *extrovert*?

3 Why is it a bad idea to label people too quickly?

4 Which type of personality is likely to be attracted to:

a boxing? **b** gymnastics? **c** rugby? **d** cross-country running?

e weightlifting?

11.4 Stress

Stress

Stress is what we feel when we cannot meet the demands that we have from our environment. It can be physical or psychological. In this unit we deal with the psychological side.

Have you ever reached the point where you have simply had enough and you feel you can't cope, or everything is just getting too much for you? If you have, you have experienced STRESS!

The amount of stress we feel varies from one day to the next or in sport from one competition to the next. We can use a continuum to illustrate this:

Calm	Tension	Anxiety	Stress

Increasing PRESSURE

Where on this continuum would you place yourself now?
Imagine yourself playing sport and the situation could be a lot different.

Some causes of stress

There are lots of things that can cause stress in sport and it is very much an individual thing. What causes you stress may not affect your team-mates in the same way. Stress can be caused by:

◎ **The number of players in your team**
The pressure/stress you may feel could vary according to whether you are playing on your own, with a partner or in a team. Some people feel more pressure if they are competing alone, whereas others feel that playing with other people is more stressful as a poor performance will let the team down. A doubles pair in ice dancing may feel more anxious as they often have a very close working relationship and if one skater makes a mistake they will be badly affecting their partner.

The pressure is on this player as he has no-one to turn to for support if he needs it.

If one of these players has a bad game, will he have let the others down?

◉ Performing in front of an audience

Imagine what it must be like to perform inside a packed stadium, with people watching your every move. It would be very exciting but for some people, extremely stressful. They would need to control their arousal if they were to perform well, as we saw on page 143.

With all this pressure from the crowd, this player must practise selective attention to help him control his stress level.

◉ Competing against different opposition

Playing against someone much better than yourself might be a cause of stress. However opposition that is too easy can be boring. Either way, if you're not careful you could lose and that might also cause you stress!

◉ Competing in different competitions

A certain amount of tension is expected when you start a competition. This arousal can help you perform well. Imagine how you would feel, however, if you were competing at County or National level rather than just for your class or school. This could be much more stressful.

How do you think you would feel the first time you competed for your country?

How to recognise stress

Because stress is such an individual thing, there is no set way of recognising it in anyone. Some people feel a sense of helplessness, others feel physically sick. Some people get angry and aggressive, others withdraw and get very quiet. In the short term stress causes increased heart rate as well as faster breathing and sweat rate. But so does participating in sport so it is impossible to use these as signs of psychological stress. It is important to recognise how YOU suffer from stress so that you can recognise it when it starts and take steps to control it.

QUESTIONS

1 What do we mean by *stress*?

2 What would be the possible signs of someone suffering from stress?

3 a What might be the possible causes of stress in sport?

  b For each of these, explain why they might cause stress.

4 If an athlete is feeling anxious, what might they do to calm themselves down?

Questions on chapter 11

1 Below are some reasons for taking part in sport.
   Match each item i to iv to a letter A or B.
   A extrinsic motivation
   B intrinsic motivation
      i   wanting to please a parent or teacher
      ii enjoying the movements in sport
      iii wanting to win the gold medal
      iv wanting to improve your skill

2 You probably have several motives for playing your
   favourite sport and they may have changed over the years.
   a Write a list of all the motives you have ever used.
   b Now place them in order of importance.
   c Beside each, write down whether it is intrinsic or
       extrinsic.
   d Which are the more important to you, intrinsic or
       extrinsic?
   e Has this changed since you were younger?

3 **a** What do we mean by a goal when we talk about goal
       setting?
   b Here are two different goals:
      i   To do my best in this event.
      ii To do 2 more press-ups today than I did yesterday in
          the same time.
   Which is the better goal? Explain why.

4 A good goal can be summed up by the word SMARTER.
   a What does each letter stand for?
   b Explain what each term means.

5 Look back to pages 90 and 91.
   a What do you think are the motives behind Jane's
       training programme?
   b Which of them are intrinsic and which extrinsic?
   c Set three goals to help Jane with her programme.
   Repeat the above questions for Dale's programme.

6 Copy and complete each statement using one term from
   this list. You must use a term once only.
   • an object
   • indirect aggression
   • direct aggression
   • aggressive attitude
   • jogging
   a A rugby tackle is an example of _____
   b An overhead smash in tennis is an example of _____
       _____.
   c There is not much obvious aggression in _____.
   d In weightlifting, athletes direct their aggression against
       ___ _____.
   e A hockey player making a hard but fair tackle shows an
       _____ _____.

7 Consider the activities you are being assessed in for your
   exam.
   a What type of aggression is present in each of them?
   b Give an example from each activity.

8 If you were the manager of a team, how would you
   encourage your players to avoid direct aggression outside
   the rules of the game?

9 People can broadly be divided into extroverts and
   introverts, depending on their behaviour.
   a What qualities would you expect in an extrovert?
   b What qualities would you expect in an introvert?
   c For each sport below, say whether it is more likely to
       attract extroverts or introverts:
       • football
       • skiing
       • sprinting
       • pot-holing
       • netball
       • judo
       • orienteering
       • discus
   d For which sports did you find it difficult to decide?
       Explain why.

10 Personality type is sometimes used to decide what sport a
   person might be good at. Do you think this is an accurate
   measure to use? Explain your answer.

11 Things affect people in different ways. One person may
   stay calm whilst another person in the same situation
   becomes stressed.
   a Name three things in sport that might cause stress?
   b Write an account of an occasion when this has
       happened to you.

12 We can use a continuum to describe levels of stress.
   Explain the difference between tension, anxiety and stress.

13 Stress can be harmful and it can affect your performance.
   Describe three ways in which an athlete could control and
   reduce stress.

THINGS TO DO

Goal setting

Setting goals can help you in all areas of life, not just sport. This shows a form for recording your goals and checking how well you met them.

My goals for:_____

Goal 1: _____

Goal 2: _____

How I did _____

Try this out for different kinds of goals. For example:

a your next piece of homework. Your goals could be about the time you spend and how many mistakes you make.

b your next sports training session.

Investigating arousal

1 a Choose one person from the class to be speaker. Allow the person to relax. Take his or her pulse for 15 seconds. Then send the person out of the room.

b The class chooses a topic on which the speaker will make a speech. For example it could be a sport or a favourite TV programme.

c Tell the speaker the topic. Allow five minutes to prepare the speech, which should last four minutes.

d Take the speaker's pulse before the speech.

e After the speech, take the speaker's pulse again.

f What conclusions can you draw about the speaker's arousal level?

2 Choose someone who likes strong coffee but has not drunk any within the last 24 hours.

a Take the person's pulse.

b He or she now drinks a strong cup of coffee.

c 20 minutes later, take the person's pulse again.

d Has there been a change? Explain why.

3 This is to investigate the effect of an audience on arousal. You need two groups of five people to do wall squats, and a person to act as timer.

a Group A does wall squats in private. The timer records how long each person holds the squat.

b Group B does the same thing in front of the class, who watch quietly without any comment.

c Which group does better? Can you explain why?

Investigating motivation

You will ask three groups of people to do standing broad jumps. Each group will need a start line marked on the floor, and someone with a tape to measure and record the jumps.

a Randomly choose three groups A, B and C, with 6 people in each group. Each person will do 3 jumps. The longest of the 3 will be recorded.

b Group A goes first. This group does the jumps in private, away from the class, and gets no feedback of any kind.

c Group B goes next. This group also works in private. But before starting the group is told that the two best performers will get a prize. Say what the prize is, e.g. a Mars bar.

d Group C goes last. The group jumps in front of the class. There is no prize, but the class is very encouraging and gives friendly and positive feedback, e.g. they can cheer.

e The average jump for each group is calculated, by adding the 6 longest jumps and dividing by 6.

f Compare the results of the three groups. What do you notice? Explain it using the idea of motivation.

Which kind of motivation worked best?

A relaxation technique

This method of relaxation is called centering.

1 Stand comfortably with your feet apart and your knees slightly bent.

2 Relax your face, neck, arm and shoulder muscles, until you feel all the tension has drained from them.

3 Still remaining relaxed, take a deep breath. Concentrate on your diaphragm. Move your chest as little as possible.

4 Now breathe out slowly and let yourself go. You will feel heavier as your muscles relax.

5 Practise this for just 1 minute a day for two weeks, in front of a mirror if possible.

Once you have learned this technique, you will be able to use it to calm down any time you feel nervous.

Visualization (mental rehearsal)

What is your next important event? It could be a sports event or an exam. Visualization will help you prepare.

1 Sit or lie down comfortably.

2 Close your eyes and breathe deeply until you feel really relaxed.

3 Now go through the event in your mind, step by step.

Imagine you are in control and performing very well. Notice how you are feeling. Notice the different problems that arise and how well you deal with them.

Do this several times a day before the event. Think of all the problems that might arise and how you deal with each of them.

The technique is also useful when you are learning a new skill. You go through it lots of times in your mind, step by step.

12.1 Leisure and participation in sport

What do you do in your spare time? Why do you do it? How does it affect your health and fitness?

Leisure

Leisure is how you spend your free time, when you can do as you please. Perhaps you like to watch TV, or play computer games, or abseil down a cliff face. What you choose to do will depend on your culture and upbringing, your social class, and the facilities available. For example most homes have a TV, but you need to be rich or have rich friends to play polo.

The growth in leisure

As a society, we have more and more time for leisure. (You may not have noticed!) There are several reasons for this:

◎ Improvements in technology mean that machines are taking over more of our work. This leaves more people unemployed or in part-time work, or forced to take early retirement.
◎ Labour-saving devices also cut the time for household chores.
◎ Improvements in health care and the standard of living mean we are living longer. The number of healthy, active, retired people is increasing.
◎ Some people choose to work less, to reduce the stress in their lives. Some choose to **job-share** with another person.

This is a challenge to the government which must provide facilities for leisure: parks, playing fields, swimming pools and so on. It is also a challenge to the leisure industry which provides holidays, theme parks, bowling alleys, ice rinks, cinemas, theatres, rock concerts and fitness centres, with the aim of making a profit.

Why participate in physical activities?

There are lots of good reasons for taking up a physical activity. It is useful to look at them in three groups: health, leisure and vocation.

Health. You might take up jogging or swimming for health reasons. As you saw on pages 8–9, participating in physical activity helps you to prevent illness and relieve stress. It helps to improve your shape. You look and feel better and will probably live longer.

Leisure. You might take up an activity as a hobby because you enjoy doing it. This may give you the chance to meet new people and make new friends. Activities such as skiing and Sunday league football can be very sociable and participators spend as much time socialising as they do actually participating in the activity!

Vocation. This means that it is your job either full time or part time. Professional and semi-professional sports people get paid to participate in their sport.

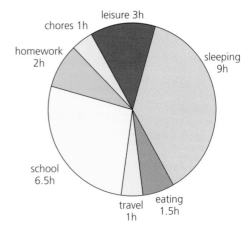

How the day is spent.

Factors affecting participation

We have seen why people take part in physical activity but what encourages people to choose a particular activity? What makes one activity more popular than another? There are many factors at work.

Peer group

Your peers are the people you mix with who have similar interests and backgrounds and are roughly your age. Your peer group has a big influence on the way you behave and the things that you do. This is not always expressed in words. If you wear the 'wrong' clothes or do the 'wrong' things you can very quickly feel left out. If your peers approve of an activity, you will feel encouraged to do it. Sadly, peer-group pressure can also force people to give up sports even though they enjoy them.

Family

Your family can have a similar effect on you. We pick up many of our habits and values from home. If your family enjoys sport and gives you the opportunities to participate, then it is likely that you will. Most young people depend upon parents and family for kit and help with travel to sports events. The opposite again is true. If your family has a negative attitude to physical activity it is likely that you will too.

Gender

There is a mistaken belief held by some people that sport is a man's world. There certainly seem to be few barriers put up to prevent men from participating in physical activity. Far more men participate in physical activities than women. You can find out more about this on page 182.

Race

People from minority ethnic groups can be discriminated against when it comes to physical activities. Many people have the mistaken belief that they are physiologically different because they are a different colour, and this means they will be good at some activities and not others. For example, some people believe that all black people are fast runners and they cannot swim very well. This belief could be the reason why we see so many black runners and few black swimmers.

Socio-economics

The activity you participate in may be determined to a large extent by what you can afford. Activities like sailing, golf and riding can be very expensive and so many people from lower socio-economic groups are excluded from them. There are also many activities that cost very little. A kick-around in the park with a group of friends, for example, and sport at school are mostly free. Unemployed people are in a difficult situation: plenty of time to fill but not much money. To encourage them, sports facilities often charge less, especially at quiet times of the day.

Support from family and friends is important.

Eric 'the eel' Moussambani of Equatorial Guinea at the Sydney 2000 Olympic Games.

QUESTIONS

1 What is *leisure*?

2 We have an increasing amount of leisure. Why?

3 How can your participation in sport be affected by:

a your peer group? **b** your family?

12.2 Further factors affecting participation

There are many other factors that affect why people participate and in what activity. Each has positive and negative effects.

Age

Young people are encouraged to participate at school and have plenty of free time to take up a sport. It also depends on the activity. To be a good gymnast you need to be young and flexible. Today, however, with computer technology not all youngsters want to spend their free time playing sport and not all sports are open to very young people, e.g. to compete in a full power-lifting competition, you have to be 14. People tend to take part less in physical recreation as they get older as they often have more responsibilities and less free time to spend on sport. Stereotyping can mean that older people are discouraged from being physically active. Some older people stereotype themselves and believe that they are too old to take part in physical activity. However, there are many sports that you can enjoy into your old age. All you need is the motivation to do it, the right facilities and no barriers to prevent you.

It's important for all age groups to have access to an activity they enjoy. Bowls has always been popular among older people.

Disability

A disability may restrict your activities and other people's prejudice can be a barrier to your participation. But disabled sport has received a much higher profile since the Paralympic Games in Sydney, and the efforts of disabled athletes like Tanni Grey-Thompson have provided disabled people with excellent role models. Many sports have changed their rules to suit the needs of disabled people and have set up coaching and competitions for them. Facilities must now include ramps and lifts and special changing rooms so that disabled people can have full access.

Access

If there is a sports facility near to where you live, and there is a good road system and public transport in place, then getting there is made easy. However, many people do not live within easy reach of sports facilities, and the public transport system is poor, so participation is made more difficult.

Popularity, promotion and role models

Participation in many sports varies. Because of media coverage during Wimbledon fortnight, tennis courts across the country are heavily used, as seeing role models perform on TV encourages people to play the sport themselves. Not all sports attract media attention, however, and not all media attention is positive (see pages 178–181). Some sports have increased their popularity by operating national schemes. Basketball, for example, is much more popular since the Basketball Outdoors Initiative of the 1990s. Thousands of free facilities began to appear in parks and school playgrounds across the country encouraging more people to play.

Environment and climate

Participation in some activities also depends upon the environment and climate. It is very hard to become a top skier if you live in a hot country and, if you want to practise mountaineering and you live in Holland, you have got to travel. So it is not hard to understand why countries like Switzerland and Canada produce very good skiers. Britain is traditionally good at sailing because it is an island and surrounded by water.

Tradition and culture

Tradition and culture also affect participation. For example, some cultures disapprove of women taking part in physical recreation in public or in mixed company. This is one reason why many sports centres operate 'women only' sessions. Most sports have had a tradition of being male only. Women have had to work hard to be allowed to participate.

Education

Your education has a big effect on your attitude to sport and physical recreation. If your school is keen on sport you will be encouraged to participate and if you enjoy it, you are likely to continue after you leave. The opposite is also true, however, for those who dislike PE. It is known that there is a drop in participation at the age of 16 when youngsters leave school. This is known as the post-school gap and is perhaps caused by the desire to leave all school-based activities behind you when you leave. Thankfully, many young people then see the benefits of physical activity and return to it a little later in their life.

Politics

The extent to which people take part in a physical activity also depends on their politicians! All governments get involved in sport for one reason or another. For example, facilities cost so much to build that the government usually has to pay at least something towards them. A government may promote sport for all in an attempt to cut the cost of the health service or cut crime. It may promote excellence in sport so as to bring a sense of pride to the country and raise its standing in the outside world.

Sponsorship

Sponsorship also has an effect on participation, as it is this that brings money into sport. Even at local level, small businesses often sponsor teams and help them financially, allowing people to play. However, sponsors can decide to pull out of the deal very easily and that leaves the team needing to find another one or stop playing (see pages 176–177).

British Olympic sailors performed particularly well in Sydney 2000.

QUESTIONS

1 Give 2 reasons why people may stop participating in sport as they get older.

2 Name 2 sports that are traditionally popular in the UK.

3 Why might putting money into sport help to cut the cost of health care?

12.3   Facilities

Some facilities for sport and recreation are built. Examples are tennis courts, swimming pools, running tracks, gyms, and reservoirs used as water sports centres.

Others are natural: lakes, rivers, the sea, hills, forests and mountains. But even these must be planned and looked after. They may need car parks, rubbish bins, marked footpaths, toilets and information centres. They may need areas marked out for different use. For example fishing and water skiing don't go together. Why?

Who provides facilities?

Local authorities. Your local council probably owns most of the local sports facilities: playing fields, tennis courts, pitch and putt, swimming pools and so on. Many local authorities employ Sports Development Officers. Their job is to promote sport within their area by creating links between schools and local clubs. Some officers cover one sport over a large area, such as a whole county. Others cater for many sports in a smaller area such as a town or district. The local education authority owns most schools and their facilities. Some school facilities are dual purpose – local people also use them in the evenings. This way they get maximum use, and the links between the school and community are strengthened.

Private enterprise. Many facilities are set up and run by businesses in order to make profit. For example, private gyms and golf clubs. Some are attached to hotels but also open to the locals. Some are very exclusive and membership may cost thousands of pounds a year. Others include theme parks such as Alton Towers and holiday facilities such as Center Parcs.

Voluntary organizations. These are bodies set up to meet a need rather than make a profit. There are lots of them, including local youth clubs, Scouts and Guides; churches; and large national charities such as The Royal Society for the Protection of Birds, The National Trust and the Youth Hostel Association. All these provide recreational facilities, e.g. The National Trust owns stately homes, gardens, farms, woodland and nature reserves which it opens to the public. Local churches may offer church halls for activities such as yoga and aerobics classes.

National Authorities. The government set up sports councils such as UK Sport and Sport England. They run national facilities, which are centres of excellence, mainly for use by top-class athletes. You can find out more about these on page 158. The regional sports councils also help other organisations with advice and grants for sport facilities. See pages 162-163 for more.

The Countryside Agency is a government-funded organisation that aims to ensure that the countryside is enjoyed for recreation purposes but also protected from pollution and overuse.

Some facilities are fairly evenly spread. Others aren't. Where's your nearest water-skiing facility?

The location of facilities

Where are facilities located? It depends on several factors:

◎ **Expected use and demand.** There is no point building a leisure centre miles from anywhere, with no one to use it. You will lose money on the venture. Most facilities are built in or near towns and cities where the demand is high.

◎ **The natural environment.** Canoeing and sailing clubs need to be beside water. Facilities for climbers need to be close to the mountains.

◎ **Cost.** Land is more expensive in some areas than others. A developer may be forced to choose a cheaper area. Even in a cheaper area, a local council may be unable to afford new facilities. But there are ways round this. It could qualify for a grant from the government or the EU, or for a Lottery Sports Fund award.

◎ **Access.** A facility must be easy to get to, especially if it's out of town. That means close to good roads and within reach of public transport.

◎ **Acceptability.** Not all facilities are welcomed by everyone. Every facility needs planning permission from the local authority. Local people get a chance to express their views. They may object to a facility that will 'spoil' a beauty spot, or bring more noise and traffic to the area.

Meeting the users' needs

Some facilities cater for just one activity. Some cater for many. Some are designed for top athletes. Some are for the general user. Think of all the groups who might use the local swimming pool: mums with toddlers, families, young adults, school and evening classes, the local swimming club, and disabled, elderly and unemployed people. You must consider all the users when designing the facility, and when deciding on timetables, charges and opening hours.

QUESTIONS

1 Find two local examples of a recreational facility: **a** which is owned by the local council **b** which is privately owned **c** which is provided by a voluntary organization.

2 A local sports centre may need to cater for several different groups of users. List as many as you can.

3 How might a swimming pool cater for many different user groups.

12.4 PE and sport in school

The government has placed great importance on PE and sport in school. What's the difference between them? You take PE during normal lesson time. You play sport outside lesson time: it is **extra-curricular**.

Why are PE and sport in school important?

◎ They help you learn about yourself and your abilities.
◎ They help to develop teamwork and a sense of fair play.
◎ They help you develop a fit and healthy body.
◎ They help you develop self-confidence.
◎ They give you the chance to enjoy yourself.
◎ If you get into the habit of regular exercise at school, you are more likely to adopt a healthy lifestyle later.
◎ They might even lead to a career for you.

PE in the National Curriculum

Everyone from 5 to 16 must take PE at school as part of the National Curriculum. You are taught from a range of physical activities that include team games, athletics, gymnastics, dance, swimming and outdoor activities. You should also get the chance to take part in sport and other physical activities at lunchtime, after school and at weekends. If your school offers at least four hours of extra-curricular sport a week it may qualify for a Sportsmark award.

PE as an exam subject

You can do exams in PE and Sports Studies at GCSE, A level, CFS, and as part of GNVQ and AVCE courses. This means you can enjoy the subject and gain a qualification that will help you find a job later.

Adopting different roles

Schools encourage students to try lots of different roles in PE lessons. This way it is hoped that everyone will find some part of PE they enjoy. If you do not like actually performing, maybe you will enjoy coaching, officiating or observing. Maybe your strength lies in organising or choreography. Roles such as captain or leader will help those who like performing to take on more responsibility as well.

THE SPORTSMARK AWARD

This award is given to a school by the government. To qualify the school must:

* offer at least two hours of PE a week in formal lessons.
* offer at least four hours of sport a week outside formal lessons.
* encourage staff to take courses and gain qualifications in coaching.
* give students the chance to take part in sports competitions in school and against other schools.
* create links with local clubs to give students more opportunities for sport outside school.
* encourage students to take part in the award schemes run by governing bodies.

Does your school deserve one?

PE, health and fitness

You study health and fitness in PE classes. But these topics are so important that schools often teach them in other classes too.
Many schools hold health awareness days, with talks and workshops on topics such as smoking, alcohol, drug abuse and AIDS. Some schools are able to offer a wide range of physical activities, both indoors and outdoors.

What physical activities can a school offer?

It depends on:

◎ the expertise available. A school can't offer an activity if there is no-one to teach it.
◎ the attitude of the teachers. Many teachers give up free time at lunchtime, after school and at weekends to run sports and other extra-curricular activities. If a teacher is really keen on an activity, it makes a big difference to the school. But teachers now have less free time to give, because the National Curriculum has meant more work.
◎ the facilities available. Schools don't always have the money or space for good facilities. Lack of playing fields can be a big problem, especially in city schools.

A school can get round a shortage of expertise and facilities by using the local sports centre (this often happens for swimming), sending students off on courses for activities such as sailing and climbing and linking up with a local sports club to take advantage of its coaching and facilities.

The benefits of links with local clubs

◎ You may get the chance to play a sport for which your school does not have facilities.
◎ You get the chance to play more sport outside school hours.
◎ Clubs can provide qualified coaching so that you reach a higher standard in your sport. Some local clubs send their coaches into schools to help.
◎ When you know how a club works, you'll find it easier to join one after you leave school. Some clubs encourage school leavers by charging them less to join.

The use of media

Schools use media resources more and more to help teachers to deliver the curriculum, e.g. coaching videos and magazines, TV programmes or the Internet.

SPORT ENGLAND

In line with government policy, Sport England is making school sports a priority. For example:

- It has set up an 'active schools' programme committed to involving more people in sport.
- It promotes links between schools and clubs.
- Together with the Youth Sport Trust it is promoting curriculum and community sports programmes.

SPORTS COLLEGES

The DfES has set up sports college status for schools to help them build on their strengths and share good practice with other schools. As well as the title, schools get extra funding.

QUESTIONS

1 Write down three reasons why sport in school is a good idea.
2 Now try to think of a reason why it's a bad idea.
3 Some people think PE should not be offered as an exam subject. Do you agree with this? Why?

4 Suggest ways a school can make up for a shortage of:
a coaches for a sport b sports facilities. Come up with as many ideas as you can.
5 List three things that Sport England is doing to encourage sport in school.

12.5 Towards excellence

The government and Sports Councils are also giving priority to developing top-class athletes – the champions.

What you need to be a champion

You need talent and hard work. But you also need:
◎ top coaching
◎ top facilities
◎ financial help
◎ help from sports science and sports medicine.

The Sports Councils and other bodies are working to improve support for athletes in all these areas.

Sports Coach UK

(formerly known as The National Coaching Foundation)
This was set up by The Sports Council (now known as UK Sport) in 1983 to improve coaching skills. Most of its funding comes from UK Sport and Sport England. It works to achieve high standards of coaching from local to national level. To do this, it runs coaching courses for all levels, shares knowledge with other agencies, works closely with governing bodies and provides information and services to coaches. It is also developing a national register of coaches. This will tell you what standard of coaching each person has achieved and also whether he or she is really a coach!

Centres of excellence

The United Kingdom has six centres of excellence for selected sports. They are funded and run by Sport England.

1 **Crystal Palace** in London caters for a range of sports including athletics, swimming, boxing, martial arts and judo. It is also a national and international venue.
2 **Bisham Abbey** in Buckinghamshire is a centre of excellence for tennis. It also caters for football, hockey, squash, weight training and golf.
3 **Lilleshall** in Shropshire is a centre of excellence for football. It also caters for table tennis, cricket, gymnastics, archery, hockey and other sports, and has a sports injuries clinic.
4 **Holme Pierrepoint** near Nottingham is a watersports centre. It has a 2000m regatta lake, ski tow ropes and a canoe slalom.
5 **Plas-Y-Brenin** in Snowdonia in Wales is for mountain and other outdoor activities, including climbing, canoeing, orienteering and dry slope skiing.

These centres provide top facilities, coaching and accommodation. They are used mainly by governing bodies to run training programmes and events for their athletes. But they also cater for other users, including beginners.

Archers preparing in the grounds of Lilleshall.

Funding

Training and competing can cost a fortune. 'SportsAid' is a charity that provides grants for many talented youngsters. Some athletes manage to get sponsorship from business. The Lottery Sports Fund now provides many of our top athletes with grants so that they can pursue their sport without worrying about earning a living (see pages 168-169). Britain's success in Sydney 2000 was testimony to the help many of our medal winners received from lottery grants.

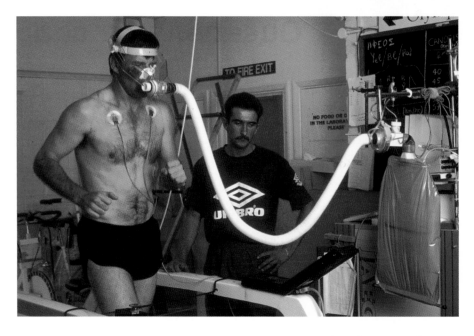

At the centres of excellence, scientific methods are used to help athletes reach their full potential or to recover from injury.

Sports science and sports medicine

For a top athlete, a change in training method, diet or attitude can mean all the difference between losing and winning. In the same way one injury can mean the end of the athlete's career. These are the areas where sports science and sports medicine will help. UK Sport has overall responsibility for sports science and sports medicine. It funds research in these areas. It also runs a network of sports scientists who advise the governing bodies and work with top athletes to prepare them for the Olympics and other events. The National Sports Medicine Institute is a network of experts, from all areas of medicine, with a special interest in sport.

The British Academy of Sport

Since it first announced plans for an Academy of Sport in 1995, the government has been debating the form it will take and its location. In 1997, Sheffield was declared to be the home of an Institute of Sport. Since then the government has allocated £160 million to its development and it will include 12 regional centres of excellence, 8 in England and the rest in Scotland, Northern Ireland and Wales. With this and the increase in National Lottery funding, it is hoped that Great Britain will continue to achieve sporting success internationally.

QUESTIONS

1 Do you think it's a good idea to develop sports champions? Why?

2 What does Sports Coach UK do?

3 Name the UK centres of excellence and briefly describe the sports they cater for.

4 Suppose you were a top weightlifter, with a heavy season of events. List all the things you'd need to spend money on for your sport.

5 How has the Lottery Sports Fund helped athletes?

6 Who is responsible for the allocation of Lottery grants?

Questions on chapter 12

1 Is it a leisure activity? Explain why.
   a playing netball at lunchtime at school
   b eating meals at home
   c going to the cinema
   d sleeping at night
   e cycling to school
   f playing cards with your friends

2 a Make a list of all the things you do in a normal week.
   b Divide your list into essential and leisure activities.
   c Divide your leisure activities into physical and non-physical.
   d Work out roughly how much time you spend on each activity in a normal week.
   e Make a pie chart to show the information.

3 This shows the results of surveys carried out in three different years. It shows the percentage of people aged 16 and over who took part in the listed physical activities:

Activity	Men			Women		
	1987	1990	1993	1987	1990	1993
Walking	41	44	45	35	38	37
Snooker/pool/billiards	27	24	21	5	5	5
Darts	14	11	9	4	4	3
Cycling	10	12	14	7	7	7
Swimming						
indoor	10	11	12	11	13	14
outdoor	4	4	4	3	4	3
Running/jogging	8	8	7	3	2	2
Golf	7	9	9	1	2	2
Keep fit/yoga	5	6	6	12	16	17
Badminton	4	4	3	3	3	2
Fishing	4	4	4	0	0	0
Squash	4	4	3	1	1	1
Table tennis	4	3	2	1	1	1
Lawn/carpet bowls	2	3	3	1	1	2
Tennis	2	2	3	1	2	2
Cricket	2	2	2	0	0	0

   a Generally women participated less than men. Why do you think this was? Give as many reasons as you can.
   b Women participated more than men in two activities. Which were they? Can you explain why?
   c Some activities seem to be getting less popular. Which ones? Can you give a reason?
   d The table shows that no women went fishing. Do you think that was true for all women in the UK? Can you explain the figure?
   e For the surveys, people were asked which activities they had taken part in at least once in the previous four weeks. Do you think the table gives a good picture of how active people are? Explain why.

4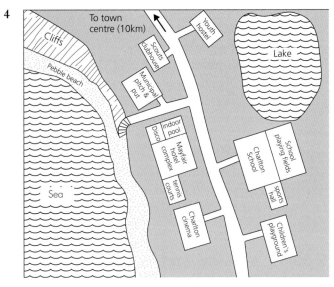

The map above shows part of a coastal town. It is not drawn to scale. This question is about the facilities for physical recreation that appear on the map. Identify:
   a two natural facilities
   b two outdoor built facilities
   c two indoor built facilities
   d one facility provided by private enterprise
   e two provided by voluntary organizations
   f two provided by the local authority

5 Suppose you are a local authority planner. You want to develop the lake in question 4 as a recreational facility.
   a Suggest some activities that could take place there.
   b List all the different groups that might use the lake.
   c Identify any conflicts that might arise between the activities. What steps could you take to avoid them?
   d If you can come up with a project that involves the local community and the school, you might obtain a Lottery Sports Fund grant. Suggest a suitable project.
   e Will you need to build anything round the lake? What? Why?

6 What factors must be taken into consideration when deciding where facilities are to be located?

7 Some people object to facilities being built in certain places. Why might this be the case?

8 Some schools offer a wide range of sports. Others offer very few.
   a Name three things that affect how much sport a school can offer.
   b What special problems might schools in inner-cities face, with respect to facilities?
   c Explain how a school could offer:
      i   tennis, even though it has no tennis courts
      ii climbing, even though it is an inner-city school
   d What might prevent the school from doing the things you suggested in c?

9 The Sportsmark Award and Sportsmark Gold Award are government awards for schools which promote sports strongly. To qualify, the school must meet a number of criteria. It can display the award on its notepaper and prospectuses.
   a List four things a school must do to qualify for the Sportsmark award.
   b Find out what further things a school must do to make the Gold award.
   c Do you think your school would qualify for an award? Explain.

10 For the Sportsmark Award, a school must run competitive sports events within the school, and with other schools.
   a Some people feel competitive sports are very good for you. In what way might they benefit young people?
   b Can you think of any disadvantages of competitive sports for young people?

11 In school you are encouraged to adopt different roles as part of your PE programme.
   a Name the different roles you could take up.
   b What are the benefits of adopting different roles?

12 In what ways do schools use the media to make learning easier and more fun?

13 a As well as good ability and effort, what four things does an athlete need to become a champion?
   b For each one, describe one way in which it is provided by British organisations.

14 In 1997, Sheffield was declared the home of a new Institute of Sport. Since then, smaller centres of excellence have been opened across the UK. Why do you think it has spread like this?

THINGS TO DO

A survey of local facilities
a list the facilities for sport and physical recreation in your area within a radius of 5 km of your school or home (Yellow Pages or the local Thomson directory will help!).
b For each facility, find out whether it is provided by the local council, private enterprise or a voluntary organisation.

A detailed survey of one facility

You may want to work with a partner for this. Choose a local sports or recreational facility. Contact the manager and ask if you can visit the facility as part of a school survey. Find out the answers to these questions.
a What activities does it offer?
b Which different groups of people use it? For example, does it welcome disabled people, or mothers with toddlers?
c What provision does it make for the different groups? For example, is there a crèche?
d How much does it cost to use? Find out all the different charge rates. For example:
   i   is it less to get in if you become a member?
   ii   how much does membership cost?
   iii are there different rates for the unemployed? families? the over fifties? retired people? students?
   iv   are there different rates for different times of day? Would a person in a wheelchair have any problems in moving around the facility? Walk around and check for ramps, swing doors and so on.
e Does the facility offer social areas such as a cafe or bar? Now write a report for the class about the facility.

Ask the manager if you can perform a survey on the customers at the centre and devise a questionnaire. Here are some examples of questions you could ask but you might want to think of some of your own:
1. Is the customer male or female?
2. What age bracket do they fit in?
3. Which of the facilities here do they use?
4. When do they use the facilities most often: morning, afternoon or evening?
5. What days of the week do they use the centre?

When you have all your results, use a spreadsheet to illustrate the information.

The manager of the centre will probably be very interested to see them.

13.1 Organisations (I)

Sport does not develop on its own. It needs hard work and planning. Here and in the next unit you can find out more about the bodies who control and direct it.

The Sports Councils

There are in fact five Sports Councils: UK Sport, Sport England, Sport Scotland, Sports Council for Wales and Sports Council for Northern Ireland.

Since being established in 1997, UK Sport's aim has been to achieve success on the world sporting stage. It does this by:
◎ looking after those areas affecting UK sport in general, e.g. coaching, sports science, sports medicine, and doping control.
◎ representing the UK on the international scene and helping bring big international sports events to Britain.
◎ supporting the UK's top performers to compete in the Olympics, Paralympics and World Championships.

It seems to have been successful. Great Britain's performance in the Sydney Olympics and Paralympics 2000 was the best since 1956. Many athletes put this down to lottery funding through UK Sport.

For the national Sports Councils, the priorities now are:
◎ to work with the governing bodies to develop sport at 'grass roots' level, especially among young people.
◎ the development of sports opportunities for women, black and other ethnic minorities and people with disabilities.
◎ to develop sports facilities for the community.

The Central Council for Physical Recreation (CCPR)

This is an umbrella organization for over 250 governing bodies and associations from all areas of sport and recreation. To make it easier to manage, they are divided into six groups. Each group elects a committee. These in turn elect the central committee that runs the CCPR. The six groups are: games and sports; major spectator sports; movement and dance; outdoor pursuits; water recreation; interested organizations.

The aims of the CCPR are:
◎ to encourage as many people as possible to participate in sport and physical recreation
◎ to represent and promote the interests of its members.

For money it depends on donations from its members, sponsorship from business, sales of its publications, and a UK Sport grant. Because it represents so many organizations, the CCPR can tackle issues of general concern. For example the 'unfair' taxation of sport, drug abuse in sport, and sport for the disabled. It provides legal and financial advice for members, and helps them find sponsorship. It also helps to promote British sport abroad.

SPORT ENGLAND

To make its work more effective, it has divided England into ten regions with an office in each: Northern, North West, Yorkshire and Humberside, Southern, South Western, Eastern, Greater London, South East, East Midlands, West Midlands.

SOME MEMBERS OF THE CCPR

The All England Netball Association
The British Horse Society
The British Judo Association
The British Ski Club for the Disabled
The British Wheel of Yoga
The Cyclists Touring Club
The Football Association
The Guide Association
The Inland Waterways Association
The Keep Fit Association
The National Council for Schools Sports
The Ramblers Association

The CCPR shares many of the aims of UK Sport and works closely with it. But by remaining separate, as a voluntary body and completely independent from the government, it feels it's in a better position to look after the interests of its members.

British Sports Trust (BST)

British Sports Trust

The British Sports Trust is the largest sports leadership training and awarding body in the United Kingdom. The Sports Leaders Awards are intended to encourage and train people to lead and organise sporting activities in their local community. At the same time it makes it possible for participants to develop their own self-confidence and leadership qualities. The four awards are:

◎ Junior Sports Leaders Awards age 14+
◎ Community Sports Leaders Awards age 16+
◎ Higher Sports Leaders Awards age 18+
◎ Basic Expedition Leaders Awards age 18+

A planned side effect of this is that it helps to reduce youth crime by providing positive, safe activities keeping young people out of trouble.

National governing bodies

Each organized sport has a national governing body. Examples are the Football Association and the All England Netball Association. These bodies are responsible for:

◎ drawing up the rules of the sport and preventing their abuse
◎ organizing local and national competitions
◎ selecting teams for international competitions, for example, European and World Championships
◎ settling disputes within the sport
◎ managing and coaching referees and umpires
◎ helping to develop facilities
◎ maintaining links with similar organizations abroad.

The governing body usually consists of all the regional and county associations, and leagues if they exist. These elect a central council to run it. The county associations in turn represent the local clubs. The governing body has links with similar governing bodies in other countries, and with the European and World governing bodies.
(You can see how this works for swimming on page 166.)

To finance its work, the governing body raises funds from major sporting events, members' subscriptions, sponsorship, grants from UK Sport and The Lottery Sports Fund, and where possible selling broadcast rights for events to radio and TV.

QUESTIONS

1 a How many Sports Councils are there?

  b Describe the jobs they do.

2 What does CCPR stand for, and how is it organised?

3 Explain how the CCPR helps its members.

4 What is the British Sports Trust?

5 What does the governing body of a sport do?

6 Name five governing bodies of sport, including the one for your sport.

13.2 Organizations (II)

The International Olympic Committee (IOC)

This is the top committee of the Olympic Movement. It is chosen from member countries. Its main jobs are:

◎ to select the cities where the Games will be held
◎ to decide which sports will be included
◎ to work with the host city and other bodies to plan the Games
◎ to lead the fight against doping in sport.

The IOC helped set up the World Anti-Doping Agency (WADA) in 1999. In the lead up to the Sydney Olympics in 2000, they performed over 2000 out-of-competition urine tests on international athletes in 28 summer sports in 82 different nations.

For funding, the IOC depends mainly on the sale of TV rights and on sponsorship by multinationals such as Coca Cola and IBM. TV companies across the world pay billions of pounds for the broadcast rights to the Olympic Games. Sponsors are not allowed to advertise in the Olympic stadiums, but they can use the Olympic symbols on their products. They get access to exclusive hospitality at the Games, and to the best advertising slots when the games are broadcast.

The money the IOC receives is divided up between the IOC, the International Sports Federations, the National Olympic Committees, and the local Organizing Committee for each Olympics.

The British Olympic Association (BOA)

The BOA is part of the Olympic Movement. Its main jobs are:

◎ to select the British team for the Olympic Games
◎ to raise money to send the team to the Games
◎ to make all the arrangements for getting it there
◎ to work with the governing bodies to prepare the athletes
◎ to select the city which will make a bid to host the Games.

The BOA also selects the British Youth Olympic Team. This team competes at the European Youth Olympic Days and gives future stars a taste of what might be in the future for them. They also receive medical support, free use of local facilities and career and education services arranged by the BOA.

Although the BOA gets some money from the IOC, it is not nearly enough to support a team. The BOA raises the extra it needs from sponsorship (in 2001 they were sponsored by Rover), licensing its logo (for use on mugs and T-shirts for example), and donations from the public.

In keeping with the Olympic ideals the BOA steers clear of politics. In 1980 the government wanted it to boycott the Moscow games in protest at the Soviet invasion of Afghanistan. The BOA refused.

CITIUS · ALTIUS · FORTIUS

The logo of the International Olympic Committee (IOC).

The logo of The British Olympic Association.

The scoreboard at every Olympics carries this message. Do you think athletes, coaches and spectators agree with it?

The Countryside Agency helps to maintain National Trails and other routes for walkers, like this one in Yorkshire.

The Countryside Agency

The Countryside Agency looks after the English countryside and advises the government on countryside matters. It is funded by the Department of the Environment.

The Countryside Agency is not directly concerned with sport. But it plays a part in physical recreation. Its aim is to ensure that the countryside is enjoyed but also protected. It is involved in:

◎ developing and looking after National Trails for walkers, cyclists and riders. These include the Pennine Way and Cleveland Way.
◎ restoring public rights of way. There are over 190 000 km of paths through the country where you have the right to walk freely.

It also looks after the most beautiful parts of the English countryside:

◎ the seven National Parks, which include Dartmoor and Exmoor.
◎ the Heritage Coasts.
◎ the landscapes protected as Areas of Outstanding Natural Beauty. These include Pennine moorlands and the Surrey Hills.

Scotland and Wales have similar organizations: the Scottish Natural Heritage and the Countryside Council for Wales.

QUESTIONS

1 What is the IOC? What are its main jobs?

2 What is WADA? What is its main job?

3 Describe two ways the Countryside Agency helps people to enjoy physical recreation.

4 What is the BOA? What are its main jobs?

5 Suppose your job is to get the British team to the Olympics and look after them there. List all the things you'd need to consider.

13.3 Inside a sport

To run local, national and international events, a sport has to be well organized.

The organization of a sport

Let's take swimming as an example. You read about governing bodies on page 163. The governing body for swimming in England is the Amateur Swimming Association (ASA). This shows how the ASA is related to other governing bodies (gb) of swimming, and to the local clubs:

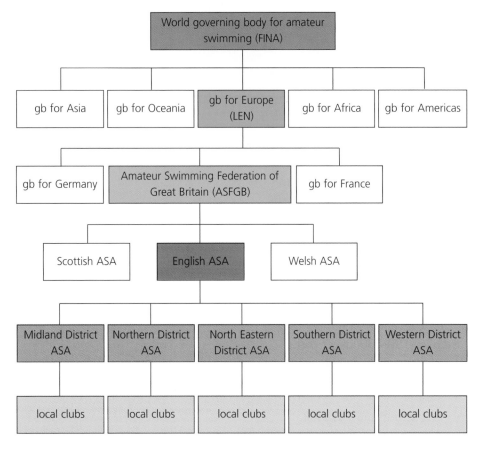

If you are a talented swimmer you start off at the bottom, competing in local events. You win and move up to regional events, then national events, and finally to international competitions.

The local clubs

The job of any local club in any sport is:
◎ to provide facilities
◎ to organize competitions
◎ to promote the sport and encourage new members.

One good way to encourage new members is to make links with local schools. This also benefits schools, as you saw on page 157. A successful club can act as a focus for the community, and give it a strong sense of pride. Can you think of any big club that does this?

Inside a club

All clubs have much the same structure, no matter what size they are or what the sport is.

Everyone who joins the club is a **member** and has to pay a membership fee. The members elect a **committee** to run the club. The committee members are the club **officials**. The committee meets regularly, for example every fortnight, to make decisions about the club's activities.

The committee

The **chair person**. This is the top official of the club. He or she represents the club and presides at meetings.
Vice-chair. This person takes over if the chair person is absent.
Secretary. The secretary arranges meetings, keeps **minutes** or written records of the discussions in them, and makes sure everyone is informed about decisions that have been taken.
Treasurer. The treasurer looks after the club's finances and manages its bank account. Cheques paid out must usually be signed by the treasurer and at least one other club official.
Other officials. Depending on its size, a club may have several other officials. For example a fixtures secretary to organize events, a membership secretary to find and enroll new members, and a coach.

Where the club gets its funding

Local clubs usually get their funding from:

◎ membership fees and match fees. For example in a squash club you have to pay a fee when you book a court.
◎ grants from the local authority or the sport governing body.
◎ sponsorship from local companies.
◎ fundraising events such as barbecues and raffles.

Big **professional** clubs such as Manchester United can raise large sums of money from ticket sales and from selling **merchandise** such as replica kit, flags and posters. Look at the box on the right.

Some large clubs are **public limited companies** or **plcs**. This means they have shareholders who put money into the company by buying shares in it, and expect a share of the profits in return. Manchester United is one example.

MANCHESTER UNITED'S EARNINGS, 2001	
	£ million
Gate receipts and programme sales	46.2
Television	31.2
Sponsorship, royalties and advertising	22.5
Conference and catering	7.8
Merchandising and other	21.9
Total	129.6

QUESTIONS

1 For your sport, what is the name of: **a** the World governing body? **b** the European governing body? **c** the UK governing body?

2 Name three different officials you'd find in any sports club, and say what their jobs are.

3 See if you can find the name of another football club that's a public limited company.

13.4 Finance in sport

It costs a lot to build and run sports facilities, organize events, buy equipment and train athletes. Who pays?

Where does the money come from?

National government. The government raises money each year from taxes and other sources. Then at Budget time the Chancellor decides how much can be spent, and divides it among the different government departments. The Department for Culture, Media and Sport is responsible for sport. It decides how much of its share will go to sport. Most of this (around £300 million is planned 2000–2004) is divided among the five **Sports Councils.** They use the money to help develop sport, improve facilities and promote excellence. In 1999–2000 UK Sport received £12.6 million from the government. You can find out more about the Sports Councils on page 162.

Local government. Your local council raises money by means of the **council tax** which each household pays, and the **business tax** paid by shops and other businesses. It uses the money to build and maintain schools and recreational facilities as well as for services such as the police, fire brigade and refuse disposal.

The governing bodies of sport. They earn money from things like selling permission for events to be broadcast on TV and radio. For example the Football Association made a TV deal worth £743 million in 1997. They also sell tickets for major events such as cup finals and Wimbledon. They then plough most of the money back into their sports.

The National Lottery. This was launched in 1994. Every week we spend an average of £5.37 per household on National Lottery tickets. From the sale of each ticket 7p goes to the Lottery Sports Fund. (It's almost the same for a scratch card.) The fund is handled by the Sports Councils who award it as grants for sports projects.

Sponsorship. This is a big source of finance for sport. For example:
◎ Adidas sponsor basketball in the community.
◎ Barclaycard sponsor Premier League football matches.

But sponsorship isn't just for big projects and big names. A local business might pay for a trophy or the strip for the local junior football team. There is more about sponsorship on pages 176-177.

Private individuals. A wealthy person may donate a large sum to a favourite club, or even buy it! Mohammed Al Fayed, businessman and owner of Harrods, is owner of Fulham Football Club.

Sales of tickets and merchandise. Clubs get money by selling tickets to events, and things like sweat shirts, scarves, flags and posters. You saw on page 167 how much Manchester United can make from these sources.

Membership fees. Small clubs like the local squash club charge a membership fee to cover running expenses.

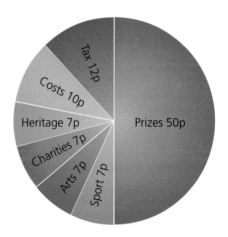

A National Lottery ticket: where the £1 goes.

Every time you buy a replica kit or other merchandise, a percentage goes to the government as VAT. Do they always spend it on sport?

More about taxation

These are the kinds of taxes we pay the government:

◎ **a tax on earnings.** Individual earners pay **income tax**. Businesses pay **corporation tax**. The more you earn the more you pay. Even bodies like the Lawn Tennis Association and Football Association have to pay tax.

◎ **a tax on spending.** A tax called **value added tax** (VAT) is included in the price of most things you buy. For example, in the price of CDs, computer games and petrol, and on your phone bill.

Each year the Treasury takes in billions from the taxation of sport. It gives nowhere near that much back to sport.

The Lottery Sports Fund

Suppose a youth club wants to build a new clubhouse. It can apply to the Lottery Sports Fund for a grant. The application goes to a panel which says yes or no. A project will receive funding only if:

◎ it will benefit the community, including disabled people.
◎ it involves building or improving something or buying equipment.
◎ it is well thought out and likely to succeed.
◎ a 'significant' amount of the total cost will be raised elsewhere.

The projects can be large or small. In 1996 Welsh Rugby Union was awarded £46 million to build a new stadium and complex in Cardiff. Average grants are usually around £40 000, however.

> **WHO CAN APPLY FOR A LOTTERY SPORTS FUND GRANT?**
>
> Organizations like these:
> - sports clubs
> - youth clubs
> - community associations
> - sports associations
> - governing bodies of sport
> - local authorities
> - schools and colleges (for facilities they intend to share with the public)

QUESTIONS

1 Explain how sport is funded by: **a** national government **b** local government.

2 When a person spends £1 on a lottery ticket, where does the money go?

3 Describe three taxes levied by the government.

4 Which bodies look after the Lottery Sports Fund?

5 Think up a sports project for a local youth club which could qualify for lottery funding. How will it benefit the local community, including disabled people? Describe it as fully as you can.

13.5 International sport

Sport brings people of all races together, regardless of their differences.

The benefits of international sport

◎ It gives players and supporters from different countries the chance to meet and develop friendship.

◎ It unites people from different races, religions, cultures and classes in a shared interest.

◎ It gives the world's top athletes the chance to compete against each other. This encourages excellence.

◎ It spreads interest in sport and encourages more people to play.

International events

Most sports hold international events arranged by their international governing bodies. For example, European and World Cup football tournaments are arranged by UEFA (the European governing body) and FIFA (the World governing body). Who do you think would organize the European and World Swimming Championships? (Check the diagram on page 166.)

Events such as the Commonwealth Games and the Olympics cover a wide range of sports. They are arranged by separate organizations with help from the governing bodies. For example the International Olympic Committee (page 164) arranges the Olympics and Winter Olympics.

Hosting international events

The host is the city or country staging the events. The venue is the stadium where an event is held. The Olympics are hosted by cities – for example Sydney in 2000. But many events are hosted by countries and spread around several centres. England was the host for Euro'96, the 1996 European Nations Football Championships. The venues were in Birmingham, Leeds, Liverpool, London, Manchester, Newcastle, Nottingham and Sheffield.

Some advantages of playing host

Countries and cities often compete fiercely for the chance to host an international sports event. Why?

◎ For prestige. It is considered an honour to host the Olympics. If the event is a success, the host city gains prestige. This can pay all kinds of ways, including an increase in trade and tourism.

◎ It unites the country and gives a sense of pride.

◎ It gives a boost to sports facilities – and other facilities. Cities build or improve their facilities to host events. The local people can enjoy these long after the events are over.

◎ The event may make a profit. Sales of radio and TV rights, tickets and merchandise can bring in a lot of money. Local shops, restaurants, hotels, taxis and other services will also benefit.

> ### THE OLYMPIC IDEALS
> The aim of the Olympics is to promote:
> * personal excellence
> * sport as education
> * cultural exchange
> * mass participation
> * fair play
> * international understanding

The opening ceremony at the Sydney Olympics in 2000. Countries line up years in advance to compete for the chance to host the Olympics.

Some disadvantages of playing host

◎ If it runs into problems in organizing an event, the country or city may lose money. Montreal made a loss of over $1 billion with the Olympic Games in 1976. The debt will take years to pay off.

◎ An event that attracts hooligans puts a big strain on the police. They may have to patrol trains and airports as well as venues.

◎ A large number of visitors means extra strain on hotels, transport, water supplies and so on. If these can't cope there will be problems.

◎ Big events are security risks. They are watched by millions, so terrorists and other groups may use them to air their grievances. They may be disrupted by bomb threats, strikes and riots, e.g. the bombing at the Atlanta Olympics in Centennial Park, where two people were killed and 110 injured.

◎ If an event does not go well the host's image suffers. The host will have difficulty attracting other events.

International sport and politics

Sport can promote peace and understanding. But where countries are already enemies, they may use it as a form of 'cold war'.

◎ A country may decide to boycott an event for political reasons.

◎ It may use its top athletes to prove it is more powerful than its enemy, or that its political system is superior.

The Olympic Games are the world's biggest and most spectacular sports event. Over the years they have often been used for political purposes. For example, in Munich in 1972, 11 Israeli team members were killed when Palestinian terrorists broke into the Olympic village and took them hostage. The terrorists wanted the release of 200 Palestinians held in Israeli prisons.

International sport and money

It can be wildly expensive to stage an international event. This means:

◎ poor countries just can't afford them.

◎ even the rich countries can't afford major events without sponsorship and the sale of broadcast rights. For example, it cost over $2 billion to stage the Sydney Olympics.

Some people think that the Olympics are now too commercial, with entertainment and profit as important as sport. What do you think?

THE SYDNEY GAMES 2000

- 28 sports
- 300 events
- Over 10 000 athletes
- Cost: over 2 billion Australian dollars
- Profit: around 400 million Australian dollars

QUESTIONS

1 Write down two benefits of international sport.

2 Name a city that has hosted: **a** the Summer Olympics **b** the Winter Olympics **c** the Commonwealth Games.

3 Your city plans to host an international football event. List all the things it will need to consider.

4 **a** Write down two advantages of hosting an international sports event. **b** Now write down two disadvantages.

5 Do you agree that the Olympic Games encourage: **a** excellence? **b** mass participation in sport? Explain why.

Questions on chapter 13

1 What do these initials stand for?
   a IOC
   b BOA
   c CCPR
   d BST

2 a How many sports councils are there and what are they called?
   b Name three things the sports councils do to promote excellence.
   c Name three things the sports councils do to increase the number and quality of sports facilities.
   d Since 1994 the sports councils have been able to give out more grants for sports facilities. Why?
   e What kind of work does UK Sport do?

3 a What is the British Sports Trust?
   b What are the Sports Leadership awards it offers?
   c What 5 aims do the BST hope to achieve?

4 The bodies that control sport often have well-known people on their committees. See if you can name one well-known person who is an official in:
   a Sport England
   b UK Sport

5 This question is about the Central Council for Physical Recreation (CCPR)
   a It is an umbrella organisation. What does that mean?
   b Name five organisations that belong to the CCPR.
   c Give two reasons why the CCPR is a useful body.

6 The Football Association (FA) is the governing body for football in England.
   a Name the World governing body for football.
   b Name the European governing body.
   c List four functions of the FA.

7 Funding is essential if athletes are to become top performers. Name five sources of funding.

8 This shows how much the local tennis club expects to spend in the coming year:

	£
Redecoration of the club house	1800
Repairs to courts	800
New nets	1700
Coaching fees	800
Groundsman	1000
Insurance	550
Post and phone	450
	7100

   a The club has 70 members. It charges £30 a year for membership. How much money does that bring in?
   b it costs £1 to book a court. Last year there were 1000 bookings. How much did that bring in?
   c Suppose the bookings remain at the same level next year. How much more money will the club need to find, to cover its costs for the year?
   d You are the club treasurer. You are determined that the club will not make a loss next year. Write a list of suggestions for ways to raise money, which you will present at the next committee meeting.

9 This chart shows where each £1 from a lottery ticket goes. You can assume that the money from scratch cards is divided in the same way. (It is very similar.)

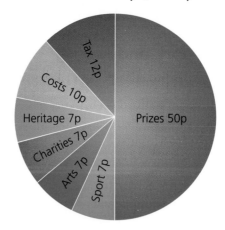

   a How much from each £1 goes on sport?
   b Where does most of the money go?
   c Write a paragraph in favour of the National Lottery, showing how it benefits society. Give examples.
   d Now write a paragraph describing its harmful effects.
   e Overall, are you in favour of the Lottery or against it?

10 Organisations can apply for Lottery Sports Grants.
  a What kind of organisations can apply?
  b What conditions must they meet before a grant is awarded?

11 a Even though you don't earn, you still pay tax now and then, for example when you buy a CD. Explain this.
  b Working people pay a tax that depends on the size of their income. What is it called?
  c Households also pay a tax.
    i What is this tax called?
    ii Who collects it?
    iii Name three things the money is used for.
  d Give four examples of how the government makes money from sport.

12 The Sydney Olympics in 2000 were described by many people as 'The best Olympic Games ever'.
  a Why was this the case?
  b Do you think that this was a fair statement to make and why?

13 Critics of the Olympics have suggested these changes:
  • no national uniforms for athletes
  • no national anthems or flags during medal ceremonies.

  a What positive effects might these changes have?
  b Can you think of any negative effects they'd have?

14 Countries and cities go to great lengths to become hosts of international events. Hosting these events costs a lot of money but profits can still be made.
  a What are the costs involved? Write a list.
  b How can a host make money from the event?

THINGS TO DO

Competitions

Competitions can be organised in different ways. Get your class to organise some using each of these three methods.

Ladder:
All the competitors are placed in rank order according to ability. Each player can challenge players 1 or 2 places above him or her. If he or she wins he or she goes up a place, if he or she loses the positions stay the same. The winner is the person at the top of the ladder after a certain amount of time.

League:
Like a football league, each team plays all the other teams once or twice. Points are awarded for a win or a draw. The winning team is the one with most points at the end of the competition.

Knockout:
Like Wimbledon, a draw takes place to decide who plays whom in the first round. The winners go through to the next round and so on until there are only two players or teams left who then battle it out in the final.

Use of information technology

1 Many organisations have been described in this chapter. Divide them up amongst the members of your class and look for more information on the Internet about each one.

2 a Search the Internet to find out about the history of the Olympic Games. Your research should include:
    the ancient Olympic Games and why they were held;
    the Frenchman who started the modern Olympics;
    the participation of women in the modern Olympics;
    some of the problems associated with the games.
  b Write a short essay on the history of the games. It should be no more than two pages.

3 Now find out when and why the Commonwealth Games were started. Write about half a page on their history.

14.1 Amateur or professional

How do you tell who's amateur and who's not? The term **amateur** was originally a sign of social class. It meant you were a gentleman who could afford to play a sport just for pleasure. There's more about this on page 187.

◎ Amateurs do not get paid for playing their sport. The theory is they do it for love of the sport.

◎ Professionals play full time and get paid for it. It's how they earn their living.

◎ Semi-professionals are like professionals but play only part time and have another job too.

Who decides?

The rules about amateurs and professionals, and what they can and can't do, are made by a sport's international governing body.

◎ Many sports divide players clearly into professionals and amateurs, with the professionals at the top. Football is an example. Amateurs and professionals don't usually compete together, except in specific events. For example, amateur, semi-professional and professional football teams can compete in the FA Cup.

◎ In some sports most athletes, even the top ones, are 'amateur'. Swimming and athletics are examples. The athletes can't accept money for playing their sports. But see below for ways around this!

◎ Some sports are open. Amateurs and professionals can compete freely in most events. Horse racing, golf and tennis are examples.

Are top amateurs really not paid?

To be a top athlete you need to devote yourself full time to your sport. But if you're not allowed to earn money from it, how do you survive?

Scholarships. In America young athletes get scholarships to colleges with a good reputation for their chosen sport. Scholarships can cover everything: food, board, books and tuition. The athletes train with top coaches in top facilities. They don't have to worry about money. The same thing is also beginning to happen here. Several UK universities now offer sports scholarships.

'Jobs'. In many countries athletes are given token 'jobs', for example as PE instructors in the army or police force, so that they can train full time. This often happens in developing countries.

Special training camps. Promising young athletes may be sent to sports schools and then training camps, where they remain long past the age when most people get a job. This is usual in China.

Trust funds. Since 1983, athletes in athletics can accept prize and appearance money. But not directly. It is paid into a **trust fund** in order to preserve their amateur status. Money from the fund is used to cover the athlete's training and living expenses. He or she gets the rest on retirement. (Rugby Union also used this system until 1995.)

SOME FOOTBALL TEAMS

Professional
Newcastle United
Tottenham Hotspur
and similar league teams

Semi-professional
Woking
Accrington Stanley
and similar non-league teams

Amateur
Your local Sunday team

SOME OPEN SPORTS

angling	mountaineering
bowling	squash
cricket	tennis

Grants and sponsorships. Amateur athletes can seek grants from Sports Aid, for example, or sponsorship from business. The governing bodies must approve these.

Why keep the distinction?

As you can see, top 'amateur' athletes get 'paid' indirectly in all kinds of ways. So the distinction between amateurs and professionals is a fuzzy one. Why not just drop it and make all sports open?

The fear is that money would then become the main reason for competing, with athletes aiming to win at all costs and by any methods. The ideal of fair play might go out the window. Governing bodies might lose control of their sports to commercial organizations.

Amateurism and the Olympic Games

The Olympic Games were meant for amateurs. Tennis was dropped in the 1920s because of doubts about the players' status.

But over the years it has been obvious that many competitors are not truly amateur, and many winners are rewarded when they get home, for example with cars, jobs and houses. In 1981 the term 'Olympic amateur' was dropped from the rules. Tennis, with professional players, was allowed back in 1988. But the only prizes offered at the Olympics are the Olympic medals.

The final decision about who can take part in the games is now left to the International Sports Federations. Some sports uphold the amateur ideal more strictly than others. For example professional footballers can now take part in the games but professional boxers cannot.

The story of Rugby League and Rugby Union

Rugby began at Rugby School. The rules were laid down in 1846. By 1881 Rugby Union governing bodies had been set up in England, Scotland and Wales.

But in 1895 Rugby League was born when 22 northern clubs broke away. Their players wanted compensation for the time spent away from work training and playing. Rugby Union had refused them.

Rugby League became the professional game, and developed its own rules over the years. Then in 1995, a hundred years later, Rugby Union finally backed down and let professional players in.

Technically an amateur but still able to earn money from sport.

Being fully professional means these players don't have to have another job to earn a living.

QUESTIONS

1 What is an *amateur* athlete? Name one top athlete who has amateur status.

2 What is a *professional* athlete? Name four.

3 What is an *open* sport? Name four.

4 To remain 'amateur', athletes must not earn a living from their sport. Describe three ways round this.

5 Are the Olympic Games still strictly for amateurs?

6 When and why did Rugby League form?

14.2 Sponsorship

What is sponsorship?

Without a sponsor, many athletes couldn't carry on with their sport. **Sponsorship** is where a business provides support (usually financial) for an event or team or athlete. Watch sport on TV and you'll see sponsors' brand names on players' clothing and hoardings around the venues.

Why sponsor sport?

◎ It is a way to advertise. The sponsor's name is displayed before the spectators all through the event.
◎ Sport has a healthy, positive image. Businesses like to be associated with this.
◎ Sponsorship is often **tax-deductible**. This means the business does not have to pay tax on the amount it spends on sponsorship. (That is one way the government helps to promote sport.)
◎ TV sports events are seen in millions of homes. So is the sponsor's brand name. An event like Wimbledon or a Cup Final reaches millions of TV screens round the world. This means a sponsor's logo reaches places that may be very difficult or expensive to reach with other kinds of advertising.
◎ When a local business sponsors a local team, it gains the good will of the local people.
◎ In exchange for sponsorship a sponsor may get the best seats at an event, or the use of luxury executive boxes. The sponsor can use these to entertain clients.

Disadvantages to the sponsor

◎ The sponsor expects the athlete or team to behave well, or the event to go smoothly. This cannot be guaranteed. If an event is disrupted by hooliganism or the weather, or an athlete is caught doping or cheating, or gets involved in a scandal, the sponsor won't be happy.
◎ The sponsor also hopes the team or athlete will be successful. That can't be guaranteed either.

Forms of sponsorship

Sponsorship may be for:

◎ a sport. Norwich Union sponsors British Athletics.
◎ a single event. Flora has sponsored recent London Marathons.
◎ a team. Vodafone sponsors Manchester United. So do several other companies, as you'll see if you check out the players' kit.
◎ an individual. Tim Henman has been sponsored by Adidas and Dunlop, among others.

Sponsorship is not always money. A car manufacturer may provide free transport, and an airline free flights. A company that makes sports goods may provide clothing and equipment. Sponsorship for a young person could be in the form of a scholarship to a centre of excellence.

The 2000 London Marathon, sponsored mainly by Flora. You can usually tell from the size of the banners which company has provided most sponsorship.

Finding sponsorship

It can be hard for an unknown young athlete to find sponsorship. Sponsors like a safe bet! Athletes, coaches and agents spend a lot of time calling on companies and very often the answer is no.

A sport may have difficulty finding sponsorship if it doesn't have a slot on TV. Big sponsors like high profile TV sports. Far more people watch sports on TV than at live venues.

It can be especially difficult for female or black athletes. Sponsors who make computers and upmarket cars aim their ads at the spectators with most spending power. These tend to be youngish, white and male. The sponsors go for the favourite sports, events and stars of this group.

But if you're a sports star you'll have no problem getting sponsorship. Companies will queue up to pay you to endorse their products: to wear their clothing, drink their soft drinks or drive their cars. Top athletes can earn more from these deals than from their sport.

The benefits and drawbacks for sport

Benefits for sport
- To promote and develop a sport you need to stage events. This can be very expensive. Sponsorship makes it possible.
- Sponsorship also helps talented athletes to train and compete when they couldn't otherwise afford to.
- For top athletes, it can be very lucrative. This is useful because their careers may be short.

Drawbacks for sport
- A deal lasts only a certain time. It does not give a team or an athlete long-term security.
- A sponsor may be bad for a sport's image. Sponsorship by alcohol and tobacco companies is not allowed for events for the under-18s. There is also pressure on TV companies to stop broadcasting events that are sponsored by tobacco companies.
- Sponsors may want to dictate the timing of sports events to suit their own purposes. For example to coincide with peak viewing time on TV. This might not be best for the athletes.
- Teams and athletes may feel exploited by sponsors. This can lower their satisfaction with sport and their motivation to succeed.

Sports stars can earn a lot of money just by taking a sip from a sponsor's soft drink during a match. Wearing a sponsor's clothing or sports shoes can earn them a whole lot more.

QUESTIONS

1 What is *sponsorship*?

2 Describe two benefits to the sponsor.

3 Now describe two possible problems for the sponsor.

4 Give two other real-life examples (not used here) of sponsorship for: **a** a team **b** an individual

5 Female rugby teams have particular difficulty in obtaining sponsorship. Try to explain why.

6 Give one benefit and one drawback of sponsorship for:
   a a team **b** an individual

7 On balance, is sponsorship a good idea? Why?

14.3 Sport and the media

The **media** are all the means by which information is delivered to you: books, newspapers, magazines, radio, TV, cinema and video.

How the media affect sport

The media have an enormous impact on sport. This is particularly true of TV. Some of the effects are good, some not!

Positive effects

◎ The media help to promote sport. Sporting events are seen, heard and read about by millions of people.
◎ They create sports 'stars' who may inspire young athletes. Denise Lewis and David Beckham are examples.
◎ When a sport gets a lot of media attention, more people get interested in playing it.
◎ Sports that get a lot of media coverage, especially on TV, find it easier to obtain sponsorship.
◎ The media can educate and inform you about sport. For example, through documentaries, coaching programmes and discussion of current issues.
◎ TV companies pay large sums to the governing bodies of sport for the right to broadcast events. This is used to develop the sport.

Dance and other activities also benefit from the media in these ways.

Some drawbacks

◎ Media exposure may foster the desire to win at all costs rather than play for enjoyment.
◎ There is more pressure on managers and team captains to get results. The media may hound them out of their jobs if they fail.
◎ Sports stars lose privacy. Their private lives get reported on.
◎ TV may force changes on a sport. In 1996 Rugby League changed from being a winter game so that TV viewers could see it all year round. The tie break in tennis was introduced to appeal to a TV audience.
◎ The media may over-sensationalise events. Why would they do this?

How the media present sport

When you read about something in the paper, or watch it on TV, or listen on the radio, it is *not* like being there yourself. The event has been 'packaged' for you by the people working in the medium. They have decided what to put in, what to leave out, and what point of view to take. For example, in TV sports the camera operators and video editors decide which shots you see and from which angle. The producers decide who should be interviewed. The interviewers decide which questions to ask. What you see is often *more* exciting than the actual event, thanks to close-up shots, slow-motion replays, interviews and a dramatic commentary. In real life you would not hear a player's thoughts before a match, or see the pain on a manager's face as his team loses.

Media attention focused on David Beckham of Manchester United and England has made him a household name.

In all of the media, the way an event is packaged depends on how much time, space and money is available. But it also depends on which of these things the media makers intend to do:

◎ entertain you
◎ inform you
◎ educate you
◎ 'hype' an event
◎ attract attention (and sales) by being sensational
◎ please the sponsors
◎ express a particular point of view.

Newspapers

Newspapers like sport because it helps to sell them. It also helps to attract advertising. Some companies prefer to advertise their products in the sports pages.

The **tabloid press** includes *The Daily Mirror*, *The Sun* and the *Daily Express*. The **quality press** includes the *Independent*, *Times*, *Guardian* and *Daily Telegraph*. Both cover sports, but there are differences:

Cathy Freeman, an object of intense media interest: as much for being an Aborigine as for being an athete.

The tabloids tend to . . .	The quality press tends to . . .
go for sensational headlines	go for in-depth coverage and comment
take a strong line of approval or disapproval	do more thoughtful analysis
pay little attention to minority sports	give more coverage to minority sports

Information technology

Increasingly people are using information technology in their homes as well as at school or work. You probably use it at school and you may use specific software to help you with certain subjects. Software is available to help you with sport. There are programmes designed to teach you about both the practical and theoretical aspects of many sports and PE. The Internet is a huge source of information. You will be able to access information about your sport including:

◎ recent events and results
◎ details of upcoming events and fixtures
◎ details of how and where you can take up a sport

QUESTIONS

1 What is meant by the media?

2 List three ways in which media coverage helps sport.

3 Describe three drawbacks of media coverage.

4 Several people play a part in selecting and shaping the information you receive in a sports programme. Name three of them.

5 Give one example of a TV sports programme designed mainly to entertain.

6 Name: **a** one tabloid **b** one quality paper.

7 Find a newspaper article about sport which:
   a is sensationalist **b** just gives the facts.

8 Why is video a useful medium for sports?

14.4 More about sport and TV

How sport benefits TV

Of all the media, TV has the biggest impact on sport – and vice versa!
You saw in the last unit how TV and other media benefit sport.
Now look at the way sport benefits TV:

◎ It is often shown at times when TV would otherwise have few viewers, such as Saturday afternoons. Events like Wimbledon and the Olympics are in summer, which is also a quiet time for TV.
◎ Sports programmes are much simpler to make than drama or documentaries. You just film the event and edit the film.
◎ Sport attracts sports fans to TV. Many of them might not otherwise bother watching.
◎ It also attracts advertisers. TV companies can charge more for their advertising slots during big sports events.

TV and the professional athlete

TV has had a big role in the rise of the professional athlete. Professional athletes get paid for playing sport. Without all the interest and money generated for sport by TV, many sports could not afford to pay them. Tennis and golf could not offer such big cash prizes. Football clubs could not afford such huge transfer fees. It is an upward spiral. Sport pays well to attract 'star' players. These players attract more spectators, TV viewers and sponsors. This in turn makes more money for sport. But it is only the top players who make a good living from sport. In the USA, for example, tennis players below the top 50 find it hard to get by.

Broadcast rights

In order to show a sports event, a TV company must pay for broadcast rights. Payment is usually made to the sport's governing body. If the company buys exclusive rights to a live sports event, it means no one else can film it. The company can then sell footage on to other companies. They may buy just a few minutes to show as highlights.

Different kinds of TV companies

◎ **Terrestrial.** The terrestrial companies include BBC, ITV, Channel Four and Channel Five. They transmit programmes from TV masts to your TV aerial. You have to pay for a TV licence.
◎ **Satellite.** BSkyB is an example. Information is transmitted via satellite to your satellite dish. You have to pay a subscription fee.
◎ **Cable.** FilmFour is an example. The information is carried along cables buried below the street, with a line fed into your home. You have to pay a subscription fee.
◎ **Digital.** Sky Digital is an example. You have to subscribe.

With satellite and cable, the number of TV channels is growing rapidly. Several show sport only. In 2001 BSkyB had four sports channels showing around 60 current sports as well as classic past events.

Settled in for the afternoon. Lots of people wouldn't bother with TV if it weren't for sport. (But if they watched less TV, would they play more sport?)

With the arrival of satellite TV there's been a huge increase in the amount of sport available to the viewer – if you're prepared to pay the subscription fee.

Although having more sport to watch on TV can be a good thing in that it allows more people to watch, it can have a negative effect. When big spectator events are televised live, many people prefer to stay at home and watch in comfort rather than pay for a ticket. As a result, crowd sizes go down. This can have a negative effect on the players as well as affecting gate receipts.

Competition between TV companies

With the increase in TV channels, competition for broadcast rights is fierce. The bids are getting even higher. For example in 1985 the BBC paid £4 million for exclusive rights to Wimbledon. In 2000 the cost had gone up to £50 million. In 1990 the BBC paid £11 million for Five Nations rugby coverage. In 1997 BSkyB paid £87.5 million for England's home games alone. Football clubs like Leeds United and Manchester United have their own television channels and so they may soon have exclusive rights to their own matches.

Government intervention

Satellite, digital and cable companies are ready to pay huge sums for exclusive rights to popular events such as Wimbledon and the FA Cup final. This means that people who don't have a satellite dish or cable TV might not see them at all, or at best just the highlights. Is this fair? Politicians don't think so. The Broadcasting Bill of 1996 sets out the events to which everyone with a TV set should have full access. The list will be continually updated.

LIST OF EVENTS TO WHICH EVERYONE SHOULD HAVE FULL TV ACCESS

The Derby
The FIFA World Cup finals
The FA Cup Final
The Grand National
The Olympic Games
The finals week of Wimbledon
The Scottish FA Cup Final (in Scotland)
European Football Championship Final
Rugby League Challenge Cup Final
Rugby World Cup Final

Pay-per-view

The first ever pay-per-view event in the UK was the world heavy-weight title fight in 1996 between Frank Bruno and Mike Tyson. It was shown on BSkyB. Viewers had to book in advance and pay extra on top of their normal subscription. Since then there have been a number of pay-per-view events. However they have caused controversy with people being unhappy about having to pay for an event when they already pay to subscribe to that channel anyway. BSkyB introduced pay-per-view premiership football in 2001.

Interactive TV

Interactive TV is now on the increase. It gives you more control over the information you receive. For example you can switch camera angles during a sports event, or press a button for more information about the players. You can look up the rules of the game, or scores in past matches.

QUESTIONS

1 Describe three ways in which sport benefits TV.

2 What does *exclusive rights* mean?

3 Name: **a** one terrestrial broadcast company **b** one satellite broadcast company.

4 Think of two ways in which it would benefit a satellite TV company to have the exclusive rights to Wimbledon.

5 What does *pay-per-view* mean?

14.5 Participation by women

Why do women participate less than men in sport and physical recreation? Is it because they're not interested?

Percentage participating in one or more physical activities (including walking)		
Year	male	female
1990	73	57
1993	72	57
1996	71	57

Historical reasons for low participation

◎ The traditional roles of wife and mother have left little time or energy for sport.
◎ Not many leisure centres used to offer crèche facilities.
◎ Women who didn't have their own job often didn't have the money to spend on physical recreation.
◎ There has been a shortage of role models.
◎ Little media coverage has been given to women's sports in the past.
◎ Women's sports have found it harder to gain sponsorship.

Participation is increasing

Since the early 1970s women's participation has increased. This is due to:

◎ the recognition that exercise is good for your health.
◎ greater economic freedom. More women are earning more and don't have to depend on men for money.
◎ efforts by the sports councils to promote sport for everyone.
◎ an increase in the number of facilities offering activities that appeal to women, e.g. aerobics, swimming and badminton.
◎ more role models for women to look up to.
◎ increased media coverage of women's events. The BBC will broadcast the women's FA Cup Final live from 2002.
◎ More crèche facilities at leisure centres.
◎ Increased opportunities for women. For example in 1993 there were 500 women's football teams across the UK. By 2001 there were 4500.

Women in sport

There are far more women being seen to be successful in sport and destroying some of the old myths. Athletes like Denise Lewis and Cathy Freeman are living proof that it is possible to be a successful athlete and still remain feminine.

We are also seeing more women take up non-participating roles in sport. There are an increasing number of women becoming coaches and officials, even in men's sport, and there are far more women presenting sport on TV. In football, professional clubs are now providing separate changing areas for lady officials like Wendy Toms, for example.

Denise Lewis, heptathlon gold medal winner at Sydney 2000.

QUESTIONS

1 Why do you think women participate less than men?
2 Describe four factors that have resulted in increased participation since 1970.

3 If you were the manager of a leisure centre, how would you try to attract more women to use the facility?

14.6 Challenge

One of the reasons why people participate in certain activities is because they provide a challenge. Maybe you are trying to reach a personal best performance, perhaps the challenge is to overcome a difficulty or perhaps your challenge is simply to compete and win. With outdoor and adventurous sports the challenge is often to overcome fear or to beat the forces of nature. Sometimes they are very risky!

Outdoor and adventurous activities

The number and popularity of outdoor and adventurous activities is rapidly increasing. Mountain walking and water sports like sailing and canoeing have always been popular and many people still enjoy them today. But sports like free diving, kite surfing and bungee jumping are on the increase. If you wanted to take up one of these sports, would you be able to? There are a number of factors at work:

◎ **Acceptability.** Not all of these activities are accepted as sports. Base jumping (parachuting off pylons, buildings and cliffs) is illegal in many countries. Even if they are legal, some sports involve so many risks that people may not want to participate.

◎ **Access.** If you want to go rock climbing or mountain climbing, you need rocks and mountains! Not all of us live near such facilities. Getting to such areas can be difficult and involve extra expense. Man-made climbing walls and diving clubs attached to swimming pools, for example, help more people participate in such activities.

◎ **Provision.** Organisations like Outward Bound provide courses for people to experience outdoor activities.

◎ **Environmental issues.** The British countryside is there to be enjoyed but we must also take great care to look after it. As more people use it, more erosion takes place. Organisations like The Countryside Agency look after the countryside for future generations.

A risk worth taking?

You may well be wondering why some people risk their lives to take part in these activities. The answer lies in the psychological factors. Eustress is a type of stress that people find enjoyable. You may feel nervous or anxious before you jump out of an airplane but once you have done it and your parachute opens your emotions quickly change to high excitement. For this reason people think certain risks are worth taking.

QUESTIONS

1 Why do people like a challenge?

2 **a** Name five adventurous activities.

  b What challenges do they offer?

3 What four factors affect participation in adventurous activities?

4 Some people think the countryside should be protected. Others think it should be enjoyed by everyone. What problems are associated with these different views?

5 Where is your nearest facility for outdoor and adventurous activities?

14.7 Sporting behaviour

Is bad behaviour common among athletes, or spectators, in your sport?

Sports etiquette

A sport has written rules. But it also has **etiquette** – an unwritten code of good behaviour. For example:

◎ a cricket player walks away from the crease when he knows he's out. He doesn't wait for the umpire to tell him.

◎ when a football player is injured, the ball may be kicked out of play on purpose so that the casualty can get treatment. When play resumes, it is usually given back to the team who kicked it out.

These are not *rules*. You don't have to behave this way. They are to do with a sporting attitude and a sense of fair play. What effect do you think they have among the players?

Violence among players

In some sports you hardly ever hear of athletes being rude or violent during events. Athletics, swimming and gymnastics are examples. But in other sports violence is quite common. In 1995 the Everton footballer Duncan Ferguson got a 3-month jail sentence for head-butting an opponent. In 2002 Martin Johnson, the England Rugby Union Captain, received a three-week ban for punching an opponent during a club match. Violence among players damages a sport. It is the job of the club managers, coaches and governing bodies to curb it.

The role of spectators

You can be a spectator at home in front of the TV, or at a live venue. Either way, you are important to sport.

◎ At a live venue spectators help their teams by cheering them on. The atmosphere can be really exciting. Teams are more likely to win at home than away. Why do you think this is?

◎ They help to fund their favourite clubs by buying tickets for events, and flags, posters and other merchandise.

◎ Without TV spectators, sport just wouldn't get shown on TV. Without sport on TV, clubs and athletes would have far more difficulty in finding sponsorship.

Violence among spectators

As a spectator you help sport. But you can also harm it. Football hooligans are an example. They ruin events by fighting the opposing fans. They throw stones, bottles and other weapons on the pitch. They smash up the streets and pubs around venues. In 2000 one Leeds United fan was fatally stabbed in Istanbul by a Galatasary supporter. Hooliganism is often planned in advance, even across continents. Some is linked with right-wing racist groups such as neo-Nazis. It is a problem not just for the police and clubs but for all of society.

One example of tennis etiquette. Definitely not a rule of the game!

The Heysal disaster. From the 1960s on, English hooligans gave English football a very bad reputation. The lowest point was in 1985. Liverpool were playing Juventus in the European Cup Final at the Heysal Stadium in Brussels. Liverpool fans rushed at the opposing fans. A wall collapsed and 41 Italian and Belgian fans were killed. English clubs were banned from European competitions for the next 5 years.

Combating football hooliganism

These are some of the steps taken to fight hooliganism:

◎ fences at venues to keep rival fans apart.
◎ closed-circuit TV cameras around venues.
◎ membership schemes to make it easier to ban troublemakers.
◎ a ban by some clubs on all away fans.
◎ police in different cities and countries sharing information about known hooligans, and passing on warnings about them.
◎ preventing known hooligans from travelling abroad when international fixtures are scheduled to take place.

The police play a big part in preventing hooliganism. They patrol venues, the streets around them, and the local railway stations.
They can have a match cancelled if they don't have the manpower to police it. The clubs have to pay towards police costs.

The Taylor report and all-seater stadiums

In 1989 tragedy struck at Hillsborough in Sheffield. Before the start of the FA Cup semi-final between Liverpool and Nottingham Forest, a huge crowd of Liverpool fans without tickets gathered outside the grounds. The police let them in. In the rush for the terraces, fans were trapped against the perimeter fence. Ninety-nine fans were crushed to death.

A government investigation into the disaster was set up, led by Lord Chief Justice Taylor. The result was the **Taylor Report**, which recommended that perimeter fences should be removed and venues made all-seater, with no more standing on the terraces.

As a result of the report, clubs were forced to spend many thousands of pounds improving their stadiums and making their grounds safer and more welcoming for spectators. Many fans are unhappy about the changes. They feel the atmosphere has been ruined and the excitement lost. But one good result is that football is again becoming a family sport, with more women and children attending matches.

Football for all the family, thanks to the improvements in safety and comfort at football grounds, and the success in controlling hooliganism.

QUESTIONS

1 Give two examples of sporting etiquette that are not mentioned here.

2 Cheering spectators can help their team on. Do you think they have any effect on the other team?

3 Even TV spectators help sport. Explain why.

4 What happened during the Heysal disaster?

5 Describe three steps taken to fight football hooliganism.

6 What incident led to the Taylor report?

7 What did the Taylor report recommend?

Questions on chapter 14

1 True or false? Explain your answer.
  a If you are an amateur athlete it means you are not as good as the professionals.
  b Amateur athletes in athletics can't accept prize money.
  c Appearance money is what you get for wearing your sponsor's logo.
  d Both amateur and professional golfers can compete in an open golf tournament.
  e Open sports never offer prize money.
  f If no-one wanted to watch sport there would be no professionals.

2 According to the technical definition, is the athlete below amateur or professional?
  a Venus Williams
  b David Beckham
  c Denise Lewis
  d Dean Macey
  e Tanni Grey-Thompson
  f Tiger Woods

3 a Explain how Trust Funds operate in amateur athletics.
  b Rugby Union used to run Trust Funds. It stopped doing so in 1995. Why was this?

4 a Is sponsorship always in the form of money? Explain.
  b Top sports stars are paid a lot to endorse products such as sports shoes and soft drinks.
    i What does endorse mean?
    ii Why are companies prepared to pay them for this?
  c Give one example of product endorsement by an athlete.

5 Give reasons for this.
  a Sponsors prefer to sponsor sports events shown on TV.
  b Sponsors are more prepared to sponsor men's sport than women's.
  c An unknown young athlete will find it difficult to get sponsorship.
  d A gymnastics competition is more likely to get sponsorship than a women's rugby event.
  e A sponsor is likely to cancel a contract with an athlete who is caught doping.

6 a Name two sports sponsored by tobacco companies.
  b There is pressure on TV companies not to broadcast events sponsored by tobacco companies. Why?

7 a List everything that comes under the heading *the media*.
  b Which medium has most impact on sport? Why? Give at least two reasons to support your answer.

8 The radio provides a fair amount of sports coverage.
  a What advantages does radio have over TV? List as many as you can.
  b Now list its disadvantages compared with TV.

9 a Make a table with two columns like this:

Benefits to me of watching sport on TV	Benefits to me of playing sport myself

  b Now fill in as many benefits as you can in each column.
  c Which brings more benefits?
  d What advice would you give people who spend hours watching sport on TV?

10 Sports events can sometimes appear more exciting when shown on TV than they are in real life. Explain why.

11 These are some attitudes to women in sport. For each attitude write a paragraph to oppose it.
  a Sports like football and rugby are unsuitable for women.
  b You can't be good at sports and attractive.
  c Women haven't got what it takes to be good at coaching.

12 'The main reason women don't participate much in sport is that they are not interested.' Do you agree? Explain.

13 Imagine you are a Minister of Sport, with a large budget. Describe three steps you would take to improve women's participation in sport. (They can be anything you want.)

14 Some people think boys and girls should be taught PE together at secondary school. Others think they should be taught separately.
  a What are the advantages of teaching them together?
  b What are the advantages of teaching them separately?
  c On balance, which would you recommend? Why?

15   tennis   gymnastics   swimming
      rugby   volleyball   football
  a From this list choose the two sports where you think:
    i violence between participants is most likely
    ii violence between participants is least likely
    iii violence among spectators is most likely
    iv violence among spectators is least likely
  b Do you think there is a connection between violence among spectators and the nature of the sport?
  c How could you test this theory?
  d Design a project for this purpose. Describe it as fully as you can.

16 'Football causes violence.' Do you agree? Explain why.

THINGS TO DO

Amateur versus professional in sport

The division between amateurs and professionals had its origins in the class system. **Amateurs** were gentlemen who could afford to play a sport, often full time, for pleasure. **Professionals** were lower-class people who earned money from sport, often by doing something for a **wager** (bet) or by competing for prizes against others. For example, gentlemen with coaches and horses had footmen. If you were the gambling type you might choose an athletic footman, and pay him something to compete in walking races against your friends' footmen. You'd put a bet on the race.

Cricket was popular among gentlemen. In the 18th century gentlemen's cricket clubs employed some lower-class cricketers who were called **players**. They were paid to look after the grounds, coach the gentlemen and play against them in matches.

As sports became more organized, tension between the amateur gentlemen and working-class professionals grew. In 1866 the Amateur Athletics Club was set up by gentlemen. Working-class men were excluded because it was felt manual labour gave them an advantage in strength.

In 1880 the club became the Amateur Athletics Association. It redefined an amateur as someone who gained no financial reward from a sport. The working class was allowed in.

1 **a** Find out more about the early professional cricketers. Write a short essay about them.
   b Find a copy of an old poster for a match between gentlemen and players. What do you notice about the way their names are listed?
2 A famous example of someone walking for a wager was Captain Barclay. In 1800 he walked 1000 miles in 1000 hours for 1000 guineas. Try to find out more about Captain Barclay. Who put up the money? Where did he walk?
3 Find out more about the Amateur Athletics Club. Who started it? In what sports did it compete, and where? Write a short essay about it.

Sponsorship

4 **a** Make a table with these headings:

Sport	Team or individual	Sponsor	Nature of sponsor's business

   b Now fill it in for as many sports and sponsors as you can.
   c Look at the last column for each sport. Can you see any relationship between the sponsor's business and the sport? If yes, explain it.

Media coverage of sport

5 The work in this activity should be shared among the class.
   a Six people each collect one newspaper a day for a week (Monday to Saturday). The papers should be a mixture of tabloids and broadsheets (quality papers). One person collects the *Guardian*, another the *Sun* and so on.
   b For each newspaper make a table like the one started here:

Name of newspaper: *The Independant*		
Sport	Type	Number of articles
Football	Men's	IIII III
	Women's	II
Rugby	Men's	III
	Women's	

   c Go through all the sport pages in your set of papers. (A new person can take over for each copy.) For each article on sport, put a tally mark in the table.
   d Now add up the tally marks for each sport. Put the results in a table like this:

Total number of articles in *The Independant* for the week		
Sport	Men's	Women's
Football	54	

   e Show the results as a bar chart. Put the women's sports at one end of the chart and the men's at the other. Put each in order, the sport with most coverage first.
   f Study the bar chart. Which sports get most coverage? Which get least? How well are women's sports covered? Write a report on what you have discovered.
6 Now compare the bar graphs for the different papers.
   a Do the same sports get most coverage in all of them? Which sports are these?
   b Is it true that the quality press provides more coverage of minority sports?
   c Which paper covers most women's sports?
   d Overall, how does coverage of women's sports compare with that of men's? Try to express it as a percentage.
7 Now pick the main sports event of the week. Compare coverage of this event in a quality paper and a tabloid.
   a What differences do you notice?
   b Do you agree with the statements in the table on page 179?

Index